Visions of Emancipation

Piazza San Carlo, Turin.

Visions of Emancipation

The Italian Workers' Movement Since 1945

Joanne Barkan

PRAEGER SPECIAL STUDIES • PRAEGER SCIENTIFIC

New York • Philadelphia • Eastbourne, UK
Toronto • Hong Kong • Tokyo • Sydney

Library of Congress Cataloging in Publication Data

Barkan, Joanne.
  Visions of emancipation.

  Bibliography: p.
  Includes index.
  1. Trade-unions—Italy—History—20th century.
2. Labor and laboring classes—Italy—History—20th
century. I. Title.
HD6709.B355   1984   331.88′0945   84-6762
ISBN 0-03-059626-2 (alk. paper)

Photo Credits

Photographs on pages vi, 4, 30, 138, and 187 courtesy of Fiat, *Centro Storico* (Turin).
All other photographs © Paola Agosti (Rome).

Five of the interviews included in this volume first appeared, in slightly different form, as
part of the article "Eight Hours a Day at Fiat: Conversations with Italian Auto Workers"
in the July-August 1980 issue, vol. 14, no. 4 of *Radical America* (38 Union Square, Somerville, MA 02143).

Published in 1984 by Praeger Publishers
CBS Educational and Professional Publishing,
a Division of CBS Inc.
521 Fifth Avenue, New York, NY 10175 USA

© 1984 by Joanne Barkan

456789 052 9876545321

Printed in the United States of America
on acid-free paper

Preface

In October 1978, I visited the city of Turin, one of the largest centers of Italian industry, for the first time. I had always wanted to see Fiat, especially the giant Mirafiori plant, which had become something of a legendary symbol of the workers' movement—from the strikes during the last months of Mussolini's regime and during the German occupation to the insurgency of 1969 and the early 1970s. While I was in Turin, I met a journalist, Gianni Montani, who proposed a visit to a new welding department that had generated a lot of publicity. The department was located in Fiat's Rivalta plant about a half-hour outside Turin. Montani arranged the tour through the company's press relations office, and we were chauffeured to the plant along with a press official who acted as a private guide.

As we made our way up and down the long aisles between assembly lines in a bubble-topped minibus, Montani, who is a former Fiat worker, mentioned that the atmosphere had changed a good deal since the height of the workers' movement in the early years of the decade. Then, Fiat often had trouble taking tourists through the plants. The workers, angry in general and irritated by the curious stares, pelted buses with whatever was at hand, jeered at outsiders, and simply did not conform to the kind of image Fiat's management wanted to project. But in 1978, the ambience at Rivalta seemed fairly relaxed. There was nothing extraordinary until we arrived at *robogate*, the new department where side panels, roofs, and floors were welded together to make body shells. I had this first view of *robogate* about a half-year before the media began to report extensively on the technological revolution of computerized manufacturing. I was certainly not prepared for what I saw. There were no human workers in the department. It looked not like an assembly line but like the set for a science fiction film.

Light poured through the glass roof into a large, open space. There were eight turquoise welding stations in a line. About a dozen yellow, dollylike carriers glided along stripes on a green floor. They were following unseen electromagnetic tracks. Each carrier held up the components of a single car body, and they slid into the stations one by one. Then four robots leaned forward from the corners of each station and began welding. The carriers coasted from one station to the next until the robots had completed 330 different welds. *Robogate* was turning out 400 completely

The automobile assembly room at Fiat in Turin, 1908.

Robogate, a completely automated welding department at Fiat Rivalta, outside Turin. The department was opened in 1978.

welded bodies in seven hours. This was three times as fast as the next
most recent technology at Fiat.

What I saw at Fiat Rivalta prompted me to investigate the impact of
the new computerized technology on the labor force. How was this going
to change not only the employment situation but also the work process
inside the plants? I returned to Turin in May 1979 to do interviews with
workers and others around Fiat—managers, supervisors, unionists, and
party activists. At that time, the city was extremely tense. The national
government had fallen, an electoral campaign was underway, and yet no
one expected the vote to resolve the political impasse. The terrorist organizations had stepped up their activities with the goal of disrupting the
campaign as much as possible. Every morning the local newspapers listed
fires and bombs set off in Turin the night before. With its high concentration of workers and capital, Turin had become a favorite target of terrorists. In addition, the national contract for all metal and mechanical
workers had expired so that the labor force at Fiat and at every other
steel, auto, and electronics plant around Turin was in constant agitation.

Beyond the specific events of that May, there were more long-term
transformations taking place both at Fiat and within the Italian labor
movement. The radical and militant struggles which began in 1969 had
been a watershed. They changed the nature of labor relations in Italy and
conditioned economic and political developments for a decade. By 1979,
however, new forces were challenging the vitality of that movement.
Young workers with different experiences and values were entering the
labor force; political and economic obstacles were undermining the gains
of the previous years; production was being restructured—both inside the
factories and offices with new technology and in the system as a whole
with decentralization and the growth of the underground economy. Italy
was clearly in a transition, and many of the changes taking place there
were relevant to transformations in the United States.

When I returned to the States, I began planning a book that would
be a general introduction to the postwar labor movement in Italy. Since
the history of Italian labor is bound up so closely with political and economic developments, it was clear that this study would actually be a survey of postwar Italy with an emphasis on workers and their unions. I
wanted the book to analyze what people there called the *caso Italiano*—
the Italian case—the particular characteristics of Italy's workers' movement that differentiate it from labor in other industrialized countries
around the world and even from other European countries. I also wanted
to write something that would be as current as possible because no up-to-
date, general overview of the postwar Italian labor movement existed in
English. Finally, I hoped to find a way of going beyond the institutionally
focused accounts of trade unions and leaders, which make up the bulk of

many labor histories. The protagonists of the book were to be the workers—not just as statistics or abstractions, but as subjects whose opinions and experiences could be known more directly.

These concerns determined the final shape of the text. The introductory chapter provides a brief profile of the structure, membership, and political nature of the unions, the composition of the labor force, the economy, and government for readers who are new to the subject of postwar Italy. The next 11 chapters, which make up Part I, present the history of the labor movement since 1945 in the context of political and economic developments. The subject is obviously a vast one, and the account in this book is an overview. Part I gives greatest attention to the period from 1969 to the present. It also examines in some depth several "extralabor" issues that have had an important impact on working people and the trade unions. These include feminism, terrorism, and the Communist Party's historic compromise policy. Part I follows industrial workers most closely. Although agricultural workers have played a significant role in the history of Italian labor since the nineteenth century, the years after the Second World War were a time of rapid industrialization. The workers inside plants and on the assembly lines have been central to that story.

In Part II, the actors—workers, unionists, managers, politicos—speak for themselves. This section includes an introduction to Fiat and Turin and 20 of the interviews that I conducted in that city in 1979. The year when the interviews were done is not an irrelevant or arbitrary factor. As described earlier, 1979 was a time of economic and political transition for the labor movement. The people interviewed recount their daily lives, past experiences, and hopes for the future. They are able to translate into personal terms events that have been described in the historical chapters of the book. They are not, of course, a representative sample of the entire labor force. But they do reveal the differing perspectives and opinions of individuals who work for a company and dwell in a city that have been closely identified with the workers' movement. They present Italian labor from the point of view of those who have lived through or, in some cases, have helped to create its history.

Contents

Acknowledgments

Many thanks to the following people who read the first draft of this work or parts of it. Their comments and suggestions were of great value to me: Stanley Aronowitz, Paola Ciardi, Aniello Coppola, Victoria De Grazia, Jon Friedman, Margaret Gibson, Temma Kaplan, John Low-Beer, Philip Mattera, Alessandro Pizzorno, Ida Regalia, Marino Regini, Itala Rutter, Mario Telò, and Peter Weitz.

There are others to whom I am deeply grateful. They are: Lynda Sharp of Praeger, for her help and interest in this project from the start; Susan Alkana, Barbara Leffel, and David Stebbing, for their fine work in seeing the manuscript through production; Rose Marie Norton, for the endless typing; Irving Barkan and Jonathan Bricklin, for their expert proofreading and the many days they spent working with me; Paola Agosti, for her photographs and for her collaborative spirit as we worked in Turin; Noris Morano, formerly of the press relations office at Fiat headquarters in Turin, for her thorough and patient help in setting up interviews and factory visits; Gianni Montani, for "introducing" me to *robogate* and for thoughtful answers to hundreds of questions; Ruth Milkman, for the many kilos of documentation and research material she brought from Turin; John Low-Beer, for his generosity and willingness to give of his time and expertise; Jon Friedman, for his unfailing patience, creative suggestions, and sustained enthusiasm for this project—these were indispensable to me; and the many unionists, party activists, and journalists who helped me arrange interviews, drove me to the plants and outlying dormitory towns, and spent hours explaining their views.

Finally, special thanks to the Fiat workers who shared their personal histories, experiences, hopes, and fears. Many of them also shared their food, coffee, and *grappa*. They took me into their homes, introduced me to their relatives, showed me around their neighborhoods. I think often of them and the others in Turin whom I learned from and enjoyed.

List of Tables

List of Abbreviations

ACLI — Associazioni Cristiane dei Lavoratori Italiani / Christian Associations of Italian Workers

ASAP — employers' association for the state-controlled companies of ENI

cassa integrazione — cassa integrazione guadagni / wage supplement fund

CGIL — Confederazione Generale Italiana del Lavoro / Italian General Confederation of Labor

CISL — Confederazione Italiana Sindacati Lavoratori / Italian Confederation of Workers Unions

CISNAL — Confederazione Italiana dei Sindacati Nazionali dei Lavoratori / Italian Confederation of National Workers Unions

CLN — Comitato di Liberazione Nazionale / Committee of National Liberation

Confindustria — General Confederation of Italian Industry (private sector employers)

CUB — Comitato Unitario di Base / Unitary Base Committee

DC — Democrazia Cristiana / Christian Democracy (Christian Democratic Party)

DP — Democrazia Proletaria / Proletarian Democracy

EEC — European Economic Community

ENI — Ente Nazionale Idrocarburi / National Hydrocarbons Agency

FGCI — Federazione Giovanile Comunista Italiana / Italian Communist Youth Federation

FIM — Federazione Italiana Metalmeccanici / Italian Federation of Metal and Mechanical Workers

FIOM — Federazione Impiegati Operai Metallurgici / Federation of Metallurgical Employees and Workers

FLM — Federazione Lavoratori Metalmeccanici / Federation of Metal and Mechanical Workers

GNP — gross national product

Intersind — employers' association for IRI and other state-controlled companies

IRI	Istituto per la Ricostruzione Industriale / Institute for Industrial Reconstruction
lavoro nero	black labor (unrecorded, illegal labor)
MLD	Movimento di Liberazione della Donna / Movement for Liberation of the Woman
MSI	Movimento Sociale Italiano / Italian Social Movement
NATO	North Atlantic Treaty Organization
PCI	Partito Comunista Italiano / Italian Communist Party
PLI	Partito Liberale Italiano / Italian Liberal Party
PR	Partito Radicale / Radical Party
PRI	Partito Repubblicano Italiano / Italian Republican Party
PSDI	Partito Socialista Democratico Italiano / Italian Social Democratic Party
PSI	Partito Socialista Italiano / Italian Socialist Party
PSIUP	Partito Socialista Italiano di Unità Proletaria / Italian Socialist Party of Proletarian Unity
scala mobile	sliding scale (national wage indexing system to offset the effects of inflation)
UDI	Unione Donne Italiane / Union of Italian Women
UIL	Unione Italiana del Lavoro / Italian Union of Labor
UILM	Unione Italiana Lavoratori Metallurgici / Italian Union of Metallurgical Workers

Modern Italy

Introduction:
Labor, the Economy, and
Government in Profile

Italy is a democratic Republic founded on labor.

Article 1 of the Italian Constitution

Work and workers play an unusual role in the 1948 Italian Constitution. Most such liberal democratic charters safeguard basic civil rights, but the originality of the Italian document is to establish as well a series of economic and social guarantees. According to the Constitution, Italian workers have the right to a decent wage that will permit them to lead free and dignified lives. Women are to receive equal pay for equal work and the means to care for their children. Injured, sick, and disabled workers are pledged whatever they need to live. Labor unions are free, independent, and empowered to represent their members in collective bargaining. The right to strike belongs to all workers.[1]

The Constitution as a whole reflects the differing political orientations of its authors who included leftists, moderates, conservatives, and former partisan fighters in the armed Resistance against fascism. The progressives among them envisioned a state that would provide some measure of economic as well as political democracy and would "protect labor in all its forms and applications." But putting the ideals of the Constitution into practice turned out to be a very different and difficult matter. In large part, the history of the postwar labor movement has been an ongoing struggle to implement and expand Italian democracy.

1

The Political Nature and Structure
of the Labor Movement

Unlike most trade unions in the United States, Italian labor organizations see themselves as representing the working class as a whole and not just union members or workers belonging to a particular industry or craft. In part, this attitude is linked to the open-shop organization of the workplaces which will be discussed further on. But more significantly, it is bound up with the political nature of Italian trade unions, their more clearly delineated ideological positions, and the greater self-consciousness about social classes and class boundaries in Italy. Labor unions are not regarded as just one of many narrowly self-interested pressure groups within society. Rather they operate as an integral and influential part of the political system. When they bid for the allegiance of the working class, they are appealing for political allegiance as well as organizational support.

Italian union leaders function not as business agents focused primarily on day-to-day problems of members as they generally do in the United States, but more as political leaders. During the early postwar years, high-ranking Italian unionists were in fact political party officials performing trade union duty. Parties and their allied labor organizations then shared the same policies. The relationship was one of binding cooperation referred to as the "transmission belt." The result was a subordinate position for labor unions in relation to the parties. Since the 1960s, the autonomy of the unions has increased substantially—although there are still periods when the old ties reassert themselves. In general, the last 20 years have shown that the greater the autonomy of the labor movement, the more unified and effective its leadership has been.

The organizational structure of the Italian labor movement reflects both its class orientation and its political divisions as they have evolved since the Second World War. At the workplace level, there are councils made up of delegates elected from each shop, work team, or office. The council represents all employees in a workplace—union members and nonmembers, regardless of their job description or blue- or white-collar status. Every worker, including those without union cards, can vote for a council delegate, and the delegates need not be union members. (There is no labor structure in the United States that operates in this way.) The Italian councils represent the work force to management; they organize job actions and implement contracts.

Outside the workplace, the labor movement is organized into a system of unions that has two branches: one based on divisions by economic sector and one based on geographical location. The first branch of the system is made up of separate unions representing either agricultural workers or workers in commerce, a service, or one area of industry. These unions are called category unions. The largest and most influential of the industrial categories is the metal and mechanical workers, which comprises auto workers, steel workers, electrical workers, and anyone else who works with mechanical systems or metal. Two other important industrial categories are chemical workers and textile workers. The various service sector categories include, for example, hospital employees and school employees. There are category unions at the local, provincial, and national levels. The national-level category unions are called federations.

The second branch of the system is made up of bodies that bring together all the category unions within a given geographical area. These intercategory or geographically based structures exist at the local and provincial levels. The Italian chambers of labor (*camere del lavoro*), for example, are provincial-level intercategory bodies. At the national level, there is an "umbrella" structure called a confederation. All category unions and all intercategory bodies belong to the national confederation. (Although the structure of Italian unions is quite complex and different from that of U.S. unions, it should be remembered that the United States too has its version of a dual system. State and local central labor councils are intercategory bodies. They bring together various industrial and craft unions. The AFL-CIO is a national confederation.)

In 1948, political differences splintered the Italian labor movement along ideological lines. Since then, there have been three competing national confederations, each with its own network of category and intercategory structures. The three confederations are the CGIL (Italian General Confederation of Labor) made up of Communists, Socialists, activists of the New Left tradition, and independent leftists; the CISL (Italian Confederation of Workers' Unions), which includes members and supporters of the Christian Democratic Party, independent Catholics, independent leftists, and some Socialists; and the UIL (Italian Union of Labor), which brings together Socialists (now the dominant element), Social Democrats, and Republicans. None of the three confederations has a complete system of category and intercategory structures at the local and provincial levels. Labor organizations are present where there are sufficient numbers of workers and adequate support. The largest confederation—the CGIL—has had the most extensive network.

In addition to the three major confederations and their affiliated unions, there are also autonomous unions, company unions, and fascist unions. The autonomous unions, which are not affiliated with any confederation, have been strongest among civil service workers, teachers, and some highly skilled employees such as airline pilots. These unions represent narrow, sectoral (corporatist) interests. The workers who belong to them often promote their particular demands at the expense of a

A worker in the mechanical department at Fiat's first plant on Dante Boulevard, Turin, 1900.

classwide perspective. The three confederations regard the autonomous unions as a threat to their own power and goals. In general, autonomous unions in Italy gain support when workers are dissatisfied with confederation policies. In the past, the influence of management-controlled unions (*sindacati gialli* or yellow unions) depended on the relative weakness of the confederal unions and the labor movement as a whole. Management-controlled unions were common during the 1950s. Compared to the major labor organizations, the fascist unions in the postwar period have been quite weak.

Union Membership and Rank-and-File Participation

Precise membership figures for the three confederations are difficult to obtain. Membership fluctuates, and the unions have often inflated their numbers. The generally accepted figures in 1981 were about 4.5 million members for the CGIL, slightly under 3 million for the CISL, and a little over 1 million for the UIL. The labor force in Italy (employed and unemployed workers) numbered 23.1 million.[2] Thus about 37 percent of the labor force was unionized in 1981. (In the United States, the level of unionization was 20.9 percent in 1980.)[3]

One of the most important features determining the character and the mode of operation of the Italian labor movement is the *open-shop* organization of the workplace. No worker is obliged to join a union. This is true even if every other employee has signed up. In fact, both the *closed-shop* arrangement (everyone must join the union) and the U.S. *union shop* (nonmembers must pay initiation fees and dues) seem highly undemocratic to many Italians.

A worker who decides to become a union member can choose from among the various union affiliates present in a particular workplace—CGIL, CISL, UIL, autonomous, management controlled, or fascist. In some categories, the three major confederations have also set up unitary structures which the workers can join. The result is an extremely fluid situation which differs from workplace to workplace. In some plants and offices, the level of unionization may be above 90 percent. In others, there may be no unions at all or just a minimal presence. At Fiat, for example, membership was just over 41 percent of the work force in 1980. Some 87 percent of the union members belonged to the unitary metal and mechanical workers' federation.[4] Although the level of unionization at Fiat was above the national average, the figure was actually low compared to other companies in the metal and mechanical category. Within Fiat, the figure varied from plant to plant.

An assembly-line worker at Fiat Mirafiori in Turin, 1979.

For many workers, joining a union is a political choice and an affirmation of an ideological position. It is similar to signing on with a political party. This was especially true during the 1950s when discrimination against leftists and union activists was harsh. Today, many young workers join unions with less deliberation, but for others membership is still a self-conscious and careful decision.

Just as union membership is neither automatic nor perfunctory in Italy, rank-and-file support for the unions vacillates considerably. Many workers feel no obligation to respond to a strike call if they disagree with its purpose or if they disapprove of union policies. Thus every strike or vote on a platform or call to a rally becomes a plebiscite measuring the rank and file's approval of the unions. Since the labor organizations negotiate directly with the government in many instances and take positions on party and government policies, each strike, vote, and rally is also an assessment of working-class attitudes toward the various political forces. The unions often cannot predict what kind of response they will receive from the rank and file. One month, participation in a strike may be low, registering as a political setback; the next month, a strike called for similar reasons may succeed. With the open shop, it is possible for a union in a minority position to lead all the workers in a plant out on strike just as it is possible for a majoritarian union to fail to mobilize the rank and file. The labor organizations must rely on the support of nonmembers in order to pressure management and the government effectively. In addition, union membership is variable. Workers who are fed up with union policy may decide not to rejoin. They may even quit the union in protest. Fluctuating loyalties obligate the unions to campaign for members and for approval among nonmembers. The situation is further complicated by the rivalries between the different unions. When the labor confederations are badly divided among themselves and competing for popularity, they split rank-and-file support and diminish labor's chances for success.

Strikes and Collective Bargaining

The use of the strike in Italy differs quite a bit from its use in the United States. First of all, the vast majority of strikes are short, lasting from less than an hour to a single day. In part, this is because there are no strike funds in Italy to sustain prolonged work stoppages. But equally important are the frequency of strikes and their more varied application. Workers strike not only at the time of contract renewals but also during the life of a contract. In the latter case, they might try to win different work rules, changes in scheduling, or added jobs; they might protest lay-

offs, plant closings, noncompliance with the contract, or excessive overtime. The no-strike clause, which prohibits work stoppages during the life
of a contract, is standard in the United States. In Italy, however, the no-
strike policy is not accepted. (Some people argue that the no-strike clause
conflicts with Article 40 of the Constitution, which guarantees the right
to strike.) Since there are nationwide interconfederal and category contracts as well as company agreements, workers can legitimately strike at
the company level to improve upon a national contract. Support strikes
(one group of workers going out to aid the struggle of another group) are
common.

In addition to strikes around all issues covered by labor contracts,
the Italian workers' movement undertakes frequent political strikes. The
focus of these ranges from protests against government economic policy
to demands for social reform to questions of foreign policy, such as opposition to the Vietnam War or calls for multilateral nuclear disarmament.
Italian courts and public opinion in general accept work stoppages for
"non-trade-union" political purposes. Such strikes are rare in the United
States. Even in countries like West Germany and Britain, they are less
common than in Italy. This kind of protest has been a powerful weapon
for Italian labor and is another expression of the political character of the
workers' movement. A massive political strike can bring down the national government or force through a significant change in policy.

The labor movement in Italy uses a variety of strike forms such as
rotating and intermittent strikes, which will be examined in Chapter 4.
During contract negotiations, the national unions often decide how
many hours of strikes there will be, while the individual plants decide
exactly when and how to conduct the strikes. Picketing is usually militant, and workers will use force, if necessary, to keep strikebreakers from
entering the plants. In order for a strike to be legitimate, a union does not
have to issue the call. Worker-initiated actions (often referred to as spontaneous strikes) are fairly common, especially during periods of intense
labor protests or when the unions are out of touch with the rank and file.
Since the unions cannot afford to remain aloof from the workers or ignore their demands without suffering a loss of support, they often end up
endorsing spontaneous strikes.

Collective bargaining takes place at several levels. There are interconfederal agreements that cover all sectors of the economy and deal
with issues like the national wage indexing system and severance pay.
From 1945 until the early 1960s, this kind of contract was the most important collective agreement. It included a wide range of issues such as
dismissals, wage differentials, and grievance procedures. After 1960, the
national category contracts came to play the central role in bargaining.
These agreements cover all aspects of labor relations—work conditions,
wages, benefits, access to information, and so on—within a single cate-

gory. One of the most valuable innovations after 1969 was the widespread implementation of company-level contracts. They cover the same areas as category contracts but give the employees in a particular workplace the chance to improve upon a national-level agreement.

As long as the no-strike clause is not accepted, labor can bring up new demands at any time. After 1969, this created a situation of "continuous bargaining." At the national level, the unions negotiate frequently with Confindustria (the national confederation of industries which represents most private industrial employers); individual employer associations for the major categories; Intersind and ASAP (which represent many state holdings); and the government. At the local level, the executive committees of the workplace councils are involved in negotiations along with the unions. Most contracts come up for renewal every two or three years. The rank and file usually ratifies a negotiated agreement at assemblies open to all workers.

The Labor Force

The labor force (employed and unemployed individuals) has consistently seemed small in Italy relative to the population as a whole. In 1981, the population had reached 57.2 million while the labor force counted 23.1 million. The participation rate (labor force as a percentage of population) was about 40 percent. In comparison, the 1981 participation rate in the United States was about 48 percent and in West Germany about 44 percent.[5] Italy's apparently low participation rate depends in part on the existence of an extensive, illegal underground economy which will be examined in Chapter 9.

Italian society exhibits many of the characteristics typical of late capitalism. The agricultural sector contracted steadily from more than 48 percent of the active population in the early 1940s to 14.9 percent in 1979. Industrial expansion has lost its dynamism. After increasing for two decades, the percentage of the Italian labor force employed in industry began to decline in the 1970s and stood at 37.5 percent in 1979. The service sector has expanded rapidly and accounted for the remaining 47.6 percent of the working population. (The average figures in 1977 for the European Economic Community [EEC] including Italy were: 8.2 percent in agriculture, 39.9 percent in industry, and 51.9 percent in services.)[6] The majority of Italians are dependent workers who receive salaries or hourly wages for their labor. In 1976, they made up 77 percent of the labor force as compared to 59.1 percent in 1951.[7]

Since the last century, women have often been a dynamic and militant force within the Italian workers' movement. For many decades, however, their presence within the labor force diminished steadily. The decline could be seen in both the proportion of the entire labor force that was female and the proportion of the female population that was in the labor force. In the 1970s, the presence of women began to grow somewhat stronger, but the statistics still lag behind those for women in other Western industrialized countries. In 1979, women made up 32.9 percent of the total labor force in Italy.[8] In 1980, just 26.0 percent of all Italian women were working or looking for work.[9] (This figure was 52.7 percent for women in the United States in 1982.)[10]

Female employment in Italian agriculture dropped dramatically after the Second World War, and employment in the tertiary sector grew. Of all women in the labor force in 1982, 15 percent worked in agriculture (this was still higher than in many European countries), 28 percent in industry, and 57 percent in the tertiary sector.[11] In general, there is a higher incidence of precarious and part-time employment among women than among men. Women often get the lowest-level blue- and white-collar jobs and earn less money. In 1978, female earnings in blue-collar industrial jobs in Italy were just 74.1 percent of male earnings.[12] Women also have more difficulty finding jobs. The unemployment rate was 13.1 percent for women in 1980 as compared to 4.8 percent for men.[13]

Another population characteristic of postwar Italy was the mass migration from the poorest regions (the South, islands, and Northeast) to the industrial Northwest and abroad (mostly to northern Europe). Between 1945 and 1970, 5 or 6 million Italians abandoned their birthplaces and homes in order to find work. The economic retrenchment of the 1970s halted this trend. In fact, the 1981 census showed that the population of the South had increased substantially more than the population of northern and central Italy during the 1970s.

Italy's class structure is fragmented and reflects its precapitalist past as well as its industrial and recent postindustrial (or late capitalist) development. The traditional middle strata—shopkeepers, artisans, and small farmers—are unusually strong. The ruling class is made up of the top corporate managers and financiers, the more powerful independent entrepreneurs, and the political and military elites. As the working-class sector of the population shrinks in industry and agriculture, an underclass of poor people excluded from the official labor market is growing.

Italy's Economy and Government

Italy has a mixed economy with the state-controlled sector accounting for about 40 percent of the gross national product (GNP). The most important industries are machinery, chemicals, food and tobacco, textiles, autos and other transport equipment, and clothing and shoes.[14] Three northern cities—Milan, Turin, and Genoa—delineate the area of greatest industrial activity, which is called the "industrial triangle." Italy has practically no oil or coal and so must buy virtually all its energy supplies abroad. In terms of regional differentiations, a great disparity in industrial development, economic infrastructure, and wealth has traditionally divided North from South. The postwar expansion did little to close the gap. In general, wealth is unequally distributed. The poorest 10 percent of Italian families receives just 2 percent of the total income while the wealthiest 10 percent takes 30 percent.[15]

A new constitution established Italy as a republic in January 1948. The territory is divided into 20 regions, 95 provinces, and over 8,000 *comuni* (cities, towns, and villages of every size). As for government structure, Italy is a parliamentary democracy, meaning that the executive must be approved by and is politically dependent upon Parliament. Parliament is made up of two houses: the Senate and the Chamber of Deputies.

The president of the republic chooses a party leader to put together a cabinet (also called the Council of Ministers or the government). If the cabinet wins a majority vote of approval in Parliament, it becomes the executive. The individual who puts together the government becomes president of the Council of Ministers (also called the prime minister). If at any time the government loses its majority support in Parliament, it falls. If the prime minister or someone else enlisted by the president of the republic cannot form a new government that wins Parliament's approval, then Parliament is dissolved, and national elections must be held. The regional, provincial, and municipal governments have parallel structures. At the municipal level, for example, the city or town council must approve the choice of mayor and government, which is called a *giunta*. The *giunta* is made up of the equivalent of ministers called *assessori*.

Members of Parliament and the councils at every level of government are elected by proportional representation. Each party's share of the total votes determines how many seats it wins. Ten or eleven parties usually elect members to Parliament, and no one party has won an absolute majority of seats since 1948. Thus the national government (and this is true of most local governments as well) is made up of a coalition of parties that maneuver and bargain among themselves for power and privilege. The result has been extreme factionalism, political intrigue, and cabinet instability. There were 44 national governments between 1945 and 1983. At the same time, however, Italy has had a stable regime. The Christian Democratic Party dominated every government of the postwar period and maintained an exclusive hold on the post of prime minister until 1981.

Notes

1. *Constitution of the Italian Republic*, Articles 36, 37, 38, 39, and 40.

2. Michael Davenport, "Italy," *World Economic Outlook* 4, no. 1 (May 1982):95.

3. Courtney D. Gifford, ed., *Directory of U.S. Labor Organizations 1982–83 Edition* (Washington, D.C.: Bureau of National Affairs, 1982), p. 1.

4. *Fiat 80*, edition no. 10033/80 (Turin: Fiat, 1980), catalog, p. 267.

5. Davenport, "Italy," *World Economic Outlook*, p. 95; Derek Ford, "United States," ibid., p. 33; Davenport, "Germany," ibid., p. 73.

6. Centro Studi Investimenti Sociali, *XIII Rapporto/1979 sulla situazione sociale del paese* (Rome: CENSIS, 1979), pp. 31, 228.

7. Gabriella Pinnarò, "Introduzione," in *L'Italia socio-economica 1976–77*, ed. Gabriella Pinnarò (Rome: Riuniti, 1978), p. 11.

8. "Lavoro donna, donna lavoro," *Il Manifesto* (Rome: June 1980), p. 2.

9. Milan Women's Collectives, "La Crisi" (Document prepared for the conference *Produrre e riprodurre*, Turin, Italy, April 23–25, 1983), mimeographed, p. 8.

10. U.S. Department of Labor and Bureau of Labor Statistics, *Employment and Earnings* 30, no. 9 (September 1983):7.

11. "Raccolta dati sulla forza lavoro femminile" (Document prepared for the conference *Produrre e riprodurre*, Turin, Italy, April 23–25, 1983), mimeographed, p. 5.

12. Commission of the European Communities, Directorate-General Information, *Women in Statistics, Women of Europe*, Suppl. 10 (Brussels, 1982), p. 22.

13. "Raccolta dati," p. 19.

14. Paolo Forcellini, *Rapporto sull'industria italiana* (Rome: Riuniti, 1978), p. 25.

15. Carmela D'Apice, "Le indagini sul reddito delle famiglie," in Pinnarò, *L'Italia socio-economica*, p. 154.

I

The Workers' Movement, Politics, and Economics Since 1945

1

Reconstructing After the War

Italy emerged from the Second World War a semi-industrialized Catholic country faced with the task—and opportunity—of rebuilding politically, economically, and culturally after more than 20 years of fascism. There was a constitution to write, people to feed, and bombed-out cities to reconstruct. Workers were occupying the factories in the North while armed Resistance fighters moved to fill the political and administrative vacuum created by the German withdrawal. Peasants in the South were claiming the right to own land. A new period of history was opening, but at the same time, the legacy of past decades reasserted itself in political life, in the reordering of the economy, and in labor relations. As far as the Italian working class was concerned, liberation raised hopes for a radically different society. The destiny of those hopes is the central theme of the early postwar years.

Parties and Politics at the Close of the War

The political lineup of postwar Italy took shape between 1943 and 1945 during the Allied campaign against the Germans and the partisan Resistance. The Committee of National Liberation (CLN), which directed the antifascist struggle, brought together Communists, Socialists, Christian Democrats, members of the Action Party, Liberals, and Labor Democrats. While the CLN carried out military actions against the Germans, the workers set up agitation or protest committees (*comitati di agitazione*) in the factories of the North. They went out on strike despite threats of deportation to Germany or execution. The strikes were both economic and political (antifascist and antiwar) in nature and included a massive general strike in March 1944—the only such action in all of occupied Europe.

The vast majority of activist leaders in the factories belonged to the Italian Communist Party (PCI). In Turin, for example, the composition of the agitation committees in the fall of 1944 was 241 Communists, 14 Socialists, five Christian Democrats, two independents, and one anarcholibertarian.[1] The PCI also played a major role in the CLN. For many workers, the antifascist Resistance was but the initial stage of a larger revolutionary process that would bring socialism to Italy after the war. In general, the Resistance interwove two different and sometimes conflicting orientations. One was a cross-class, antifascist impetus that included even some members of the bourgeoisie. The other was a militant working-class perspective whose demands were in conflict with the basic choices of the capitalist ruling class.

In March 1944, Palmiro Togliatti, head of the Communist Party, returned from exile in the Soviet Union. He soon announced that there would be no socialist revolution in Italy at the close of the war. The objective conditions for a revolution did not exist. Both Britain and the United States saw the left in Italy as a serious menace. They were determined that the country be made safe from Soviet influence and be integrated economically and politically into the capitalist bloc after the war. They were prepared to use their overwhelming military strength to obtain this objective. Meanwhile Allied troops were making their way up the peninsula, occupying the liberated zones. In addition, the armed Resistance movement was limited to the northern half of Italy, and even there, only part of the population wanted to make a revolution. Finally, the Soviet Union had no intention of battling the United States and Britain over Italy and did not support an attempt at insurrection. But given the international disposition of forces at the end of the war, the alternative to revolution was Italy's inclusion in the Western bloc under the economic and military hegemony of the United States. The Bretton Woods accord on international monetary policy in 1944, the establishment of such institutions as the World Bank and the International Monetary Fund, and the activity of the Marshall Plan initiated in 1947 secured U.S. dominance in Western Europe.

With revolution off the agenda, Togliatti elaborated a substitute strategy for the PCI in the postwar period. The party was not to be a small group of professional revolutionaries and highly trained cadres. Instead it was to become a mass party, organizing and recruiting in the working class while reaching out to peasants and middle class strata as well. The PCI counted some 1.7 million members soon after liberation. By 1947, the number had grown to more than 2.2 million.[2] The Communists planned to help build a "progressive democracy" in Italy. Through structural reforms, they would ensure the full participation of the working class in governing the country. Over time, this could open the way for a gradual and democratic transition to socialism.

The strategy came to be called "the Italian road to socialism" (la via Italiana al socialismo). Central to the entire conception was a policy of alliances. In theory, the PCI would forge social and political alliances at the grass-roots level with various class strata, organizations, and movements. In specific terms for the immediate postwar period, the Communists would participate in a national unity government of antifascist parties and would collaborate with those political groups in the reconstruction of the economy, the development of a democratic political system, and the renewal of social structures. The Communists put particular emphasis on cooperation with the Christian Democratic Party (DC) and other Catholic forces.

During the first two years after the war, the fear of political isolation shaped many of the PCI's decisions. The leadership's overriding concern was to remain in the coalition government. Cooperation and compromise characterized the party's policies. Even working-class sacrifices in the short term were not considered an excessive price to pay for continued political participation. The PCI also wanted to keep up close ties with the Soviet Union and the international communist movement although these relations soon began to aggravate tensions with other political forces.

In terms of economic programs, the PCI called for active government intervention and general reforms such as collaborative economic planning, nationalization of the large monopolies, and land redistribution. But the party made these proposals in the context of support for medium-sized and small private enterprises. The PCI suggested no general program to transform property relations in Italy. In the name of national reconstruction, the party also pushed for raising productivity in industry and agriculture by curtailing labor's demands and by imposing discipline in the workplace.

The economic and political policies of the Communist Party had a tremendous impact on labor relations in the early postwar years. The PCI enjoyed more support within the working class than any other party and exercised a strong influence over the labor movement. In addition, the Socialists—the other major left formation in Italy—were committed to cooperating with the Communists and ended up playing a subordinate role to them. The two parties renewed their unity of action pact in 1943 and again in 1946. Although many Socialists were wary of the Communists' close ties to the Soviet Union, most were still willing to collaborate until the mid-1950s.

The Catholic forces in Italy came out of the Fascist and war periods as a well-organized subculture which provided a mass base for the Christian Democratic Party. The DC quickly developed into a complex forma-

tion bringing together peasants, rural and urban middle strata, traditional petty bourgeoisie, white-collar workers, and segments of the ruling
class. Early on, the party expressed a populist orientation, but it increasingly came to represent the interests of capital in the postwar national
government. Initial support for extensive state economic intervention,
for example, gave way to acceptance of the private sector's priorities and
its demand for a free hand. From the point of view of the United States
government, the DC provided the best vehicle for U.S. interests since it
was mass-based, linked to the powerful Church, and anticommunist.
The ideology of anticommunism rapidly acquired a crucial function in
Italy.

Political party activity embraced much more than electoral campaigns and government administration. The parties zealously recruited
interest groups and organized constituencies by setting up collateral
structures. These included labor unions, cooperatives, newspapers, publishing houses, sports facilities, and organizations for young people,
women, and professionals. The result was a generally strong party presence in society. But among the diverse activities and perspectives two sub-
cultures dominated—the Catholic and the Communist. They remained
separate, competing, and largely antagonistic despite the PCI's hope of
constructing alliances with Catholic forces at the grass-roots level. This
division of a society into two major camps is one key to understanding
the political and social history of postwar Italy.

An Economy in Disarray

Of all the tasks facing the political forces at the end of the war, none
was more pressing than the reconstruction of the economy. The Fascist
era had passed on a stagnating and underdeveloped system that was
largely agrarian. Some 48.2 percent of the labor force worked in agriculture in 1941 as compared to 28.1 percent in industry. (In France in 1941,
the figures were 24.7 percent in agriculture and 36.1 percent in industry.)[3]
Industrial development was both partial and regionally unbalanced. The
level of technology was fairly low, and industries accustomed to the protectionist policies of the Fascist state had grown sluggish. In addition, the
South, Sicily, Sardinia, and the Northeast were much poorer and less
developed than northwest and central Italy. Political repression of the
working class had kept wages down. Taking 1913 wages as a base of 100,
real wages in 1942 were just 99.1.[4] Other legacies of the Fascist years were
a number of state-controlled industries and high structural unemployment.

The war—Allied bombings and the struggle between German and
Allied troops—destroyed about one-third of Italy's national wealth and

economic infrastructure. Compared to the destruction in other European countries, the peninsula was in an intermediate position. When the fighting finally ended, there were shortages of food, fuel, raw materials, and equipment. Industrial production plummeted to one-quarter of the prewar level, and inflation soared wildly. Taking 1913 prices as 100, the cost of living was 10,398 in 1945 and 19,888 in 1947.[5] Immediately after the war, job dismissals were prohibited. But once the ban was lifted, unemployment mounted. By 1948, between 1.5 and 2.5 million Italians were jobless in a labor force of slightly less than 20 million. In addition, an even greater number were underemployed.[6]

The early postwar debate on how to deal with the economy centered around the question of control. The left parties and the left wing of the labor movement wanted some form of democratic participation. Given the circumstances at liberation, it seemed that both popular pressure and the impetus of the antifascist struggle would have been sufficient to win reforms in favor of the industrial and agricultural working classes—land redistribution, some public control over production for national needs, some worker participation in plant management, and a more decentralized and democratic public administration. The partisans had great support among the people; the workers had control of the factories; and the left parties were in a strong position in the Committee of National Liberation. But within just two years, the business elites and officials of the old state bureaucracy had regained the upper hand. They succeeded in imposing their version of reconstruction on the country.

Several factors determined this outcome. The ruling class in Italy, although divided on many questions, was adamant about maintaining control over the economy and had the weight of the Church and the Christian Democrats on its side. Representatives of the United States government intervened actively in the debate in support of the business elites and the more conservative political forces, and Washington kept U.S. troops on Italian soil until December 1947. The United States also controlled the supply of desperately needed raw materials, equipment, and credit. Furthermore, the left parties and the trade-union leadership held to their policies of conciliation and compromise.

The position prescribed by Italy's ruling class was quite clear. The private sector was to have full authority over economic reconstruction. The state would play a subordinate role, removing unwanted obstacles and providing requested support for the leading industrial sectors. The ruling class rejected most reforms which it saw as threats to its own initiative and privilege. With regard to the workers, employers demanded immediate labor peace, a strict nationwide policy on salary structure that would curb demands, increased productivity, and the right to dismiss excess workers. The goal of the most dynamic industrial sectors (steel, chemical, machinery, and automobile) was to launch Italian products on the international market. To do this, industry had to modernize, develop export goods, and have Italy's trade barriers abolished. The policies of Italy's industrialists and financiers conformed to the U.S. government's program for Europe. The United States wanted the countries in its sphere of influence to get inflation under control, keep their balance of payments in equilibrium, and open their borders to trade and investment.

The Rebirth of the Labor Movement

While German troops patrolled the streets of Rome in late 1943 and early 1944, representatives of the Communist, Socialist, and Christian Democratic parties met clandestinely and planned the refounding of a free labor movement for after the war. Just before the Allies liberated the capital in June 1944, the three parties signed the Pact of Rome establishing the Italian General Confederation of Labor (CGIL) and the principles for a nationwide, nonpartisan trade-union structure. The CGIL was to represent workers in every sector of the economy—agriculture, industry, and services. In addition to the national "umbrella" confederation, there would be category unions for major groups (metal and mechanical workers, chemical workers, teachers, and so on) at the national, provincial, and local levels. (The national-level category unions were called federations.) There would also be intercategory bodies at the provincial level bringing together the various categories of workers. The Pact of Rome made no special provision for union structures inside the workplace.

The agreement attempted to insure internal democracy by providing for the election of officials, minority representation, and freedom of expression for all political tendencies and religions. In theory, the CGIL was to be independent of the political parties, although the pact clearly stated that the trade unions would not be apolitical. They would take positions on issues concerning the working class and would ally with political forces that could further the interests of labor and safeguard "popular liberties." The signers of the Pact of Rome were well aware of their significant ideological differences, but they hoped to preserve unity by clearly establishing the trade unions as politically autonomous. To insure freedom of expression and to maintain unity, the pact stipulated that the three major political groups would have equal representation on the executive body of every labor organization.

Fragile though it was, the unity of the newly formed CGIL was not a mere façade. Rather it reflected the same antifascist impetus that brought together the various political parties in the Committee for National Liberation and in the postwar national unity government. According to the Communists and Socialists, only the solidarity of the masses could safeguard Italy from a resurgence of fascism and insure the development of democracy. For the Christian Democrats, an alliance with the left provided the advantage of a base within the working class and the possibility of a less contentious reconstruction period. The CGIL also expressed the unitary nature of the struggles in the northern factories before liberation. In the early postwar years, the trade-union confederation focused as much on the national objectives of the Resistance as on specific demands for the working class.

In January 1945, the first CGIL congress for the liberated zones of Italy took place in Naples. The platform adopted called for a role for the CGIL in postwar economic planning, nationalization of the monopolies, land reform, higher wages, and a cost-of-living salary adjustment to compensate for inflation. The congress demonstrated that the Communists were going to be the dominant force within the labor movement. They had the support of over 40 percent of the meeting's delegates. The Communists were led by the popular Giuseppe Di Vittorio who remained the PCI's principal trade-union leader until 1957. By the time of the first postwar national congress in 1947, the CGIL counted about 5.7 million members of a labor force of slightly less than 20 million. The Communists could claim 57.8 percent of the delegate votes at the congress; the Socialists 22.6 percent; the Christian Democrats 13.4 percent; the Liberals (a conservative lay party) 2.2 percent; and the Republicans (another conservative lay party) 2 percent.[7] Yet despite the powerful presence of the Communists, trade-union unity still made sense for the smaller factions as long as unity also prevailed in the larger political context of the postwar government.

While labor unity had a temporary grounding in the political realities of Italy, the CGIL's claim to political autonomy was illusory. The leadership of the three major parties set up the CGIL as an extension of their activities within the working class and within the domain of labor relations. They organized the confederation from the top down. Each party feared the political manipulation of its opponents within the CGIL, but no party was willing to break its ties and help develop the labor confederation's autonomy. The executive leaders of the unions came directly out of the party hierarchies. In fact, unionists were really party leaders and party activists doing union duty. Many held high positions in both organizations, and some were also members of Parliament. For the remainder of the 1940s and well into the 1950s, labor leaders echoed and carried out the policies of their respective parties. The party–union relationship was known as the "transmission belt." Since the unions were subordinate to the parties, it was really the latter that organized and mobilized the working class during the early postwar period. Thus the unions exhibited a strong political character, but their politics were not autonomous. When the parties first accepted the imperatives of the private sector for reconstruction, the labor movement had no cohesive, alternative policy of its own to use in a counteroffensive. The unions could not or would not rally the working class as a whole against the government.

Between 1945 and 1948, the political differences within the CGIL grew into major disputes and irreconcilable divisions. The issues of greatest contention were political unionism, the program for economic reconstruction, and party ties. The more conservative factions—Christian Democrats, Republicans, and Liberals—opposed political strikes and labor involvement in struggles that went beyond traditional trade-union concerns. They were willing to support ruling-class positions on reconstruction and on concessions from labor. These groups accused the Communists and Socialists in the CGIL of creating dissension and turmoil by allowing a subversive PCI to dictate union policies.

From the start, the Church and the Christian Democrats had their doubts about the viability—and advisability—of a unitary labor movement. As early as 1944, Catholic Action with the approval of Pope Pius XII organized the Christian Associations of Italian Workers (ACLI), a collateral organization which brought together Catholic workers and their families for entertainment, sports, education, and religious events. That same year, the Christian Democrats set up a national confederation of small farmers called Coldiretti which claimed over 3.5 million members (representing over 8 million persons) by the early 1960s.[8] Coldiretti regularly pulled in a massive rural vote for the DC. The ACLI provided the Christian Democrats with their own labor network. Both the Coldiretti and the ACLI helped build an autonomous mass base for the DC. Thus if unity with the left became too troublesome, the Christian Democrats were prepared to go it alone.

Labor Relations 1945 to 1948

Unlike collective bargaining in the United States, which takes place at the plant or company level (and sometimes at the level of multiemployer bargaining units within an industry), the system of bargaining in Italy after the war was extremely centralized. Just one key accord at the national level covered all industrial workers, union members and nonmembers alike. The CGIL negotiated this accord with Confindustria, the national confederation of industrial employers. This so-called interconfederal contract was not a pattern accord or general framework for more specific sector or company contracts. It was a detailed document that covered all aspects of labor relations from wages and dismissal procedures down to vacation schedules and holiday bonuses. On questions of salary, in fact, most members of Confindustria vehemently refused to negotiate other agreements. The centralization of collective bargaining worked to the advantage of the employers by constricting labor's ability to maneuver at the grass-roots level and in the individual workplace. For years, the limitation on salary negotiations also undermined the strength and relevance of the fledgling national category federations.

This form of collective bargaining was not new in Italy. Centralization was another legacy both of the first decades of the twentieth century and of the Fascist system. In the early years after the Second World War, many party and union leaders believed that the centralized system corresponded to the need for a national perspective on reconstruction. Italy's most pressing problems, they maintained, were national in scope. They also argued that in an overall situation of misery and economic dislocation, it was best to protect the weakest segments of the working class and to insure minimally acceptable circumstances for everyone.

On a series of issues negotiated with Confindustria in late 1945 and 1946, the labor confederation demonstrated its willingness to accommodate business interests. The single salary structure agreed upon by labor included rigid wage differentials by region, industrial sector, skill, sex, and age. This meant that a worker in the South doing exactly the same job as someone in the North earned less according to an established scale. These scales were called *gabbie salariali* or salary cages. The payscales for women and young people were set at a lower level than those for adult males despite the constitutional guarantee of equal pay for equal work. The CGIL also signed six-month salary truces in October 1946 and May 1947. In compensation for stabilized salaries, the employers agreed to a national wage indexing system called the *scala mobile*. It offered limited protection from inflation by adjusting wages as the cost of living rose. At the end of the war, the workers abolished the hated piecework system which many considered to be superexploitative. The following year, however, the employers' associations argued for reinstating piecework as a way for employees to improve upon their low base wages. The economic situation was so dismal that the CGIL agreed to the restoration.

With the collapse of production after the war, dismissals were blocked in order to prevent mass expulsions from the workplace. Then in January 1946, the CGIL agreed to revoke the ban completely over time. The full effect of this was felt after the summer of 1947 when budget minister Luigi Einaudi imposed restrictive policies including a drastic squeeze on credit and devaluation of the lira. The measures quickly resulted in a drop in investment and consumption. Workers were dismissed.

Einaudi's policies proved to be central in shaping the country's reconstruction. Using the power of the Bank of Italy, he made credit available on a selective basis, favoring industries with competitive potential and letting the others go under. Einaudi's longer-range goals were the restructuring and modernization of Italy's productive base, increased productivity, and the growth of internationally competitive industries. The expansion of internal demand was not a priority. For the working class, the by-product of these policies was a debilitating level of unemployment which did not begin to drop until the latter part of the 1950s. Unemployment was a key factor in the labor movement's weakness.

Inside the factories, the workers quickly lost the autonomy and leverage they held at the moment of liberation. At that time, most of the owners and managers abandoned the workplaces. They feared a general upheaval or reprisals for collaboration with the Fascists and Nazis. The workers took responsibility for keeping order and for starting the process of reorganizing production. Despite the position of power of workers in many northern plants, the left and CGIL leadership had no intention of pressing for permanent worker control. (Nor did the Allied Military Government intend to let this happen.) Just as the left leaders were committed to a policy of collaboration in the government, they envisioned a system of management–labor collaboration or codetermination in the workplace. Thus they had two goals: to help shape basic economic choices in the interests of the working class and to set up stable mechanisms for employee participation in workplace management. At the end of the war, the Committee of National Liberation called for the establishment in all factories of joint-management councils (*consigli di gestione*) to be made up of owners, supervisors, technicians, and workers. The purpose of these councils was to solve technical problems and to devise methods to stimulate and rationalize production. By late 1947, there were 500 joint-management councils in Italy, about 300 of them in the northern region of Lombardy and most of them in large plants.[9]

Italian industrialists, however, had no intention of collaborating with their workers to shape production. Led by Confindustria, they carried on a vociferous public campaign against the joint-management councils. They had the support of the conservative parties in Parliament, so the government never granted official recognition to the councils. Meanwhile, in the hope of reviving economic activity, the antifascist forces had invited the owners and former managers back into the factories where they soon refused to cooperate with labor. In the course of a few years, the joint-management councils lost whatever function they once fulfilled, and by the early 1950s, they had for the most part disappeared.

In exchange for participation in national economic policy making, the left and labor leadership was willing to restrain the rank and file. The Communists and Socialists were also concerned to keep the CGIL in one piece and to preserve the unity of the national government. Thus in spite of agonizing inflation, unemployment, and poverty, the CGIL and the political parties discouraged strikes and other forms of protest in the first years after the war. In June 1947, PCI Secretary Togliatti claimed before the Constituent Assembly that the workers "have moderated their movement, they have restrained it, they have contained it within the limits in which it was necessary to contain it in order not to disturb the work of reconstruction."[10] At the grass-roots level, however, the workers did not always abide by the national confederation policy of restraint. Their struggles were particularly intense during the summers of 1945 and 1946. At times, local unions supported or even led strikes. This aggravated tensions between the leadership of the CGIL and the base of the unions and between factions of the CGIL hierarchy. The conservative parties accused the left of instigating labor conflict and jeopardizing economic recovery.

The lack of effective union structures inside the workplaces became an ever greater liability for the Italian working class. Aside from the joint-management councils, the only representation for labor in the plants was on the internal commissions (*commissioni interne*). Internal commissions had existed before the Fascist period and were revived in 1943 after Mussolini was deposed. After the war, they mediated between the work force and management on a routine basis; they dealt with grievances over schedules, promotions, and incentive pay; they also implemented the national contract. The commissions were not, strictly speaking, union structures since all workers—union members and non-members—voted for representatives and could run for election. As management regained control in the shops, the duties and effectiveness of the commissions declined. The employers denied formal contractual power to the commissions, and only on occasion did a plant's management agree to negotiate a contract with these bodies. The commissions were badly divided because each political group presented its own candidates for commission elections. The posts were filled according to a system of proportional representation. Given the weak position of the commissions, the workers could not rely on them for adequate protection.

U.S. Policy and the Splintering of the Labor Movement

The labor movement in Italy was edging toward a major defeat. One source of the problem lay in the tactical choices of the CGIL leadership and the left parties as they responded to attacks by conservative forces. But the goals and policy decisions of the United States government also determined the outcome of the uncertain situation during the first three years after the war. In addition to setting up an expanded system of world trade favorable to U.S. interests and brandishing economic aid as an instrument of persuasion in foreign policy, the U.S. government intervened directly in Italian domestic affairs. The objectives were to isolate the left, to secure a friendly and like-minded regime in Rome, and to demobilize the labor movement. Washington saw the situation in Italy as a microcosm of the developing East-West confrontation. The left, under the leadership of the Communists, had to be defeated.

For the U.S. government, the first positive sign of "normalization" came in December 1945 when a Christian Democrat, Alcide De Gasperi, took over the post of prime minister from Ferruccio Parri, a partisan leader. De Gasperi dissolved the High Commission for Sanctions Against Fascism in early 1946 and turned its functions over to the courts. Most of the judges presiding over the courts, however, were those who had served under the Fascist regime. As a result, there was no thorough investigation of collaborators, and substantial parts of the old order were restored. Many business leaders, civilian and military bureaucrats, academics, and journalists who had made their careers under fascism simply reassumed or held on to their positions.

In the June 1946 elections, the population chose a republican form of government over the monarchy by a small margin. The simultaneous voting for the Constituent Assembly to draft the new constitution yielded these results:

Party	Percentage of popular vote
Christian Democrat	35.2
Socialist	20.7
Communist	19.0
Liberal	6.8
Any Man (a rightist grouping)	5.3
Republican	4.4
Monarchist	2.8
Others (including regional parties)	5.8

In the first part of 1947, right-wing Socialists who opposed the unity of action pact with the PCI broke away from their party. With the help of secret financing from the U.S. government, they founded a new anticommunist organization which later took the name Italian Social Democratic Party (PSDI). (The Socialists allied with the PCI took the name Italian Socialist Party—PSI.) In January 1947, Prime Minister De Gasperi made his well-known trip to Washington where officials of the Truman administration guaranteed generous aid if the Communists and Socialists were expelled from the Italian government. De Gasperi went home with an initial loan of $100 million and the promise of ships, coal, and grain. In May 1947, he formed a new government excluding the two major left parties. The more conservative groups—Social Democrats, Liberals (PLI), and Republicans (PRI)—remained in the coalition.

The contest that sealed the political fate of Italy's government was the parliamentary election held in April 1948. Washington wanted to see the Christian Democrats secure ongoing control without any threat from the left. No effort was spared to influence the outcome of the election. The United States undertook a massive propaganda campaign to link economic aid to an anticommunist vote in the minds of the electorate. According to the *Boston Herald* of April 8, 1948, the U.S. government would end up spending $20 million on this task.[11] With the help of the conservative political forces in Italy, the campaign included "Voice of America" broadcasts, signs on Italian trains that read "This train runs thanks to American coal," postage stamps printed with the slogan "American aid—Bread and Work," aircraft showering leaflets and food, films, and photo displays. The Vatican and the local churches were also active in the antileft campaign. A month before the election, the U.S. State Department announced that Italians who joined the Communist Party would never be permitted to emigrate to the United States and that all economic aid would be cut off if the left won. U.S. troops remained on Italian soil until the last day allowed by the peace treaty, and there were public pronouncements about the willingness of the United States to demonstrate its "resolve and military strength" in the event of a left victory. The Communist takeover in Czechoslovakia in February 1948 intensified fears on both sides of the Atlantic.

In the spring, CGIL officials met with U.S. unionists from the CIO and asked them to support aid for Italy no matter what the outcome of the elections. The CIO representatives refused and allied themselves with State Department policy. The issue of aid from the United States created serious difficulties for the Italian left. It was no secret that economic assistance came with many strings attached. But Italy desperately needed aid, and what the United States was offering looked attractive to many Italians.

External pressure combined with internal economic and political factors yielded excellent results for the Christian Democrats on April 18. They took 48.5 percent of the vote and 305 of 574 seats in the Chamber of Deputies. The other members of the so-called centrist coalition attracted just a small part of the electorate: 2.5 percent for the Republicans, 3.8 percent for the Liberals, and 7.1 percent for the Social Democrats. The Communists and Socialists in an electoral alliance polled only 31 percent. They were effectively cut off from national power until the mid-1960s.

With the government secure, the conservative forces in concert with U.S. policy had just one more task: to split the CGIL. They hoped to ostracize the left, drawing away as many members as possible. U.S. unionists and government officials pressured the minority factions of the CGIL not to delay the rupture. They also promised financing for a new labor confederation. Before long, an opportunity presented itself. On the occasion of a strike in July 1948 to protest the attempted assassination of PCI Secretary Togliatti, the Christian Democratic faction broke away from the CGIL. In May 1949, the Social Democrats and Republicans split off. This left the Communists, Socialists, and their supporters in the original organization.

After a year of quarrelsome negotiations and various recombinations of forces, a group of Social Democrats, Republicans, and autonomous socialists founded the Italian Union of Labor (UIL) in March 1950. That same month, some unaffiliated unions, veterans' groups, and workers' organizations with monarchist leanings formed the Italian Confederation of National Workers Unions (CISNAL) which came to be known as the neofascist union. Although it tried to deny this characterization, the CISNAL espoused the fascist corporative model and had links to the neofascist party. In April 1950, the Christian Democrats along with a much smaller number of Social Democrats and Republicans organized the Italian Confederation of Workers Unions (CISL). The DC's prominent trade-union leader, Giulio Pastore, became secretary-general. In addition to the proliferation of confederations, autonomous unions began to appear in various sectors, especially among public employees and teachers.

The events of 1948 completed the isolation of the left and ended the politics of compromise and cooperation. In order to rally the support of their bases and clarify their opposition to the centrist government, the PCI and PSI emphasized protest tactics. The CGIL led strikes and rallies in 1949 and 1950 against job dismissals, inflation, the government's economic measures, and Italy's cooperation with U.S. foreign and military policies. The struggles were militant, but given the CGIL's weakened position, they were without significant concrete results. During this time, the CGIL won the allegiance of many peasants, sharecroppers, and agricultural day laborers through committed support of their struggles for land.

Contrary to the hopes of the Italian ruling class and its U.S. allies, the splintering of the labor movement provoked no mass exodus from the CGIL. Each departing faction took its own cadres, but the vast majority of members remained in the original confederation. This was only a small consolation to the left. The rupture still disabled the labor movement as a whole, and it was the workers who suffered the consequences during the years of repression that followed.

The Question of Women: Emancipation and Protection

During the reconstruction period, women grappled with the inequities and limitations of their circumstances. Like much of the working class, they had celebrated liberation as an opportunity to improve the quality of their lives at work and at home. Many women hoped to achieve, for the first time, equal status in the new postwar society. But a long history of oppression was not easily overcome, and even the debate over the nature of that oppression was not fully developed for many years.

The evolution of Italy's economy during the first half of the twentieth century had not created new space for women in the labor force. In fact, the long-term trend was moving in the opposite direction. The employment profile of women looked worse at midcentury than it had 50 years earlier. In 1901, the female share of the total population was 50.2 percent, and women made up 32.4 percent of the active population (everyone employed or looking for work). In 1951, 51.3 percent of the total population was female, and women accounted for just 24.9 percent of the active population.[12] The labor force participation rate for women also continued to drop (Table 1.1). Although these figures do not reflect the significant number of women doing illegal and highly exploitative work in the underground economy, they do demonstrate how the proportion of women in the regular labor market was steadily diminishing.

There were a variety of reasons—economic, ideological, and cultural—why women found it difficult to enter and to remain in the labor market. Some of the sectors where they were traditionally employed had shrinking work forces. Agriculture was an important example of this. Industry did not absorb large numbers of new workers until the late 1950s. When companies did hire, they preferred men, and there was an ample pool of unemployed males willing to work for low wages. In addition, the chronic lack of social services, especially day care, made it difficult for

TABLE 1.1.: Labor Force Participation Rate for Italian Women

1901	1951	1961	1971
52.3[a]	30.6[a]	26.5[b]	21.7[b]

[a]Women working or looking for jobs as a percentage of the female population between 15 and 64 years of age. *Source:* George H. Hildebrand, *Growth and Structure in the Economy of Modern Italy* (Cambridge: Harvard University Press, 1965), p. 136.

[b]Women working or looking for jobs as a percentage of female population. *Source:* Donald C. Templeman, *The Italian Economy* (New York: Praeger, 1981), p. 338.

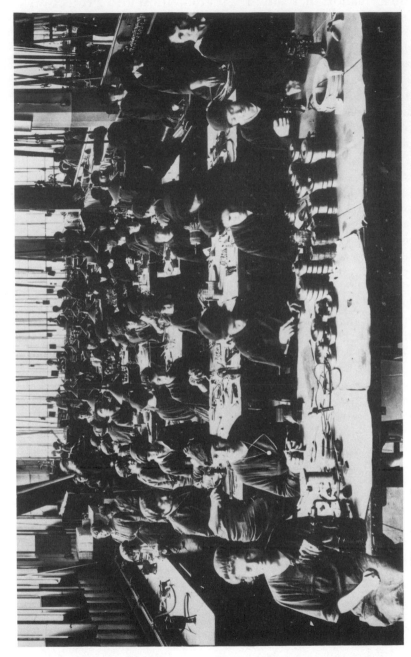

The electrical instrument department at Fiat's plant on Dante Boulevard, Turin, 1917.

women with young children to hold down jobs. Beyond economic factors, there was the deep-rooted conviction that a woman's primary place was in the home, as wife and mother. These female roles were to be preserved and protected by society even when a woman defined her needs differently. As a result, employers were able to make a regular practice of firing women when they married or became pregnant. Legislation held over from the Fascist period prohibited women from doing night work or taking specific jobs that were considered physically or morally perilous.

The difficulties did not cease when a woman managed to find and keep a job. She faced serious economic discrimination which was built into the legal wage structure. For comparable work, women received a lower base rate of pay than men; many bonuses and added allowances were also set at a lower rate for women; cost-of-living adjustments were smaller; and women had to retire at an earlier age with smaller pensions. With less training and fewer skills, they had jobs at the lower end of the pay scale, and many had no choice but to take positions that were precarious or temporary. They also worked as domestic servants or did home labor, both of which paid low wages. In the immediate postwar years, the CGIL agreed to the wage structure which discriminated against women. At the same time, the labor organization adopted a general policy of protecting the worst-paid workers. Although this policy ended up diminishing wage differentials between the sexes somewhat, the gap remained quite wide into the 1970s.

Even before the Second World War ended, women in Italy began to build a movement for emancipation. Their goals were to eliminate discriminatory practices and to help women achieve full status in society. Most of these women were active in the Resistance. They believed they had a role to play in shaping postwar Italy as well as in defeating the Fascists and Nazis. They wanted access to all jobs, equal pay, and the vote. In 1944, they began setting up an organization, the Union of Italian Women (UDI), that was open to all antifascist women—independents and party members. By 1949, UDI had one million members.[13] But the ideological antagonism that divided parties and labor unions also divided women. Those who joined UDI were leftists—Socialists and, in greater numbers, Communists. Catholic women joined the organizations set up by the Church and the Christian Democratic Party. These groups attracted equally impressive numbers through the 1950s. (The female branches of Catholic Action counted almost 1.9 million members in 1963 but then rapidly shrank in size.)[14]

The divisions that marked every aspect of political life in Italy after the war undermined the struggle for women's equality. On the one hand, there was strong sentiment in favor of equal rights legislation and special concern for women as workers; on the other hand, there was the commitment to preserve the existing status of women and to promote their roles as wives and mothers. Nowhere is the tension between these two orientations more clearly and succinctly presented than in the first part of Article 37 of the Italian Constitution. It reads:

> The working woman has the same rights and, for equal labor, the same remuneration which are due to the working man. The conditions of labor must permit the fulfillment of her essential family function and assure to mother and child a special adequate protection.*

It was certainly possible (and desirable from the point of view of many women) to insure equality in wages and in access to jobs and at the same time to provide support such as maternity leaves and day care. Yet Article 37 raised several problems. Despite the declaration of equality, a woman's place at home took priority; it was where her "essential" functions were carried out. But Italian women did not have equal status within the family. Legally (in terms of property rights and authority in familial relationships) and culturally, men had far more power. To reaffirm women's existing role in the family was to reassert their inferior status. There was also tension between the commitment to full equality and the commitment to special treatment and protections for women. By establishing limits on when, where, and how women could work, there was the risk that they would always be separated from the male labor force and isolated in female job ghettos. This situation would make it much easier to maintain rigid divisions of labor and to limit women's access to traditionally male jobs. Special protection for women could also imply that men were to accept the status quo. For example, if the law barred just women from dangerous jobs and unhealthy conditions, it followed that such jobs and conditions were permissible for men. If only women could take leaves of absence to care for infants, the traditional and secondary role of men in parenting was reconfirmed.

The tensions and ambiguities implicit in Article 37 of the Constitution reflected in part the division between conservatives and leftists. Yet the left forces themselves—PCI, PSI, UDI, and CGIL—held ambiguous and contradictory positions. PCI Secretary Togliatti maintained that the inferior status of women was due to the uneven development and backward nature of both Italian capitalism and social relations. These made the Italian family particularly oppressive for women. Emancipation, he argued, had to be the concern of all women. It was not an issue limited to one class or one party. At the same time, the PCI defended the family and

---

*Author's translation.

emphasized women's special roles as wife and mother. The Church and the Christian Democratic Party accused the PCI of wanting to destroy the family in favor of free love and libertarian life styles. But when the Communists insisted on their support for the family and motherhood, it was not simply a reaction to the assault from the right. There was a strain of social conservatism and puritanism in the PCI and in the Italian workers' movement.[15] The perception of women was traditional in many ways, and among male party members and male workers, there was hostility to the idea of women's emancipation.

As organizations, of course, the PCI and CGIL officially supported emancipation and equal rights legislation as well as protective measures. The position of the Socialist Party was essentially the same. Women were expected to join the major campaigns of the left and the CGIL which included the struggles for peace, jobs, land reform, and a ban on atomic weapons. There was greater emphasis on women adopting these general themes than on the development of an analysis, full program, and campaigns that dealt specifically with the condition of women in Italy. Like the CGIL, UDI came under the dominant influence of the Communist Party. The women's organization received funding from the PCI, and UDI's line echoed that of the party. Despite some effort to assert a more independent position in the 1950s, UDI did not begin to develop significant autonomy until the 1970s.

With the left and labor on the defensive, with Christian Democrats in control of the political arena, and with business leaders opposed to economic concessions, there was little hope of rapid progress for women. But even in this adverse context, several important gains were made. In 1946, women voted in elections for the first time. In 1950, Parliament passed a strong maternity protection law which improved upon an existing law. The new measure mandated longer compulsory leaves for women before and after birth with a substantial portion of wages paid. Employers had to provide work breaks for nursing mothers and nursery space for one year after birth. In addition, employers could not fire pregnant women or women with children under one year of age. After this law was passed, the left forces pressed for a labor agreement on equal pay. For ten years, they had no success. Then in 1960, the confederations signed the first pact abolishing separate wage scales for women. Over the next few years, the principle of equal pay for equal work was applied to women in nonindustrial as well as industrial workplaces. Although these agreements went some way toward equalizing wages for men and women, large discrepancies in pay persisted. Women were still caught in the lowest-level jobs, and the various bonuses and salary adjustments beyond the base wage still favored men. Finally, in 1963, Parliament passed a law prohibiting employers from firing women for one year after they married.

Each of these significant measures was a victory that improved conditions for women or diminished the level of inequality in a tangible way. But their sum total was still small. Even a decade and a half after liberation, the basic situation of women in Italy had not changed a great deal. Furthermore, the analysis of women's oppression was quite primitive. Neither UDI, nor the labor unions, nor the left parties seized upon some of the most fundamental and controversial issues such as patriarchy and the sources of women's oppression independent of the capitalist system, a critique of the family, the links between family and Church, female sexuality, birth control, abortion, divorce, and necessary changes in women's consciousness. It was not until the development of an autonomous feminist movement in the 1970s that these themes generated new analyses and action.

Notes to Chapter 1

1. Raimondo Luraghi, *Il movimento operaio torinese durante la Resistenza* (Turin: Einaudi, 1958), p. 218.

2. Marzio Barbagli and Piergiorgio Corbetta, "Partito e movimento: Aspetti e rinnovamento del PCI," *Inchiesta* 8, no. 31 (January–February, 1978): 11.

3. Maurice F. Neufeld, *Italy: School for Awakening Countries* (1961; reprint, Westport, Conn.: Greenwood Press, 1974), p. 527.

4. Ibid., p. 540.

5. Ibid.

6. Francesco Silva, "I fattori dello sviluppo: il 'miracolo' economico italiano," in *Problemi del movimento sindacale in Italia 1943–1973*, Annali, no. 16, ed. Aris Accornero (Milan: Feltrinelli, 1976), p. 450. The lack of reliable statistics or a commonly accepted definition of unemployment during the early postwar period makes estimates of total unemployment approximate.

7. Daniel L. Horowitz, *The Italian Labor Movement* (Cambridge: Harvard University Press, 1963), pp. 208–9.

8. P. A. Allum, *Italy—Republic Without Government?* (New York and London: W. W. Norton, 1973), pp. 97–98.

9. Liliana Lanzardo, "I consigli di gestione nella strategia della collaborazione," in Accornero, *Problemi del movimento*, p. 345.

10. Author's translation. Palmiro Togliatti, *Discorsi alla Costituente*, 2d ed. (Rome: Riuniti, 1974), p. 194.

11. Roberto Faenza and Marco Fini, *Gli americani in Italia* (Milan: Feltrinelli, 1976), p. 283.

12. George H. Hildebrand, *Growth and Structure in the Economy of Modern Italy* (Cambridge: Harvard University Press, 1965), p. 136.

13. Giulietta Ascoli, "L'UDI tra emancipazione e liberazione (1943–1964)," *Problemi del socialismo* 17, no. 4 (October–December 1976):123.

14. Yasmine Ergas, "1968–79—Feminism and the Italian Party System: Women's Politics in a Decade of Turmoil," *Comparative Politics* 14, no. 3 (April 1982):257–58.

15. Ascoli, "L'UDI," p. 130.

2

Economic Boom and Labor Defeat

The decade that followed the shattering of the unitary labor confederation was a grim period for the workers' movement in Italy. It was a time of divisions and defeats, errors and repression, which later came to be called the *anni duri*—the hard years. On one level, the statistics for economic expansion and profits looked better and better. But overall, the pattern of development aggravated the imbalances of the economy and deepened the inequalities between social classes and geographic regions. The working class bore most of the burden of reconstruction, and the price paid was high in human as well as economic terms.

The Economic Successes and Failures of Reconstruction

The context of Italy's economic reconstruction was expanded world trade. Success depended upon abandoning the kind of protectionist policies that characterized the Fascist era and integrating the economy into the international market system. Therefore, despite the opposition of less forward-looking members of the bourgeoisie, the government passed measures in 1951 to diminish import barriers and to facilitate Italy's participation in world trade.

In the economy as a whole, both private sector and government policies boosted the development of industry, especially large scale industry in the North, at the expense of agriculture, the South, and small businesses. Within industry, however, certain manufacturing sectors benefited much more than others. The division became sharper between highly productive industries able to compete internationally and stagnating, antiquated, and inefficient industries. The principal growth sectors during the 1950s were those producing (or contributing to the production of) durable consumer goods and luxury goods for export: automobiles, motor cycles, office equipment, home appliances, steel, rubber, artificial fibers, and petrochemical products. The traditional and nondynamic industries produced goods such as food and textiles. In general, the state gave the private sector maximum freedom in manufacturing choices, but it did intervene directly to rationalize and modernize steel production which then provided a strong base for expanding industries. The policies of the Marshall Plan, which the left protested vigorously, promoted this model of development. Between 1948 and 1951, 70 percent of the plan's loans went to the metallurgical, chemical, electrical, and mechanical industries.[1]

Modernization and rationalization meant the introduction of new technology. Since Italy's previous level of technological development was low, the gains to be made in productivity were greater than in many other capitalist countries. For the first time in Italy, the assembly line and scientific management (the fragmentation of the work process into small, discrete, repeated tasks) became widespread. This transformation of work (also called *Taylorization*) had taken place in countries like the United States decades earlier. The change in Italy during the 1950s meant that much work inside the factories became less skilled. Management used technology and the new organization of labor to speed up production and to hold down the number of workers employed.

As important as government policy, the international market, and modernization were in the 1950s, the fundamental mechanism for financing Italy's reconstruction was low wages. By keeping salaries down, employers were able to finance new investments and expansion out of high profits. Statistics published in 1957 by the Catholic workers' organization, ACLI, provide a clear picture of what was happening in Italy. Between 1948 and 1955, industrial production rose 95 percent, productivity per worker-hour increased 89 percent, and profits (1950–55) went up 86 percent. For the same years (1948–55), the number of hours worked and real wages each climbed a mere 6 percent.[2] Some ten years after liberation, about 10 percent of the labor force was still unemployed.[3]

Despite the unmet needs of vast numbers of people, much of the ruling class continued to oppose comprehensive economic reforms. Between 1948 and 1953, however, the government felt sufficiently pressured by mass protests and land seizures to respond to the most potentially explosive demands. Two important government programs of the period were land reform and the Fund for the South (*Cassa per il Mezzogiorno*). The goal of the land reform program was to divide large estates that were not being farmed intensively and to distribute the land to poor peasants. According to the plan, over 8 million hectares of land (20 million acres) were to be redistributed by 1960. But when the target date arrived, the government had expropriated only 8 percent of the land. A decade later, not much more had been done.[4] In addition, the landowners held on to the best properties. Most of the farms created were so small and inefficient that they were barely self-supporting.

The purpose of the *Cassa per il Mezzogiorno* was to provide funds for irrigation, fertilizer, technical aid, roads, railways, and housing in the South. The *Cassa* had some positive results, but the effort was neither large enough, nor adequately planned, nor immune from the distortions of political patronage. Conditions in the South, rather than improving, deteriorated relative to those in the North. In the second half of the 1950s, the government did even less in terms of reform programs and entrusted the economy to the play of market forces and private interests.

Anticommunism and Coalition Politics in the 1950s

As the economy expanded, the centrist and conservative political forces (DC, PSDI, PLI, and PRI) tried to consolidate their bases of power within the state and economic institutions and among voters. Anticommunism gave them a common ideological ground and an excellent tool for organizing against the left and the CGIL. In the Cold War crusade, the Catholic Church proved to be an invaluable ally. From the Vatican down to the local parish, religious leaders used their authority to persuade the faithful to shun whatever was communist or PCI influenced. Pope Pius XII excommunicated all Communists in 1949. The centrists and rightists accused the PCI of totalitarianism, disruption of Italian life, and domination by a foreign power. The workers' movement came under fire because militant strikes, demonstrations, and most political and economic demands were categorized as subversive agitation aimed at crippling the state and the economy. Meanwhile, the U.S. government continued to play its part in the antileft campaign. During the 1950s, U.S. strategic services spent between $20 and $30 million each year to finance anticommunist political parties, unions, newspapers, and other institutions in Italy.[5]

International events—especially the 1956 Hungarian uprising and Nikita Khrushchev's revelations about the Stalin era—provided the center and the right with more ammunition. They also generated dissension within the left and labor movement. By the mid-1950s, the Socialist Party had already begun to assert its political independence from the Communists and interpreted cooperation between the two parties as being nonbinding. The relationship between the Communists and Socialists grew more competitive as the PSI staked out its own territory and made overtures to the Christian Democrats about possible participation in the national government. The Socialists condemned Soviet foreign and domestic policy and softened their opposition to NATO. These positions widened the breach between the PCI and the PSI. Although Khrushchev's revelations and the Soviet invasion of Hungary upset many Communists, the party continued to defend the Soviet Union. At the same time, Secretary Togliatti affirmed that the PCI determined all its policies autonomously and that the party would pursue its own democratic and Italian road to socialism.

The Christian Democratic Party dominated the government after the 1948 defeat of the left. The party garnered the support of those who benefited from the economic expansion and rise in national income. The DC used its governmental position to set up a vast patronage system that reached down into the smallest villages and towns. By trafficking in jobs, subsidies, and favors, the Christian Democrats strengthened their electoral machine and secured the loyalty or obligation of a variety of interest groups, from small farmers to professionals, from shopkeepers to bankers. The DC's power base came to include the state industrial holdings, the swollen state bureaucracy, and the political and economic network of the Church. The party also won the support (sometimes tacit) of many military and police officials and members of the legal establishment.

In addition to securing a constituency for the DC, the state bureaucracy functioned as a barrier to reforms. Legislation could easily be lost in the huge labyrinth of the state. Implementation could be delayed indefinitely. The power brokering and patronage deals that grew out of government domination soon led members of the DC into illegal activities. The party became so embroiled in financial and political scandals that Christian Democratic government eventually came to be associated with corruption and inefficiency.

Despite their grip on state and economic institutions, the Christian Democrats feared a substantial loss in the 1953 parliamentary elections. Vast numbers of Italians saw little improvement in their lives, and some were turning to the left and to the far right. The centrist parties had not done well in some earlier local contests. So to insure a comfortable majority in Parliament, the four government partners pushed through a law establishing that any coalition of parties winning 50 percent plus one of the popular vote would take almost two-thirds of the seats in the Chamber of Deputies. The maneuver, which matched the tactic used by Mussolini in the 1924 elections, outraged both the left and some members of the centrist forces. They focused the 1953 campaign against the infamous "swindle law" (*legge truffa*), and the government parties fell just below the 50 percent mark. The DC's share of the vote plummeted to 40.1 percent in the Chamber of Deputies, and its coalition partners lost proportionately even more. De Gasperi, who had held the post of prime minister since 1945, retired. The government repealed the swindle law the following year. The 1953 elections were a testament to growing dissatisfaction with the government. In spite of the relentless anticommunist drive, the PCI gained support (22.6 percent), and taken together, the Communists and Socialists won a total of 35.4 percent.

After 1953, the national government coalitions became more divided and unmanageable. The separate interests of each party took precedence over the need for compromise and cohesion. The cabinet arrangements grew more unstable, and the government was often paralyzed. This was not a passing state of affairs. Narrow group interests and fragmentation became the hallmarks of the Italian political system.

The Trade Unions: Policies of a Divided Movement

The labor movement faced long years of defensive struggles after 1948. In addition, there was debilitating competition between the labor confederations. Management exploited the divisions effectively so that the movement had to devote much of its energy to protecting basic democratic rights and to insuring the survival of the unions. But in addition to the employers' offensive and the complicity of the government, union errors undermined the position of labor.

All three major confederations suffered from highly centralized structures and the critical lack of a union presence in the workplace. They operated in a top-down fashion, offering the rank and file little opportunity to participate in union affairs. Over time, the absence of real democracy and direct involvement of the base created a gulf between the hierarchies of leadership and the rank and file. Most often worker participation amounted to responding to calls for strikes and demonstrations. These took on the character of plebiscites measuring the workers' commitment to a union. But the strikes rarely produced substantial improvements, and they often ended with reprisals by management.

Without an ongoing presence in the shops and offices, the unions were increasingly out of touch with daily conditions. They did not pay sufficient attention to the transformation of the work process taking place inside many plants. Employers often seized the opportunity to undermine the internal commissions even further. Fiat, for example, refused to give commission members time off the job to perform their duties. Other enterprises followed Fiat's lead until the policy became widespread. The status of the internal commissions varied from workplace to workplace. Occasionally a commission was able to negotiate a contract, but in many other instances, management simply ignored the existence of the commission.

Like the centralized structure of the unions, centralized collective bargaining also handicapped the labor movement. No nationwide contract could possibly respond to the variety of problems in every shop and office in every company. So the unions could not adequately negotiate on workplace issues such as schedules, hiring procedures, promotions, eating facilities, piece rates, work loads, assembly-line speeds, and incentives. The combination of inadequate contracts and no union presence in the workplace to counterbalance management left the workers exposed to numerous abuses, from speedups to excessively long hours to safety and health hazards. The national category federations tried to improve upon the interconfederal contracts, but their strikes were rarely successful. Management sometimes dragged out category negotiations for years. A comparison of numbers of contracts is revealing: In the United States in the late 1950s, there were approximately 150,000 collectively bargained agreements in force. In all Italy, there were just several hundred.[6]

The fierce animosity between the labor confederations was a great advantage for management. The CISL and UIL collaborated with employers to isolate the CGIL. They were willing to exclude the left confederation from negotiations and sign separate agreements with employer associations. Since there were no laws governing collective labor relations,* nothing obliged management to negotiate a contract except the strength of the workers' movement. When the CGIL formulated demands and called a strike, it was never certain how many workers would go out. The CISL and UIL did not support CGIL work stoppages and often tried to thwart them. At the same time, the two nonleft confederations were in competition with each other. Each hoped to set up a privileged relationship with employers and become the primary representative of labor. In fact, until 1954, the CISL and the UIL spent a good part of their energies opposing each other. That year, they worked together in negotiations with Confindustria on a new wage structure. Wages in Italy were made up of an extremely low base rate and a large number of special allowances and supplements. The goal of the bargaining was consolidation (*conglobamento*) and rationalization of the unwieldy structure. When the CISL and UIL signed the important consolidation accord, the CGIL was excluded.

The willingness of employers to use the CISL and UIL to undermine the CGIL was not based on a desire to strengthen those confederations. On the contrary, the objective was to defeat the labor movement as a whole. Whenever possible, Confindustria refused to give in to any union's demands. At the plant level, management often tried to win workers over to company-controlled or collaborationist unions (*sindacati*

---

*For years after 1948, Parliament postponed the legislation necessary to implement many provisions of the Constitution, including the provisions relating to labor.

gialli). Businesses that enjoyed a high rate of profit sometimes offered wage increases beyond the levels established in the interconfederal contracts. This was a form of paternalism. The employers hoped to win the loyalty of the workers and demonstrate that management—and not the unions—had the workers' interests in mind.

In competing with each other after 1948, each confederation tried to carve out its own space in the labor movement based on a particular identity that would attract as many workers as possible. Thus the confederations formulated different analyses and presented different strategies.

The CGIL was stronger than its competitors among blue-collar industrial workers and farm laborers but had some members in most sectors of the working class. Between 1948 and the mid-1950s, the left confederation gave its greatest attention to international issues, national economic goals, and classwide concerns. The CGIL organized antigovernment protests and national strikes against the atomic bomb and NATO, against the negotiations for the European Common Market, for peace in Korea, and in support of the Rosenbergs in the United States. This line corresponded to Communist Party policies and provided support for the party. The protests generally involved large numbers of workers, but they also generated some frustration in the long run—the antagonists were far removed, the objectives were difficult to attain, and economic and workplace grievances were left unresolved.

In late 1949 and early 1950, the CGIL proposed a broad public spending and reform program called the *piano del lavoro* (labor plan). Its goal was to transfer more control over the economy from private capital to the government in order to create jobs and strengthen the economic infrastructure. The plan called for expansion and nationalization of the electrical power industry; a national agency for the development of agriculture tied to a program of agrarian reforms; a national agency for the construction of housing, schools, and hospitals; and a vast public works program for roads, sewers, lighting, telephones, and aqueducts. Within the left, there were criticisms of both the assumptions and specific points of the plan, but those critiques remained somewhat academic since there was no chance that Parliament would adopt the program. It had some propagandistic value for the CGIL. The confederation could point to an alternative to government policy and could try to organize around the program. But as time went on, the confederation proved unable to better the circumstances of the workers significantly or to protect its own activists from political repression. Confidence in the CGIL began to erode, and support among the workers dropped.

During the early 1950s, the CGIL was firmly opposed to company-level contract negotiations. The confederation argued that such negotiations would divide the working class and pit one group of workers against another. Then in 1955, the metal and mechanical workers' federation of the CGIL (FIOM) lost its majority in the internal commission at Fiat. This major defeat set off a serious self-examination within the CGIL. The confederation admitted that it was out of touch with the rank and file, that it had not analyzed the impact of changes in the work process, and that its program was too vague. The CGIL placed new emphasis on the importance of building effective union structures inside the workplace. In a shift of policy, it also recognized the necessity of company-level negotiations. The confederation saw that industrial expansion in the North and the improving employment situation there would make salary increases in many plants possible if negotiations were decentralized. Finally, the leadership of the CGIL hoped that the new policies would enable its unions to compete successfully with the CISL in plants and offices.

This period was particularly difficult for the CGIL because of international events. Both Khrushchev's revelations and the Hungarian uprising in 1956 placed the CGIL in an awkward situation. The Communists in the confederation had to juggle their party's pro-Soviet position with the opposing position of the Socialists within the CGIL. In the case of Hungary, the Communist and Socialist labor leaders agreed to a declaration of support for the insurgents. The PCI took a different stand. This made it necessary for the Communist unionists to explain why they held one position in the CGIL and another in the party. They justified the contradiction by saying that they compromised within the CGIL in order to preserve confederation unity.

From the time of its formation, the CISL suffered from its image as the government union. It maintained a close association with the Christian Democratic Party, and many of its leaders were prominent in the party hierarchy. Concerned not to contradict government policy, the CISL rejected most militant actions and moderated labor demands. It embraced the notion of a restricted, nonpolitical role for trade unions. A little over half of the CISL's members were public employees.[7] Most of the others worked in large factories or were agricultural laborers.

In the early 1950s, the CISL chose company-level bargaining as the keystone of its program. (This was several years before the CGIL.) Many CISL leaders argued that the nationwide interconfederal accords set wages and benefits at a level that met the needs of the least efficient and most marginal companies. The more productive and successful enterprises were making extremely high profits without necessarily increasing wages for workers. In addition to presenting a solution to this problem, the demand for company-level collective bargaining also served the organizational purposes of the CISL. By operating on the company level and emphasizing what it considered to be strict trade-union economic issues, the CISL hoped to project an image of autonomy and credibility.

The confederation wanted to avoid national-level questions which would inevitably involve unacceptable conflicts with the government. The CISL took U.S. unions as its model for nonpartisan, company-oriented unionism. Moreover, the CGIL was weak at the company level, and the antileft policies of management were successful there. These factors seemed to give the CISL a better opportunity to build up its organization at the expense of the CGIL at the workplace level.

The economic program of the CISL linked wage increases to productivity gains. The confederation argued for modernizing production in Italy. The resulting efficiency would generate higher profits which in turn would create greater margins for meeting working-class demands. This reasoning grew out of the CISL's assumption that the needs of both the bourgeoisie and the workers could be met if Italy would only transform its archaic economy in accordance with a modern capitalist model of development. For the first half of the decade, the CISL based its analysis on the possibility of class reconciliation and the acceptability of collaborating with management. Later, the confederation acknowledged that collaboration restricted its freedom to act on behalf of the workers. Because of the employers' intransigence, the CISL's policies on wage increases and company-level negotiations bore no fruit in the early 1950s.

The UIL initially tried to stake out territory equidistant from what it called the communist union and the government union. It hoped to attract workers who saw the CGIL as tainted by totalitarianism and the CISL as collaborationist. The UIL was interested in building a strongly anticommunist organization, focused on a rather narrow conception of trade union issues. Linked to the small, centrist lay parties (the Republicans and Social Democrats), the UIL also had an anticlerical orientation. Despite its attempts to forge an autonomous identity, the UIL ended up endorsing most of the Italian government's economic and foreign policies along with the CISL. The UIL, however, did not place company-level negotiations at the center of its program during the early 1950s. For a time, the union advocated bargaining at the sector level. (In Italy, a sector is usually defined as a subdivision of the economy centered on one kind of product such as petrochemicals or automobiles.)

The organizational structures of the three confederations remained weak. Outside Rome where the national headquarters were located, the provincial-level intercategory structures were the heart of the Italian labor movement. (These structures were called provincial chambers of labor in the CGIL, provincial unions in the CISL, and provincial union chambers in the UIL.) They carried on the bulk of the work which was not national in scope, such as organizing and leading strikes, maintaining contact with workers, research, and supplying technical information. They also had to balance the needs and wishes of the national offices with those deriving from the local situations. In general, the provincial structures were underfinanced, understaffed, and overburdened. According to the CGIL, just one-third of its chambers of labor provided a full range of services. The figure was smaller for the other confederations. As for the local and provincial category unions, they functioned well only in large cities with substantial concentrations of workers. Of the national category federations, only the metal and mechanical, chemical, textile, farm workers', and sharecroppers' unions were reasonably strong in the CGIL. In the CISL, only the first three of these, and in the UIL, only the chemical workers' union, were well organized.[8] In spite of a more positive attitude toward plant-level representation in the late 1950s, the efforts of all three confederations to launch new workplace structures ended in failure.

Financing was still another serious problem for the unions. Employers did not permit dues checkoff, so worker volunteers collected membership payments. There was always a substantial number of members who did not pay their dues. Altogether the confederations collected only 30 to 40 percent of the money owed them.[9]

The Cold War in the Workplace

It was not only economic hardship and arduous labor conditions that made the 1950s "the hard years." There was also systematic political repression in the workplace. Employers oriented their policies toward two goals with respect to the labor movement. The first was to disarm the workers of their fundamental weapon, the capacity to strike. The second was to rid the factories of leftists and union activists.

Management retaliated against workers who went out on strike by firing a certain number and then threatening the rest. Reprisals became increasingly easy to carry out as fewer and fewer workers were willing to strike. Another tactic was to reward those who did not participate in work stoppages. In March 1952, for example, the FIOM (the metalworkers' union of the CGIL) called a strike in the industrial triangle for higher wages. Fiat responded by firing several activists. When the CGIL countered by announcing a 24-hour protest strike, the company promised a sum of money to everyone who would not go out. Management used this combination of reprisals and incentives after many of the political strikes called by the CGIL, such as the protest against General Eisenhower's visit to Italy in 1951 and the strikes against the swindle law in 1953. Antistrike bonuses were common in workplaces all over Italy. Every six months or so, companies would pay a supplement to each worker who had not gone out on strike during the previous bonus period.

In addition to employers' tactics, some union policies undermined the strike. As a general practice, the unions did not call workers out while contract negotiations were going on. Instead they used work stoppages to get employers to the bargaining table. This greatly diminished the usefulness of the strike as a weapon. It also encouraged management to drag out bargaining as long as possible. Federations were in and out of category negotiations for years. (Between 1949 and 1956, for example, the metal and mechanical workers were unable to win a new contract.) The delays made the unions look ineffectual in the eyes of many workers.

Employers also devised techniques to rid their establishments of leftists and union activists. Undesirable workers found themselves being transferred from one department to another and from one facility to another. In this way, they could never form relationships with co-workers or do effective organizing. In 1952, Fiat set up the first "isolation" or "exile" department (*reparto confino*). The company transferred some 100 blue- and white-collar workers—Communists, Socialists, and FIOM activists— to the same department where they were isolated from the rest of the labor force. Over the next several years, Fiat established at least nine more exile departments to sequester objectionable employees.[10] A number of other companies followed Fiat's example.

When workers lost their jobs for political reasons, employers often claimed the justification was "inability to do productive work." In most cases of discrimination and repression during this period, protests failed to alter management's decision. According to a 1956 CGIL report, 674 of its internal commission members and 1,128 of its activists had lost their jobs during the previous year.[11] Between 1948 and 1955, there was also systematic collaboration between the police and private industry in controlling the political orientation of workers. The police departments sent printed forms to personnel directors to obtain information for their files on the moral and political conduct of every employee.

Isolating, firing, and keeping records on undesirable workers was just a partial solution. It was equally important for employers to control who was hired. When companies began taking on new workers, they carefully screened each prospective employee. The parish churches played an important role in the process. Many workers were able to get factory jobs during this period only with the recommendation of a priest who would vouch for the applicant's anticommunist politics and willingness to work.

Meanwhile, the government was determined to oppose the mass mobilization of the left parties and the CGIL against its policies. This determination did not stop short of violence. The government rarely hesitated to call out the police to confront a demonstration. Between 1948 and 1954, some 75 Italians were killed during protests and over 5,000 more were wounded.[12]

The United States government sustained and even renewed its anticommunist efforts in Italy when Clare Boothe Luce became U.S. ambassador to Rome in 1953. Luce was a fervid crusader who made it clear—publicly as well as privately—that if Italian political leaders and entrepreneurs wanted U.S. favors, they had to demonstrate sufficient vigor in combating communist influence. In 1954, Vittorio Valletta, Fiat's chief executive, assured the ambassador that his company kept its work force informed of the "hidden intentions" of Communist activists when strikes were called. He also declared that Fiat regularly fired Communists who attempted to create disorder.[13] That same year, Fiat laid off 636 workers from its Aeritalia facilities, also known as "Little Stalingrad" because of the Communist presence there.[14] Along with the U.S. Defense Department in 1955, Ambassador Luce developed an existing attitude into explicit policy. No offshore procurement contracts (for the production of military equipment to be supplied by the United States to its allies) would go to any Italian factory where the CGIL had a majority in the internal commission. Since the contracts involved more than $400 million each year in Italy, the United States had found a useful instrument for influencing its ally.[15]

The Cold War intruded upon almost every aspect of labor activity. The elections for internal commission representatives were treated like significant East-West showdowns. Observers interpreted a CGIL victory as a sign of mounting communist influence within the labor movement. These contests preoccupied the Italian government, employers, the unions, and the U.S. embassy. They even rated press coverage in the United States. The elections generated full-blown campaigns with rallies, speeches, pamphlets, posters, and sound trucks. This consumed a tremendous amount of political energy and material resources, considering that there were between 3,000 and 4,000 internal commission elections each year.[16]

The events leading up to the 1955 vote at Fiat are instructive. That was the year the FIOM (CGIL) lost its majority in the commission. After mass layoffs in 1954, Fiat's management began an intense campaign in preparation for the voting. Supervisors spoke to their workers one by one and warned them to consider their jobs and their families and not to vote for the left. Company watchmen in civilian clothes were stationed in working-class neighborhoods and near FIOM headquarters. For added intimidation, management transferred many workers from one shop to another and set up a new exile department. Employees opening their paycheck envelopes found a cartoon drawing inside that showed a worker exiting from a doorway marked CISL-UIL and happily entering Fiat's gates.

The combination of Cold War campaign and union errors took its toll on the CGIL. By its own admission, the confederation lost about 1.6

million members between 1954 and 1958.[17] Yet this decline did not signify a simple shift from left to center or right. Most of the workers who dropped out of the CGIL did not join the CISL, UIL, or any other union. The losses of the CGIL represented instead a process of deunionization of the Italian working class. The figures for the metal and mechanical workers' federations are particularly striking. Between 1950 and 1959, the FIOM (CGIL) lost 404,000 of its 589,000 members while the rolls of the FIM (CISL) shrank from about 100,000 to 84,000.[18] In spite of its decline in membership, the CGIL remained the largest labor confederation in Italy throughout the 1950s. Every union's figures on membership were notoriously inflated and variable, but the following gives some idea of relative size. At the start of the new decade, estimates of CGIL membership ranged from less than 2.5 million to over 4 million; estimates for the CISL went from under a million to 2.5 million; and for the UIL's membership, the figures were between 125,000 and over 750,000.[19]

The high end of these estimates is certainly much exaggerated. So it is safe to say that the 1950s came to a close with union membership at a low level and the vast majority of Italian workers unorganized. It had been a decade of hardships and defeats, and yet the economic and political conditions of repression were not static. By 1960, they had bred the forces of their own transformation.

Notes

1. Ruggero Spesso, *L'economia italiana dal dopoguerra a oggi* (Rome: Riuniti, 1980), p. 36.

2. Associazioni Cristiane Lavoratori Italiani, *ACLI Incontro*, April 2, 1957. Cited in Sergio Turone, *Storia del sindacato in Italia 1943–1980* (Rome: Laterza, 1981), p. 232; and in Peter Lange, George Ross, and Maurizio Vannicelli, *Unions, Change and Crisis: French and Italian Union Strategy and the Political Economy, 1945–1980* (London: George Allen & Unwin, 1982), p. 193. *ACLI Incontro* was the publication of the Milan branch of the Associazioni Cristiane Lavoratori Italiani. The statistics are frequently cited, but the April 2, 1957 issue of *ACLI Incontro* is missing from both the ACLI library in Milan and the Milan public library where by law it should be deposited. ACLI officials expressed no hope of finding the issue in question in other public libraries in Italy. An extended search has produced no results so far.

3. George H. Hildebrand, *Growth and Structure in the Economy of Modern Italy* (Cambridge: Harvard University Press, 1965), pp. 156–67.

4. Elizabeth Wiskemann, *Italy Since 1945* (London: Macmillan Press, 1971), p. 19.

5. Roberto Faenza and Marco Fini, *Gli americani in Italia* (Milan: Feltrinelli, 1976), p. 328.

6. Maurice F. Neufeld, *Italy: School for Awakening Countries* (1961; reprint, Westport, Conn.: Greenwood Press, 1974), p. 509.

7. Alessandro Pizzorno, *I soggetti del pluralismo: Classi, partiti, sindacati* (Bologna: Il Mulino, 1980), p. 181.

8. Neufeld, *Italy*, pp. 506–9.

9. Ibid., p. 513.

10. Renzo Gianotti, *Trent'anni di lotte alla Fiat (1948–1978): Dalla ricostruzione al nuovo modo di fare l'auto* (Bari: De Donato, 1979), pp. 55–56.

11. Sergio Turone, *Storia del sindacato in Italia 1943–1980* (Rome: Laterza, 1981), p. 211.

12. Donald L. M. Blackmer, "Continuity and Change in Postwar Italian Communism," in *Communism in Italy and France*, eds. Donald L. M. Blackmer and Sidney Tarrow (Princeton: Princeton University Press, 1975), p. 47.

13. Vittorio Foa, ed., *Sindacati e lotte operaie 1943–1973*, Documenti della storia, no. 10 (Turin: Loescher, 1975), pp. 107–8.

14. Gianotti, *Trent' anni di lotte alla Fiat*, p. 63.

15. Paul Joseph, "American Policy and the Italian Left," in *The Politics of Eurocommunism: Socialism in Transition*, eds. Carl Boggs and David Plotke (Boston: South End Press, 1980), p. 361.

16. Neufeld, *Italy*, pp. 484–85.

17. Gian Primo Cella, "Stabilità e crisi del centralismo nell' organizzazione sindacale," in *Problemi del movimento sindacale in Italia 1943–1973*, Annali, no. 16, ed. Aris Accornero (Milan: Feltrinelli, 1976), p. 645.

18. Ibid., p. 647.

19. Neufeld, *Italy*, p. 554.

3

The Reawakening of the
Workers' Movement

Fifteen years after liberation, Italy was a different country. Industrialization, television, the automobile as a mass consumer item, a new vision within the Church, and the geographic displacement of millions were all transforming the nation. There were changes in the composition of the labor force. Workers began perceiving themselves and their position relative to management differently. The cumulative result in the early 1960s was a less restrictive situation for labor. The opportunity existed for creating the workers' movement anew.

Economic and Social Conditions at the Start of a New Decade

From the point of view of the capitalist class, reconstruction based on low wages and increased productivity was a great success. Italians produced a higher average rate of economic growth than all other capitalist countries except Germany and Japan. From 1951 to 1958, gross national income in Italy increased at an average annual rate of 5.3 percent.[1] Between 1955 and 1960, exports grew in real value at an average annual rate of about 18 percent.[2] This steady growth was then the springboard for a four-year period of even more rapid expansion (1959 to 1963) called "the Italian economic miracle." The average rate of national income growth for those years was 6.6 percent.[3] The economic miracle was actually a cyclical boom set off by a sharp increase in exports in 1959, followed by a steady increase in productive investment and in internal consumer demand. The epicenter of the economic miracle was in the manufacturing industries of the North.

Impressive as the picture looked, this kind of growth—concentrated in the export industries and controlled by the private sector—came at a high price. It created greater distortions in the productive base of the economy and in the structure of employment. It also aggravated disparities between geographical regions and social classes.

As an overall trend, prices for essential items such as food and health care rose relative to the general consumer price index. Meanwhile prices for nonessential goods such as electrical appliances and autos gradually fell relative to the price index. The economy was centered more and more on auto production and gasoline consumption. The state encouraged this development by financing a system of superhighways that was second in Europe only to that of West Germany, by providing cheap steel from state-owned mills, and by lowering the price of gasoline. The result was that by 1969, private car ownership in Italy was not much below the Western European average. But the average daily per capita consumption of animal protein was only 38 grams, compared with 64 in France and 55 in West Germany.[4] The government's choice to support an automobile economy meant that fewer public resources were going into the South, health care, education, and public transportation.

As for the structure of employment, there was a significant shift of economic activity from the rural areas to the cities, from independent work to salaried work, and from agricultural production to industry. Other countries experienced these same structural transformations, but in Italy the shift produced an unusually severe distortion of the labor market. The official unemployment rate dropped from 5.2 percent in 1959 to 2.5 percent in 1963,[5] but the demand for labor did not correspond to the supply geographically or in terms of skills, sex, and age. While there was a great surplus of labor in many regions and among women and young people, there was an actual shortage of workers in certain industries and locales. Although the official level of unemployment was declining, the labor force participation rate (labor force as a percentage of population) fell from 45.0 percent in 1959 to 41.8 percent in 1963.[6] Italy's participation rate (not including the underground economy) had already been low compared to other European countries before 1959. The further drop meant that a shrinking percentage of the population was active in the official economy. This too was a structural weakness.

The disparity between North and South grew worse. In 1951, per capita income in the South was just 47.7 percent of per capita income in northern and central Italy. In 1959, almost a decade after the Fund for the South was set up, this figure had dropped to 46.6 percent.[7] The relationship of South to North resembled that of a Third World country to a more highly industrialized nation. The South provided an outlet for manufactured goods (for example, public works projects in the South used equipment made in the North) and a source of cheap immigrant labor for northern industry.

Finally, the contrasts in well-being between social classes were still glaring. As mass consumerism developed in Italy for the first time, the push to sell goods generated new needs and new desires. But the inequalities in buying power led to new frustrations. Although wealth was being created, it was obviously concentrated in relatively few hands. One example of this was housing. Millions of Italians were inadequately housed, the construction industry was booming, and yet a large proportion of the building was luxury housing and tourist accommodations.

The distortions of the Italian economy were responsible for one of the most extreme social upheavals of the postwar years—mass internal migrations. Poverty forced millions of Italians to leave their birthplaces and communities in the South, the islands of Sardinia and Sicily, and the northeast regions. Between 1951 and 1961, about 2 million emigrated from the South and the islands (11.6 percent of the regional population), and close to a half-million left the Northeast (almost 5.2 percent of the regional population). They went in approximately equal numbers to the industrial centers of the Northwest and abroad. (Emigration out of the national territory had begun in the nineteenth century.) Between 1961 and 1971, another 2 million abandoned the South and islands. About three-quarters of them stayed in Italy. Of those who did leave the country, an increasingly large proportion went to find jobs in northern Europe.[8]

Most of the immigrants to the industrial triangle were peasants and farm workers who had never before confronted an urban environment. Most spoke only their native dialects and could not understand the Italian spoken in cities like Milan and Turin. In addition to homesickness, language difficulties, and culture shock, the immigrants also faced the hostility of the natives. Many Northerners considered Southerners, Sicilians, and Sardinians to be racially inferior, lazy, uneducated, and dishonest. The immigrants suffered discrimination in jobs and housing as well as social ostracism.

In Milan, many immigrants settled 20 or 30 kilometers outside the city where they crowded into temporary shacks and half-built houses. Their chaotic settlements were called *Corea* (Korea) because they reminded Italians of recent wartime images. In Turin, the newcomers made their way from the train station to boarding houses in the most run-down parts of the city or the shantytowns on the outskirts. They rented beds by the hour. They went without heat or hot water. Some found that they could not get a job until they had a permanent address and they could not rent an apartment until they had stable employment. They managed to find work in small factories or in the construction industry where they often did *lavoro nero* (literally "black work"). This meant they were "off the books." They had no work papers, no benefits, and no protection under the law. The employers, of course, did not pay taxes or contributions to the various social insurance programs. Most often the wages were abysmal and the hours long. It was not uncommon for an immigrant to work 15 hours a day, six and half days a week, for 14 cents an hour. For many who had previously known only farm labor, the fume-filled shops and the rigidity of assembly-line rhythms were an unbearable experience.

As in most European countries, the Italian state owned or partially owned many industrial and commercial enterprises. By the early 1960s, these had become a significant part of Italy's economy. The Institute for Industrial Reconstruction (IRI), set up under Mussolini in the 1930s, had evolved into a massive holding company with operations in iron, steel, shipbuilding, merchant shipping, chemicals, civil engineering, banking, telephones, radio, television, highway construction, airlines, automobiles, electronic equipment, and electrical appliances. A second holding company, the National Hydrocarbons Agency (ENI) dated back to 1953 when the government decided to develop Italy's natural gas resources. The primary focus of ENI was the exploration, production, and distribution of natural gas and oil and the refining and marketing of petroleum products. But ENI grew to include nuclear energy, textiles, plant engineering, construction, and newspaper publishing.

Despite state ownership, there was little government coordination of economic activities, let alone comprehensive planning. Private industry competed with many public companies so that the state sector had little control over national-level production or the market. In addition, special-interest groups and systems of patronage grew up around the governing bodies of the various public companies, and corrupt practices became common.

For the first decade after the war, the state industries were part of Confindustria along with private industries. Then in late 1956, after much debate and opposition from the private sector, Parliament voted to set up a Ministry of State Holdings and to take the public corporations out of Confindustria. Organizations were later set up to represent the state holdings in collective bargaining with the labor unions. Just as Confindustria negotiated on behalf of private industry, Intersind represented IRI and other state holdings, and ASAP represented ENI. The advantage to the labor movement of this arrangement was that the solid front of employers united into one organization was broken.

Changing Work Conditions and New Attitudes for Labor

The economic and social transformations that were taking place in Italy were bound to affect the composition of the labor force. The expansion of industry brought new and younger people into the factories. Many were immigrants and former farm laborers. They tended to be less divided along traditional party lines than the previous generation. Most of them were unskilled and worked on the assembly lines. Thus they were also less divided by job classifications. Since the employment picture had improved in many areas of the Northwest, workers there were less afraid of losing their jobs. They were more willing to go out on strike. The repressive tactics used by management in the past were not quite as effective as they had been. Feeling less divided among themselves, the new workers tended toward unitary job actions. Although they were more combative, many did not join a union.

Just as the composition of the labor force changed, so did the nature of work inside the factory. Economic expansion and the need to compete in the international market encouraged investment in new plants and equipment. As discussed earlier, the stronger companies reorganized production during the 1950s by automating. They installed more assembly lines and broke up the work process into short, discrete tasks to be repeated again and again by unskilled or semiskilled workers. Before this reorganization, most of the rank-and-file activists in the factories had been skilled. Under the new system, the skilled workers were both fewer in number and more isolated. Many of them did auxiliary tasks such as maintaining and repairing equipment. Most of the semiskilled and unskilled workers were tied to the assembly lines. Yet rather than permanently estrange one worker from another, this more rigid system of production generated a new kind of solidarity. A group or team of workers in close proximity to each other and involved in similar tasks faced the same problems and came to recognize common interests.

These work groups (*gruppi omogenei* or homogeneous groups) began to play an important role in the mobilization of the rank and file as it confronted management. In the past, the national confederations and category unions had tried to activate the workers around the general demands of national contracts. The cadres of the various unions were scattered randomly in the factory. They were strong in some departments, weak in others. They had direct contact with only a limited number of workers and often were not familiar with the specific concerns of employees in other shops. In the reorganized factories, the work groups became the source of a new kind of rank-and-file mobilization. Much of it was spontaneous and took the form of work stoppages and collective protests around issues that came up day by day—speedups, temporary layoffs, changes in scheduling, or problems with piecework incentives.

The labor unions were in a state of uncertainty and organizational weakness. Most of them, especially the national-level unions, did not realize the full significance of the changes taking place. They underestimated the potential strength of the working class in the new period and its willingness to do battle with management.

At the same time, however, attitudes within some unions were slowly beginning to evolve. After years of opposing each other as fiercely as they opposed management (in certain cases, more fiercely), labor organizations gradually started making unitary demands. They called occasional strikes together and cosponsored legislation in Parliament. The impetus for this change came in large part from below—from the rank and file and from the local or provincial union apparatus. At the base level, both the specific needs of the workers and the greater power of united actions were obvious enough to overcome old antagonisms. The process was long, tentative, and often contradictory. Some of the unitary actions took place in the midst of bitter competition and mutual recriminations. The three confederations were much slower to accept unitary policies than were some of the national category federations. In 1959, the three metal and mechanical workers' unions (FIOM, FIM, UILM) went out on strike together when the national category contract came up for renewal. For the first time in years, the workers used the slogan "United, We Win" (*uniti si vince*). In Milan, there was a joint rally at which leaders from all three unions spoke. The results of the contract negotiations were disappointing to the workers, but the unitary process had a long-term positive effect in revitalizing the movement.

The most dramatic changes during the late 1950s and early 1960s took place within the Catholic workers' movement and especially within the FIM (CISL). As early as 1957, some Catholics took the position that the weakness of the labor movement and the high price paid for the postwar reconstruction were due to the fragmentation of the unions. The only remedy, according to this perspective, was unity of action in concrete struggles at every level.

The CISL itself began to change as it took in a new generation of unionists trained at the confederation's school in Florence. According to the original conception, the school was to turn out cadres who adopted the "apolitical" contract trade unionism in the United States as a model. But unexpectedly, the school's alumni gradually made it possible for the CISL to move in a more radical direction. The admission policy favored applicants from the workplace. After their training, a large number went on to the FIM. These young *Fimmini* rejected the collaboration with management that had characterized much of the CISL's policy in the past. They gave the FIM a more independent and combative orientation. In 1962, the new generation of militant unionists won a majority at the FIM's national congress. The renewed FIM played an important role because it provided a place for militant workers whose Catholic identity was strong. They found that their attitudes and objectives as workers were quite the same as those of young leftist workers. Both groups supported unitary struggles.

The Reawakening of the Movement

Historians often point to the unitary strikes of the electromechani-
cal workers in Milan during the winter of 1960–61 as the start of the renewed movement. The local unions were trying to improve upon the national metal and mechanical workers' contract of the previous year. Since
the electronics sector in Italy was expanding rapidly and productivity was
rising, the unions claimed that management's refusal to improve the contract was more politically than economically motivated. The companies
did not want to sanction decentralized bargaining—within a single sector
or with local unions. Employers were also loath to grant a victory to a
reviving workers' movement. Pressured by large unitary strikes, however,
Intersind signed an accord on behalf of the state-controlled companies in
December 1960. The workers won salary increases of about 5 percent and
a reduction in work hours. But an outstanding feature of the agreement
was recognition of a union's right to bargain on the company level and on
the sector level in order to change specific provisions of a national category contract. This kind of negotiating was called integrative contracting
(*contrattazione integrativa*). The accord with Intersind also affirmed the
unions' role as legitimate representatives of the workers in company-level
disputes.

Intense as the labor struggles of 1960–61 had been, they were just a
prelude to events of the following year. In 1962, a postwar record of almost 378 million work hours were given to strikes,[9] and management
faced the most arduous negotiations since the immediate postwar years.
In addition, 1962 marked the reemergence of the Fiat work force as a
major protagonist in the Italian labor movement.

Some 90 national category contracts came up for renewal, but the
key negotiations were those of the metal and mechanical workers. The
FIOM, FIM, and UILM called several unitary strikes and forced the state-
owned companies to sign a contract. The final agreement with Intersind
recognized the legitimacy of company-level agreements on questions such
as piece rates, job classification, incentives, and production bonuses. The
negative point was that employers imposed limits on what could be negotiated at the company level and how much could be demanded. The contract also acknowledged the unions' presence in the workplace. The
unions could post notices on bulletin boards; union representatives could
take time off the job to carry out their duties; and membership dues
would be deducted from paychecks. After a national general strike of all
industrial employees in February 1963, the metal and mechanical workers
in private companies were able to win concessions comparable to those
won in the state enterprises.

Overall, Italian workers made substantial gains in 1962. The salary increases in the various industrial categories ranged from 8 to 16 percent. Many of the contracts reduced the work week from 48 to 46 hours.[10] The metal and mechanical workers' contract also established a precedent for other industries in integrative contracting.

The 1960–63 cycle of labor struggles in Italy broke the pattern of the previous decade by transforming the content of demands and the nature of rank-and-file participation. The three major confederations finally came to agree that every aspect of labor relations was fair game for bargaining, from job classifications to safety conditions to vacation schedules. It was years, however, before the workers won control over even some of these issues. As for rank-and-file participation, many of the initial job actions began spontaneously on the shop floors. In certain cases, the workers did not inform the unions before shutting down an assembly line. During negotiations, the rank and file contributed to the formulation of contract demands. The workers maintained their own networks within the plants rather than relying exclusively on union activists to do the organizing. The marches and rallies were more spirited than in the past. The picketing became more aggressive, and strikers kept other workers from entering the plants. There were instances of workers coercing reluctant colleagues (often white-collar workers) to go out on strike. For the time being, the feeling of powerlessness diminished.

The police reacted to the new militancy of the workers with the same ferocity as in the past. They attacked demonstrators and broke up rallies. Companies called in the police to disband picket lines. During a lockout at a soap factory in 1962, the police killed one worker. In response, all the unions demanded that police be disarmed when dealing with strikers. The request was refused.

A New Political Coalition Emerges

The first signs of growing labor unity and militancy were a warning to the Italian ruling class. The techniques that had worked well until then—authoritarian control in the plants, exclusion of the left from government, and political repression—were not going to be sufficient for the coming period. Some other mechanism was needed to restrain labor while maintaining the freedom to pursue the most profitable course of economic development. Meanwhile the centrist coalition governments had become increasingly divided by warring political factions. The result was paralysis and instability. One government after another fell, but no recombination of forces was any more adequate than its predecessors.

The industrialists and financiers most interested in preserving Italy's new dynamism in the international market clearly needed a more effective arrangement to further their interests. The solution proposed by some political forces was to bring the Socialist Party into the ruling coalition. This operation was known as the "opening to the left."

The reaction to the proposal, first discussed in the mid-1950s, was mixed. Some Christian Democrats and Social Democrats argued that a center-left coalition with the PSI would have a more stable majority. It would pass enough reforms to quell discontent over the distribution of income and over the use of resources. The new coalition might also isolate the Communists more and win support for the government from the agricultural and urban working classes. Other members of the DC and the PSDI distrusted the Socialists because of their longtime attachment to the Communists. But the growing autonomy of the PSI began to counter this objection.

From the Socialists' point of view, playing a role in national government would enhance their power and prestige. They could also stake out a field of operations where they, rather than the PCI, would be the dominant left force. The risk was that the Christian Democrats might continue to control the government. The internal conflicts and strong conservative factions of that party might make significant reforms impossible. If that happened, the Socialists would be mired in the DC's system of poor government and would lose their credibility as a reform party capable of providing an alternative. Despite these risks, support grew within the PSI for the center-left proposal.

For all the political forces interested in reform, the purpose of a center-left government was to maintain a high level of employment and to improve the economic conditions of the working class. The reformers argued that the center-left would have to undertake comprehensive economic planning in order to accomplish its various goals. By 1961, the more progressive wing of the DC supported planning as did the Socialist Party.

Much of the capitalist class and the conservatives who controlled Confindustria opposed the opening to the left. But there were also powerful voices in favor, including Fiat's Valletta. These advocates of the new coalition saw the center-left as an opportunity to exchange some working-class representation in the government for consensus and collaboration. Above all, they required that the center-left provide the conditions for a continued high rate of profit and for competitiveness on the international market.

Another supporter of the center-left proposal was the U.S. government, which had come to believe that the Christian Democrats could not furnish adequate stability or legitimacy. In 1958, the United States began secret funding of the PSI, especially those party factions that wanted autonomy from the Communists and participation in the government. This position grew stronger under President John F. Kennedy. A harsh opponent of the opening to the left was the Vatican under Pope Pius XII whose attitudes were dogmatically anticommunist. But in 1958, John XXIII succeeded Pius and began creating a climate in Italy that was favorable to social and economic reforms and to a center-left government.

Another factor that helped pave the way for the center-left was the disaster of the Tambroni government in 1960. After one of the longest cabinet crises since the war, the Christian Democrat Ferdinando Tambroni pulled together a parliamentary majority with the votes of the neofascist party, the Italian Social Movement (MSI). This was a turning point since until then it had been assumed that no government would accept the support of the neofascists. Emboldened by its leverage in the government, MSI decided to abandon its low profile. The party announced it would hold its July national congress in Genoa, one of the centers of the antifascist Resistance. The neofascists added still another challenge and insult. They announced that the honorary president of the congress would be Carlo Emanuele Basile who, as prefect of Mussolini's Republic of Salò, directed the reprisals against Genoa's Resistance fighters.

The antifascist forces—both political parties and unions with the CGIL playing a leading role—called protest strikes and demonstrations until the authorities cancelled the congress. The police wounded a number of demonstrators in Genoa, and when those events set off protests in other cities, the police were equally aggressive. Five lost their lives in Reggio Emilia, and four were killed in Sicily. After a CGIL-sponsored general strike, the Tambroni government fell on July 19, 1960. For the next three years, the political parties moved step by step toward the final parliamentary vote on the center-left.

The inherent political contradictions of the center-left proposal undermined the project from the start. In 1962, the more progressive DC factions set up a government that was supposedly based on a program of economic and social reforms and on planning. Yet there was no majority sentiment, let alone consensus, among business leaders or within the centrist parties for either planning or reforms. Factional interests, the patronage system, protection of middle-class privileges, and personal antagonisms obstructed almost every proposal. The one major accomplishment of the government was the nationalization of the private electric utility companies in November 1962.

In April 1963, there were national parliamentary elections. The two protagonists of the center left, the Socialists and the Christian Democrats, each received a lower percentage of the votes. The victors in the election were the Communist Party to the left and the Liberal Party to the right. At that point, the left wing of the Socialist Party argued that the whole concept of the center-left had already lost its vitality and potential for innovation. The left Socialists feared that the PSI would do no more than provide a stable majority for an ineffectual government. But most of the leadership opted to pursue the negotiations. In December 1963, the Socialist Party finally entered the government, and Secretary Pietro Nenni became deputy prime minister of Italy. Part of the left wing resigned from the PSI. In January 1964, the dissidents formed a new organization called the Italian Socialist Party of Proletarian Unity (PSIUP).

The fears of the left Socialists were justified. As soon as the first center-left cabinet was functioning, conservatives began to block the reform initiatives supported by the left. They called for measures to hold down the cost of labor. This went on until June 1964 when the government fell over the issue of public financing to parochial schools. Then extreme right-wing military and political forces decided it was time to take matters into their own hands. General Giovanni De Lorenzo of the *carabinieri* (military police) began to develop plans for a coup d'état. The plot was aborted during the summer, but it strengthened the hand of conservative forces. The PSI leadership agreed to postpone reforms and to participate in a new government whose programs would placate the conservatives and restore the confidence of Italy's entrepreneurs. The PSI rationalized its participation by arguing that the threat from the right made it necessary to dilute the original aims of the center-left.

The Collapse of the Economic Miracle

The final negotiations for the center-left government coincided with the collapse of the economic miracle. The concurrence of the two events had a certain irony since the initial conception of the coalition had been to steer a new course for Italy by managing her resources and wealth during a period of economic expansion. But the very nature of the boom—its economic development and political consequences—prepared the way for its collapse.

Until the 1960s, salary increases in Italy had been equal to or lower than productivity gains. As a result, the cost of labor per unit produced in industry was no higher in 1961 than it had been in 1953.[11] This situation suddenly changed in 1962 (see Table 3.1), and the cost of labor began to mount.

Industrialists responded to the higher labor costs by raising prices to maintain profit levels. This produced what was a high rate of inflation for

TABLE 3.1:   Changes in Hourly Productivity and Hourly Wages in Italian Manufacturing Industries, 1962–64

Year	Hourly productivity	Hourly wages
1962	+ 8.1%	+ 15.7%
1963	+ 5.6%	+ 15.9%
1964	+ 5.9%	+ 10.6%

Source: Michele Salvati, "Politica economica e relazioni industriali dal 'miracolo' economico a oggi," in *Problemi del movimento sindacale in Italia 1953–1973*, Annali, no. 16, ed. Aris Accornero (Milan: Feltrinelli, 1976), p. 702.

Italy at the time. Between 1962 and 1963, for example, consumer prices rose more than 7 percent.[12] The expanding economy and higher wages stimulated domestic demand, and this put more pressure on prices. The cost of Italian goods went up relative to international prices, imports rose, and exports fell. The balance of payments went into deficit, and the economic miracle began to wind down. In early 1964, the government approved a sharp credit squeeze which strangled already declining investments. Fiscal measures such as tax increases began to shrink demand. The economy dropped into a recession. Tens of thousands of industrial workers lost their jobs, and others were put on a short workweek.

Measured in terms of GNP, the recession did not last long. By 1965, industrial production was climbing again. But the recession did establish several new trends so that the overall economic picture in the second half of the 1960s looked different. Statistics from the period illustrate the changes. After the recession, investment in plant and machinery as a percentage of income never attained the 1963 rate. This made Italy the only highly industrialized nation where investment as a percentage of income was lower between 1964 and 1969 than it had been between 1958 and 1963.[13] The trend of decreasing unemployment established during the economic miracle was also reversed. In addition, the low labor force participation rate in the official economy dropped further, from 41.4 percent in 1964 to 38.9 percent in 1969.[14] Meanwhile, industrial production was going up. In fact, the average rate of increase of industrial production between 1964 and 1969 was 6.8 percent, which was equal to the average growth rate of the 1950s.[15] The figures on productivity reveal one important source of industrial expansion. Between 1963 and 1968, hourly productivity in industrial manufacturing rose 50 percent.[16] In this way, industrialists succeeded, for the time being, in keeping Italian goods competitive on the international market.

Labor on the Defensive

The workers' movement of 1960–63 was not developed enough to withstand the reaction of the employers and the government. The level of militancy dropped back, and the daily lives of workers deteriorated both inside the plants and in working-class communities.

In order to raise productivity inside the workplace, management could resort to two methods. The first was to make humans and machines work faster and longer by speeding up assembly lines, reducing the work time for operations on individual machines, increasing incentive pay and overtime, and putting on extra shifts. The second method was to install new labor-saving technology. During the second half of the 1960s, Italian industrialists used both approaches although the emphasis in many industries was on the first. Management's goal was to put an end to all "dead time" in the factory. Work conditions became even worse, and the incidence of industrial accidents and nervous disorders climbed. New machinery gave productivity another boost. In some cases, the gains were awesome. At Fiat Mirafiori, for example, the assembly line for one of the sports models turned out 60 cars per shift in May 1967. In June, the line was producing 112 cars per shift with the same number of workers.[17] Skilled laborers often found that their status changed with the introduction of new technology. During this period, Olivetti installed its first computerized machines to turn out tools and dies. The highly specialized machinists who once did the work saw their skills become obsolete overnight.[18]

Outside the plants and offices, millions of Italians still contended with inadequate housing and poor social services. Immigrants continued to pour into the industrial centers of the North. Like their predecessors, they faced culture shock and discrimination. The causal relationship between industrial expansion and social dislocation did not change. One example of this was the opening of a new Fiat auto plant in 1967. The factory was located a half-hour outside Turin in the tiny farming town of Rivalta. Once it acquired its full complement of 18,000 workers, the Rivalta plant was second only to Mirafiori in size. The opening of the plant set off another wave of immigration to Turin, and the result was acute shortages of housing, schools, public transportation, and sewers. As far as the company was concerned, these issues were the business of local and national government and not private enterprise.

If one goal of employers in Italy was to wipe out the effects of the wage gains made in the early 1960s, an equally important objective was to cripple the burgeoning workers' movement. Unemployment was a useful tool. The unions were not strong enough to oppose mass layoffs in industry during the recession. Strike activity dropped after the high point in

Housing in a working-class neighborhood called Mirafiori Sud, in Turin.

1962, and the ability of the unions to deliver contract improvements also declined. The labor organizations were still not able to set up effective structures inside the workplace, so the bond between the rank and file and the union organizations remained feeble. Membership fell during the mid-1960s.

The development of labor union unity continued its slow and contradictory course. The main obstacles were the traditional political divisions, the mistrust, and the competitiveness cultivated over the years. One specific point of contention was the so-called incompatibility question. Many forces within the labor movement objected to union leaders also holding party offices or elected government posts. In 1965, the CGIL congress finally ruled that this practice was not permissible at the local and provincial levels. At the national level, however, union leaders could continue to be members of Parliament. They could also serve on party leadership bodies. That same year, the CISL adopted a similar motion on the incompatibility question.

A Change in Political Climate

Although the workers' movement stalled during the mid-1960s, the political climate in Italy was anything but static. A shift in the orientation of the Catholic Church, the war in Vietnam, new radical movements abroad, the student mobilization in Italy, the development of the New Left—all of these altered the social and political environment. They provided a new, hospitable, and even stimulating context for the workers' movement.

The papacy of John XXIII and Vatican Council II in the early 1960s had an impact on Italian society as a whole but especially on young Catholics. The greater concern for economic and social justice, the decentralization of Church power, and the revived spirit of inquiry influenced the political thinking of the faithful. Many Italians came to see social change—radical change in some cases—as integral to their religious beliefs. They no longer accepted the traditional ideology that linked all left politics to atheistic communism. As one example of this trend, the Catholic organization ACLI moved to the left during this period. At the 1966 ACLI convention, many delegates called for rejecting moderate politics. They also proposed distancing the organization from the Christian Democratic Party. The spirit affected Catholic trade unionists as well. Within the CISL, the left wing grew stronger, and the radical political orientation of the FIM gained more support.

The mid-1960s in Italy were a time of growing protest against the war in Vietnam. The Communist Party and the CGIL not only took positions against the war, they organized a mass opposition to it within the population. After a short time, the FIM came out against U.S. policy. In 1967, the Italian student movement was born into this climate of protest. Students began to analyze their own situation as well as international issues such as Vietnam. Since the Second World War, the student population at the universities had grown twice as fast as the teaching staff. Classrooms were overcrowded, the university structure was elitist and authoritarian, and teaching methods were outmoded. In many of the major universities—Rome, Turin, Milan, Pisa, Venice, Trento, Bologna— the students forced confrontations with professors and administrators. Over the next several years, they won substantial changes in admission policies, staffing, course structure, and examination procedures. High-school students picked up on what was happening at the universities and began to organize to change conditions in their own institutions. By setting a political tone for those years, by introducing new forms of struggle, and by catalyzing specific protests, the Italian student movement influenced the workers' movement in the late 1960s.

New ideas and images also came from the Chinese Cultural Revolution, the May 1968 student and worker uprising in France, the movement for community participation as well as the student movement in the United States, and the developing critique of affluent consumer societies. A reexamination began within the Italian left of the role of a revolutionary party and its relationship to the population and to autonomous social movements. The undemocratic structure of left parties came under attack as did the model of a centralized, state-controlled economy. Many leftists argued that revolution in Italy had been relegated to an indefinite future for too long. For some, China became a point of reference or even a model for the transformation of Italy. The general debate took place both within and outside the Italian Communist Party. Inside the PCI, the discussion was related to an internal power struggle between right and left tendencies. (By 1966, a middle-of-the-road position had won out.) Over the course of the decade, the debate stimulated the growth of new organizations and radical forces to the left of the party. This area of the political map became known as the New Left.

The political spectrum in Italy was shifting. This meant not only new forces critical of the Communists, but also increased support for the PCI as progressives moved farther to the left and as many young people became radicalized. These changes and the growing frustration with the center-left government became clear in the 1968 parliamentary elections. The Communists' share of the vote in the Chamber of Deputies rose from 25.3 percent to 26.9 percent. Farther to the left, PSIUP did well for a small breakaway party (4.5 percent). The Christian Democrats gained just 0.8 percent, going from 38.3 to 39.1 percent. The Socialists and Social Democrats suffered the most. Having become partners in the national government, the PSI and PSDI decided to merge their organizations. They became the United Socialists (PSU) in 1966. But the new grouping then lost about a quarter of the votes that the two parties had attracted when they were separate. The election results were a repudiation of a government that had promised sweeping reforms and had produced practically nothing. In the summer of 1969, the three-year-old PSU experiment fell apart, and the political lineup returned to what it had been (PSI and PSDI). The only noteworthy change was that some former Social Democratic trade unionists in the UIL moved to the left and switched their party affiliation to the Socialists. As a result, nearly half the UIL leadership was in the PSI.

Notes to Chapter 3

1. Mariano D'Antonio, *Sviluppo e crisi del capitalismo italiano 1951–1972* (Bari: De Donato, 1973), pp. 54–55.

2. Michele Salvati, "Politica economica e relazioni industriali dal 'miracolo' economico a oggi," in *Problemi del movimento sindacale in Italia 1953–1973*, Annali, no. 16, ed. Aris Accornero (Milan: Feltrinelli, 1976), p. 692.

3. D'Antonio, *Sviluppo e crisi*, pp. 54–55.

4. Ibid., p. 235.

5. Alessandro Pizzorno et al., *Lotte operaie e sindacato: Il ciclo 1968–1972 in Italia* (Bologna: Il Mulino, 1978), p. 298. These figures, provided by the Central Institute of Statistics (ISTAT), may underestimate the unemployment rate. See George H. Hildebrand, *Growth and Structure in the Economy of Modern Italy* (Cambridge: Harvard University Press, 1965), pp. 156–67.

6. Donald C. Templeman, *The Italian Economy* (New York: Praeger, 1981), p. 338.

7. Giuseppe Di Nardi, "Politica e sviluppo o programma di opere pubbliche?" in *L'economia italiana dal 1945 a oggi*, 2d ed., rev. ed. Augusto Graziani (Bologna: Il Mulino, 1979), p. 286.

8. Augusto Graziani, "Introduzione," in Graziani, *L'economia italiana dal 1945 a oggi*, pp. 67–69.

9. Eugenio Guidi et al., *Movimento sindacale e contrattazione collettiva 1945–1970*, 2d ed., rev. and enl. (Milan: Franco Angeli, 1971), p. 119.

10. Ibid., p. 73.

11. Salvati, "Politica economica," p. 702.

12. D'Antonio, *Sviluppo e crisi*, p. 76.

13. Salvati, "Politica economica," p. 703.

14. Templeman, *The Italian Economy*, p. 338.

15. Salvati, "Politica economica," p. 703.

16. Ibid., p. 707.

17. Sergio Turone, *Storia del sindacato in Italia 1943–1980* (Rome: Laterza, 1981), p. 345.

18. Renzo Gianotti, *Trent'anni di lotte alla Fiat (1948–1978): Dalla ricostruzione al nuovo modo di fare l'auto* (Bari: De Donato, 1979), p. 165.

4

The Workers' Revolt: Anatomy of a Movement

The events of 1968–72 altered relations between labor, management, and the national government making this period a watershed in postwar Italian history. In the course of just a few years, the nature of the working-class movement changed, and the balance of power between classes shifted. As a result, labor assumed a new role as one of the protagonists shaping developments in the economy and in the political arena.

The Rise of a New Workers' Movement

There was no single, precipitating cause of the workers' revolt in the late 1960s. Nor did the movement have a well-defined starting point. Instead, it developed in the first half of 1968 as an increase in protests and work stoppages in individual plants and companies. What characterized the actions was a new combativeness which escaped union control. Few national contracts were up for renewal that year, and those that were negotiated involved smaller categories. So the bulk of the strikes took place when the unions or the workers by themselves tried to win concessions on the company level. Although women, older people, and the very young still had difficulty finding jobs, a shortage of labor in some locales bolstered the workers' confidence.

In most cases, unions initiated the strikes, but the demands they proposed were moderate and their forms of struggle cautious. As the workers in a plant responded to a strike call, participation and militancy often grew until there was an explosion of anger. The actions of the rank and file quickly outstripped the unions' tactics. The workers prolonged strikes beyond the time periods set by the unions, and they broadened the demands. They occupied plants, organized slowdowns, and set up militant picket lines and roadblocks. They marched through cities and held demonstrations. There were many sharp, even violent confrontations with employers and the police. In some cases, the workers initiated strikes without the unions' input. There were instances of the new militancy all over Italy, but the greatest concentration was in the northern regions. During this early stage, most demands focused on wage increases and other economic improvements.

The protagonists of these struggles were often skilled workers and activists who had some previous strike or union experience. Their knowledge enabled them to respond to the unions' directives and then go beyond. The newly hired, younger, and less skilled workers not only had less experience, they also felt little attachment to the unions. They answered strike calls more reluctantly. They were aware that the unions traditionally relied on and represented the interests of the more skilled, older workers.

The militancy of the struggles caught the unions off guard. Once again, they were out of touch with the mood, needs, and potential strength of the workers. Their reaction to the rank-and-file combativeness and to the autonomous actions was mixed. In workplaces where the unions were particularly weak, they tried to adapt their tactics to the workers' level of militancy in order to win support. In workplaces where the unions had some kind of long-term presence and some loyal cadres, they felt more threatened, and there was hostility toward the spontaneous actions of the rank and file. But despite the unions' efforts to seize control of the struggles, and despite the very modest concessions from management, the movement continued to pick up momentum. What were limited and scattered events during the spring of 1968 increased in intensity and frequency during the fall.

The labor confederations led two major national campaigns in 1968—one to reform the pension system and the other to abolish the "salary cages" (regional salary differentials). Both long struggles increased the level of mobilization throughout the working class. The pension issue pitted the workers and the unions against the government because the state controlled the nationwide pension system. In early 1968, mass protests began against a new pension law which the workers claimed offered too little. The government repeatedly refused to reconsider the legislation until the three labor confederations organized a unitary general strike in November 1968 which received vast worker support. There had been no such strike in Italy for 20 years. In February 1969, the government finally agreed to a new law which guaranteed 74 percent of the average of the last several years' salaries (80 percent by 1976) to everyone who had worked 40 years.[1]

The struggle against the regional salary differentials dragged on from early 1968 to March 1969. First the state-owned industries, then the small and medium-sized businesses, and finally the large private corporations signed accords to level out wage differences over a period of two and a half to three and a half years. The pension and salary cage campaigns turned out to be significant in several ways. They brought the North and South of Italy together into unified struggles; they activated workers in regions and in individual companies that had been quiet for years; and finally, they required and achieved the unitary action of the three labor confederations.

As the labor unrest grew during the fall of 1968, the semiskilled and unskilled workers took over the leading role. They had little experience with or commitment to the predictable and relatively disciplined forms of organized labor struggles. When they joined the movement, they added a new intensity and inventiveness. They also increased the number of workers involved. Known in Italian as the *operai comuni* (ordinary workers, as opposed to skilled), they rapidly forged a collective identity and made their perspective dominant.* Most of the innovative demands and forms of struggle that rapidly emerged in late 1968 and 1969 originated with the *operai comuni*. The developing movement also began to draw office workers in industry, agricultural workers, employees of large stores, technicians, and engineers.

It is important to note that the level of unity of these different groups fluctuated over the course of several years. It also varied from workplace to workplace. Early on, few office workers in industry identified with the actions of the production workers. In many instances, there was overt hostility between the two groups. Blue-collar workers tended to see those with clerical jobs as privileged and separate. Their salaries were higher and their benefits better. They were more carefully selected by management for their loyalty. The level of unionization was even lower among office workers than among blue collars. During the early stages of the movement, it was not uncommon for production workers to shut down offices forcibly and to coerce the employees to go out on strike.

As the protests gained momentum, many office workers joined in. The sense of a common struggle was strongest at the high point of the movement in 1969. The enthusiasm and energy of the times bound the office and production workers together. The same was true of the *operai comuni* and the skilled workers. The specific interests of the latter were not necessarily served by some of the demands of the *operai comuni* (for example, the demand for equal wage increases for all). Yet most of the skilled joined the movement and supported these demands through

---

*In political analyses, these workers were also called *operai massa* (mass workers).

1969. Later the desire to preserve their privileges and to promote their more narrow interests reasserted itself. The engineers and technicians were still another group with their own orientation. In many high-technology enterprises, these employees were quite radical. They initiated innovative struggles themselves. Earlier experiences of political activism in the student movement had influenced the attitudes of some.

New Demands

Many of the individual demands that evolved out of the movement looked similar to demands made or won by workers in other countries (for example, an end to compulsory overtime or some control over the pace of work and the workplace environment). Yet what made the situation in Italy new and anomalous was the systematic extension and linking of many demands into a coherent group and their ideological motivation. The demands fell into several categories. The first and perhaps most original group related to the issue of equality. The underlying concept was that of a united working class, one no longer divided by skills categories, wage differentials, regional origins, age, or sex. In concrete terms, the workers asked for pay raises consisting of the same sum for everyone (as opposed to percentage increases which maintained salary differentials), equal fringe benefits for blue- and white-collar workers, a reduction in the number of job categories (job categories determined payscale), and some worker control over the definition of categories and over the criteria for passing from one to the next.

A large number of demands concerned control over work conditions and over the organization of labor. In reaction to the strict command and the repressive conditions maintained by employers, the workers' movement established as one of its central objectives some measure of control over production in order to alter power relations in the plants. The struggle against authoritarianism became an important theme of the period. As a first step in this long process, the workers wanted some say over the pace of work, work schedules, division of tasks, and health and safety conditions. They also sought to abolish the practice of extra pay for hazardous jobs, arguing that a worker's well-being should not be traded for money. Instead, employers should eliminate dangerous conditions for everyone. Related demands challenged the accepted notions of productivity. The workers rejected the assumption that it was management's prerogative to push workers to their limit and to make salaries dependent on how much was produced. The movement called for a 40-hour week and the abolition of piecework, other incentive systems, and compulsory overtime.

Increased worker participation and representation made up still another category of demands. In addition to general union rights to organize and represent workers, the rank and file asked for the right to hold periodic assemblies inside the workplace on company time. They also wanted the right to continue bargaining (and striking) on any issue even after a contract was signed. This group of demands reflected the determination to prolong the movement and to make rank-and-file democracy a part of working life in Italy.

As the struggles intensified and drew more and more workers, a process of politicization took place. The new militancy contributed to the growth of group ideology and group identification. The practice of holding open assemblies became more widespread. Large numbers of workers reflected on their own actions and consciously shaped them according to emerging political criteria. Central to the political orientation of the movement was a rejection of the current organization of production in Italy. Many workers were anticapitalist (or socialist in the generic sense). The nature of the struggles stimulated their thinking about alternative systems of production and politics and a better life outside the workplace. Some activists began to speculate on topics such as workers' self-management in the factories. They discussed economic decentralization and democratic planning. They conceived of a new political order that would link workplaces to communities and situate significant power at the grassroots level.

Unlike some trade unions and social democratic parties in other European countries, the labor movement in Italy rejected the notion of co-determination. The movement was not oriented toward collaborating with management in running the plants or in determining compromise labor and economic policies. Winning concessions through struggles and collective bargaining was preferred over the negotiations of high-level labor-management boards. Radical activists hoped to achieve workers' control eventually. Some of the themes heard again and again were "a new model of development," "a new type of democracy," and "workers' power." Significantly, many unions came to adopt this rhetoric so that the innovative and radical orientation was not limited to small groups of workers. It gradually infused the overall tone of the labor movement.

Certainly not every worker thought of the movement in terms of significant change in the economic and political system. But there was general agreement on the specific objectives and widespread approval of the tone and militancy of the movement. Some radical workers expected to "make the revolution" within a short period of time (and some were bitterly disappointed a few years later when this had not happened). But a majority of the activists who considered themselves revolutionaries or radicals thought in more long-range and strategic terms. The policies they were formulating then were aimed at changing power relations in Italy step by step in favor of labor and at the expense of the capitalist class. This perspective motivated several demands that became a fixed part of the labor movement's official program for almost a decade: access to information on management's production and investment plans; some control over investment, credit, and employment policies in the private and public sectors; development programs for the South.

In addition to the new politicization of large numbers of workers, another transformation was taking place—the breakdown of the old work ethic. Early in the postwar period, the traditional leaders of the labor movement—the unions, the rank-and-file vanguard, and the PCI—incorporated a strong work ethic into their value systems. High productivity became a virtue. In the first decade after the war, the Communists saw productivity as a way of defending jobs and keeping factories open. But beyond the specific difficulties of that period, the work ethic was seen as positive in itself. The Italian left assumed that hard work and high levels of productivity would be features of a socialist society. This estimation of work began to change in the late 1960s. Younger workers in particular questioned the value of time spent on the job. They disputed the worth of what they were producing and the nature of work as they knew it. They no longer assumed that, aside from better material conditions, labor would look much the same in a noncapitalist society. They examined their current alienation in terms of the separation of intellectual and manual labor. They objected to the exclusion of the working class from scientific and technical knowledge. Another criticism focused on the fragmentation of the work process into small, meaningless tasks.

The Unions Regain Control

The workers' movement found both support and stimulation in the new environment in Italy. Challenges to academic and political authority, marches, assemblies, demonstrations, and all-night discussions had become a part of daily life. There was a fruitful interaction between workers, students, and some of the New Left organizations. They debated theory and tactics and held joint assemblies. Students and New Leftists leafleted at factories, marched on picket lines, and attended labor rallies. The nonworker activists often played a positive role in the labor mobilization by encouraging political discussion and new forms of struggle. The relationship was usually strongest in large, highly visible workplaces and in those where the unions were weak. In a number of factories, activist workers who were critical of the unions set up autonomous workers' groups that promoted debate and organized protests. Some of these were called unitary base committees (CUB). The CUB were generally stronger in university cities of the northern and central regions (except Turin) where the student movement was also an active force.

Both the New Left organizations (which were able to recruit small numbers of workers) and the CUB criticized the unions for being undemocratic, removed from the daily lives of workers, and ineffectual. They reproached all the traditional representatives of the working class, and especially the PCI, for having failed to build a revolutionary movement. They argued that new forces should take over that task. But these groups were never able to mount a serious challenge to the labor unions or to the traditonal left parties for leadership of the working class. They never developed into mass organizations or into a mass political movement. Before the discontent had consolidated into a substantial threat, the unions managed to renew their relationship with the rank and file and to reassert their hegemony over the labor movement.

But the reassertion of union control did not come about effortlessly. It required extensive debate and changes in policy. Early on, when the struggles were escaping union control, the labor organizations had neither the strategy, the structures, nor the cadres to lead the workers effectively. Some union leaders defensively accused the independent workers' groups and the "outsiders" (students and New Left organizations) of acting against the interests of the working class. But the younger, more radical unionists took a very different approach. They argued that the labor organizations could not afford to be out of touch with their bases. They saw the workers' revolt as a positive occasion for the entire labor movement to renew itself. This part of the leadership, which came to be known as the union left (*la sinistra sindacale*), maintained a dialogue with the radical workers' groups. These unionists accepted the changes taking place: new demands, new attitudes, the protagonist role of the *operai comuni*, and the non-union-led job actions. The union left played a key role in mediating between the rank and file and the union hierarchies.

By 1969, many unions concluded that it was in their interest to join and try to lead the movement rather than oppose it. (*Cavalcare la tigre*, "ride the tiger," was a typical way of putting it.) This meant that the unions began to support and even to anticipate demands coming from the base. The unions could then initiate struggles themselves. In companies where they were particularly weak, the unions found that by encouraging the mobilization, they could create a base for themselves and then influence the movement. The FIM was particularly open to the innovations of the period, and the other two metal and mechanical workers' unions (FIOM and UILM) also went through a process of internal debate and adjustment. In 1969 when the national contract for that category came up for renewal, the rank and file played a major role in deciding the content of the union platform for the first time. Some 300,000 metal and mechanical workers debated the platform in 2,300 assemblies around the country.[2] The rank and file also had ample representation on the negotiating team. Unitary committees of workers which were elected in the various shops took responsibility for organizing the plant-level contract struggles. Workers in other categories had similar experiences.

The unions had notable advantages that helped them regain control over the workers' movement. They were able to coordinate, generalize, and unify struggles. For example, when the major labor organizations called national strikes in late 1968 and 1969, hundreds of thousands of workers, sometimes millions, would participate. This kind of mass action absorbed the small dissident groups, leaving them little opportunity for an autonomous response. The unions were able to generalize a demand put forward in one locale by making it part of a national campaign or a contract platform. By sustaining a high level of mobilization, the unions also found they could unify—at least temporarily—different groups of workers whose immediate interests were in conflict. When used effectively, this capacity to coordinate, generalize, and unify inspired confidence within the rank and file and won support.

When some 60 national contracts came up for renewal in 1969, the unions seized this as an occasion to rally the workers around unitary platforms that included many new rank-and-file demands. In this way, the unions channeled the movement and consolidated their own leadership position. The national contract struggles of 1969 also marked a decline in the influence of nonunion organizations among the workers.

The Hot Autumn: A Victory for the Workers' Movement

In the fall of 1969, national and local strikes exploded all over Italy, drawing 5.5 million workers—more than a quarter of the entire labor force—off the job. Rallies filled piazzas with tens of thousands; the streets were cordoned off for marches; and on the shop floors, protests could erupt at any time. This was the Hot Autumn.

Almost every major category of workers was struggling for a new contract, including the metal and mechanical, chemical, construction, and farm workers. More than 520 million worker-hours went to strikes, by far the highest figure since the first postwar years. In fact, comparable levels of participation and militancy had not been seen since the early days after liberation. On November 19, 1969, 20 million Italian citizens joined a nationwide general strike to demand reforms from the government. At the end of that month, 150,000 metal and mechanical workers marched on Rome.[3] The outcome of the Hot Autumn was a victory for the labor movement, a victory that the unions considered to be one of the most significant events of their entire history.

From the start of the contract struggles, employers took an intransigent position. They resorted to repressive tactics such as individual and mass layoffs to discourage workers. As in the past, they called in the police to confront pickets and demonstrators. Most employers could count on the support of magistrates (many of whom were still holdovers from the Fascist era) and local governments as well as the police. These forces did what they could to harass the labor movement. In the few months between September and December 1969, 13,000 Italians were arrested or charged in incidents having to do with the labor conflicts.

Both Confindustria and Intersind were particularly resistant on the issues of company-level bargaining, work conditions, and control over the organization of labor. They recognized that their autonomy and traditional privileges were at stake. Even before national negotiations formally began, Fiat suspended 35,000 workers in reprisal for company-level struggles. But rather than undermine resolve, management fed the anger of the rank and file. Solidarity was bolstered. Workers everywhere achieved an unusual degree of unity, with certain groups continuing to struggle in support of others even after their own demands had been met. The metal and mechanical workers in state-controlled plants, for example, ratified a new contract in December, but they immediately voted to give active support to the metal workers in private industry until the latter were able to sign an equally strong accord.

The contracts won in 1969 and early 1970 differed on specific points from category to category, but the general areas of improvement were the same. An overview of the metal and mechanical workers' agreement with Confindustria illustrates the nature of the 1969 victory. The provisions of this contract, which covered 1.2 million workers in private industry, included a reduction of the work week to 40 hours over two to three years; limits on overtime; recognition that overtime was an exceptional rather than a regular circumstance; schedule accommodations for workers attending school; one additional holiday; equal treatment for white- and blue-collar workers who fell ill or suffered accidents; the right to hold up to ten hours of assemblies each year on company time inside plants with over 15 workers; the right to hold additional assemblies in the workplaces before or after work hours; recognition of union representatives in the plants; eight hours a month with pay for representatives to carry out union duties and additional time off without pay; the right to post union

TABLE 4.1: Wage Increases for Metal and Mechanical Workers
and Changes in the Cost of Living, 1966–70

Year	Wages*	Cost of Living
1966	100.0	100.0
1967	106.2	102.0
1968	108.3	103.3
1969	115.1	106.2
1970	147.8	111.6

*Minimum established by contract.

Source: Alessandro Pizzorno, et al., Lotte operaie e sindacato: il ciclo 1968-1972 in Italia (Bologna: Il Mulino, 1978), p. 298.

notices on designated bulletin boards; the right to distribute union litera-ture during nonwork hours; union dues check-off;* rank-and-file ratifica-tion of union contracts; the right of every worker to a written explana-tion from management for any disciplinary action; the right of workers to defend themselves in the case of disciplinary actions; and significant wage gains that were largely egalitarian.[4] Table 4.1 shows the increases in wages earned by the metal and mechanical workers from 1966 to 1970 com-pared to the rise in the cost of living.

Remembering for a moment the repressive conditions in many Ital-ian factories—exile departments, blacklisting, political surveillance, workers summarily dismissed for talking on the assembly line or glancing at a newspaper during lunch hour—the breadth of the 1969 victory be-comes clear. In addition to improvements in wages and work conditions and some protection against arbitrary authority, the workers had reas-serted the right to organize themselves as a collective body. The unions would be able to operate openly in the plants and offices where they had been banished for years.

There was a strong sense within the workers' movement that the new contracts were just the beginning, that the conflict with manage-ment would be ongoing until power relations changed. When 43 other category contracts, including the textile workers' agreement, came up for renewal in 1970, the struggles continued. The workers were able to repeat the successes of the previous year. In some cases, they made even greater gains.

*Once a year, the company would insert a dues form in each pay envelope. The workers would check off whether or not they wanted to join a union and which one. Management would then automatically deduct union dues from the paychecks and turn the money over to the unions. A worker could decide to stop paying dues at any time.

The victories were marred, however, by the onset of a violent reaction from the far right. The targets were the workers' movement and left political and cultural forces. On December 12, 1969, neofascists detonated a powerful bomb during business hours in a bank in Milan's crowded Piazza Fontana. The dead numbered 16 and the injured 90. This intensified the so-called strategy of tension—a right-wing mission to destabilize Italian political and social life through the use of violence. What followed were long years of terrorism—of the right and the left—which continued into the 1980s. The nature of this violence and its impact on the workers' movement will be discussed in Chapter 6.

The Forms of Struggle

During the late 1960s and early 1970s, the labor movement drew upon forms of struggle that went far beyond the customary strike in which workers walk off the job and picket outside the workplace. The movement combined and modified a variety of tactics in order to maximize the impact on employers. Italian workers had employed most of these tactics at one point or another in the past, but the novelty of the late 1960s was how the tactics were used—their frequency and intensity, the high level of rank-and-file participation, the self-conscious choice of one tactic over another, their combination into a coherent strategy, and the political value attached to various tactics.

As in the past, the workers relied heavily on short actions with pre-established starting and ending points. (It often took many months to win a contract, and there were no strike funds to sustain long work stoppages.) The time-limited strike usually lasted from 15 minutes to several hours. Sometimes the workers left the factories and picketed to keep everyone outside. But there were also several types of internal strikes. For example, during the "checkerboard strike" (*sciopero a scacchiera*), one group of workers at a time stopped production for a brief period. The strike jumped from shop to shop in the plant, disorganizing the entire flow of production. The "hiccup strike" (*sciopero a singhiozzo*) involved a series of short, plantwide work stoppages, one after another. These limited, internal strikes had several advantages. First, an individual worker stopped production for only a short time, minimizing his or her pay loss. Second, there was no long truce period during negotiations when the momentum of the movement and the sense of mobilization declined. Third, the rank and file had more control over these decentralized forms of struggle.

Strikes without a time limit (*sciopero ad oltranza*) did occur, but they were relatively rare even during the height of the workers' movement. It was difficult to keep such strikes going for long with a high level of participation. As the strike faltered, the workers often became discouraged and divided among themselves. Unlimited strikes sometimes started spontaneously in situations where the unions were weak or under challenge. Many of these shutdowns took place in single departments or shops. At times, workers used this kind of strike to express frustration with slow negotiations.

Other strikes included more than single plants or companies. The general strike involved all workers in industry, commerce, agriculture, and services. Its political impact was tremendous. Such a strike could paralyze the entire country and bring down a government. The unions sometimes called a general strike for political purposes: to demand a reform program or to protest the killing of a worker or an act of terrorism. In many cases, the call to strike went out to the citizenry as a whole and not just to the working class. Variations on the general strike were actions limited to all industrial workers or to a single region of Italy.

Another category of tactics did not involve going out on strike. There were, for example, slowdowns of various kinds. In one, workers simply followed every rule to the letter (*sciopero bianco*, known as "working to rule" in English). This inevitably bogged down production, especially in offices. Another tactic became emblematic of the period. Auto workers who were painting, welding, or performing some other task on the car bodies would simply skip over every fourth or fifth piece that passed by on the assembly line (*salto della scocca*). Still another tactic was to put a particular demand into effect without waiting for negotiations or the mediation of the unions (*praticare l'obbiettivo*—putting the objective into practice). If the workers wanted shorter hours, they stopped work early; if they were demanding the right to assembly, they began holding assemblies; if they wanted better safety conditions, they set up those conditions. This form of struggle gave the rank and file a sense of its own power. The workers altered the process of production to meet their own needs. They based their decisions on their own evaluations. The tactic undermined the traditional hierarchy in the workplace and was considered a particularly aggressive form of struggle. Sabotage of equipment and machinery was yet another tactic. There had always been individual acts of sabotage in the plants which management did not publicize for fear of spreading the phenomenon. But during the early stages of the movement, some workers and political groups began to encourage sabotage as a tactic to be used regularly. There were many incidents of sabotage over the next several years, but they remained primarily an expression of frustration and anger rather than a systematic form of struggle.

The workers used other tactics to strengthen the effectiveness of a strike. One of these was the indoor or internal march (*corteo interno*). As a strike began, workers would march through the plant making sure that everyone left the machines and offices. On occasion, fights broke out with workers who did not want to strike. Managers and white-collar employees were sometimes forced out of their offices. Another tactic was to block every entrance into a plant so that no materials could be delivered and no goods taken out. The workers took turns guarding the gates. Aggressive picketing stopped those who were not sympathetic to a strike from entering a workplace.

Many forms of struggle—for example, internal strikes, internal marches, putting the objective into practice—reflected the new central position of the workplace itself in labor campaigns. Most of the tactics demanded planning and coordination. They also required combativeness and a high rate of participation in order to succeed. Management's response was correspondingly aggressive. Employers called in the police to clear away pickets. They dismissed workers and brought criminal charges against them for disrupting production and destroying property. The workers would then retaliate with a new round of job actions. The forms of struggle used during the late 1960s became regular procedures for the Italian labor movement during contract negotiations and company-level campaigns for most of the next decade.

Workers' Delegates and Councils: A New System of Representation

One of the major achievements of the Italian workers' movement of the late 1960s and early 1970s was the development of a new form of labor representation in the workplace—a system of rank-and-file delegates and councils. The new system was (and still is) unusual for an advanced capitalist country in the postwar period. It was a response to particular circumstances in Italy. On the one hand, there was an ongoing, combative, and politically sophisticated rank-and-file movement that had no durable organizational expression. On the other hand, there were national and regional labor unions that had been frustrated until then in their attempts to create a substantial presence in the workplace. The result of these circumstances was the effort to create base-level structures that would meet the partially coincident needs of the rank-and-file movement and the unions. The day-to-day struggles generated an initial system of representation that was gradually transformed to accommodate the unions.

There has always been controversy over the exact origins of the workers' delegates in Italy. Some participants in the movement and observers have claimed that the workers elected their first delegates spontaneously. Others assert that the unions proposed the idea. What seems clear is that in the early stages of the movement (1968 and early 1969), strike meetings and assemblies were open to all workers. The structures that sprang up at that time were informal struggle committees and study groups whose mode of operation was fluid and whose membership was heterogeneous. In the meantime, the unions were trying to establish a presence in some factories in a variety of ways. They tried setting up locals affiliated with single confederations, and they tried unitary locals. They also bargained with management to strengthen the old internal commissions. But none of these efforts was especially successful.

By early 1969, some factory departments and work teams were electing their first representatives or delegates. These delegates were activist leaders who headed struggles, negotiated informally with supervisors, and acted as liaisons for their work groups. But even at an early and unsettled stage, some workers opposed the idea of representation and delegation of authority. *Lotta Continua* (Struggle Continues), an organization to the left of the Communist Party, claimed that the idea of delegates was a union maneuver to channel and control the movement. For *Lotta Continua*, the election of delegates signaled the decline of direct democracy and a loss of autonomy for the movement. The organization expressed its opposition with the slogan "We're all delegates!"

In the summer of 1969, the metal and mechanical workers of the CGIL (FIOM) held a conference to discuss the possibility of extending the phenomenon of delegates during the contract struggles of the fall. The other metal and mechanical workers' unions soon agreed to the formation of unitary committees of department delegates in the factories. They were to lead the strikes and job actions along with the old internal commissions. The unions did not establish a set method for choosing the delegates. In some cases, the workers elected representatives by secret ballot or by a show of hands. In other cases, the department simply ratified the choice of the internal commission or the unions. The committees were still quite informal. They met when there was something to be decided, and they frequently took on new members.

After the contracts were signed, the delegates chosen in the fall did not disappear. They led new struggles, especially at the department level, to force employers to implement the contracts. A generally accepted system soon emerged for choosing new delegates. The workers from a homogeneous group elected a delegate by secret ballot. There was no list of nominees, so each worker simply wrote down a choice for delegate. The worker with the highest number of votes won. Union members and nonmembers all voted, and delegates did not have to belong to a union. Under this system, popular and activist workers tended to win the elections. The delegates then led struggles and spoke for their work teams or assembly lines on any issue that the workers wanted to confront. If workers were displeased with their delegate, they had the right to discharge him or her. The ratio of workers to delegates was about 50 or 60 to one.

Many of the contracts signed in 1969 stipulated that the workers could have union representatives from each confederation in the plants (*rappresentanti sindacali d'azienda*). The question immediately became whether or not these representatives had to be union members elected only by other union members. In other words, would the representatives in a plant function as a union local, or would they be delegates who represented all the workers and expressed the autonomous organizing activity of the rank and file? It was up to the union confederations to decide who their official plant representatives would be and how they would be selected. The ratio of workers to representatives was set at about 300 to one. The unions finally opted to choose their representatives from among the rank-and-file delegates. By doing this, the unions affirmed their commitment to rank-and-file activism and democracy. They also forged more solid ties to their bases. In some cases, the FIOM and FIM let assemblies of delegates choose the union representatives themselves. Unlike the delegates, the union representatives had the official recognition of management. According to most contracts, they could take time off from work for union duties, move about the plants, hold meetings, and negotiate with management. The delegates did not have these formal privileges.

As the next step in consolidating their presence in the workplace, the unions began to organize workplace or factory councils. As in the case of the delegates, many of the first councils grew directly out of the experience of specific struggles. The various activists and representatives in a workplace—delegates, internal commission members, technical committee members, union representatives, activist rank-and-filers—would all meet to decide on goals, tactics, and negotiation procedures. The unions came to believe that it would be in their interest to formalize a similar sort of factorywide or officewide representative structure. Such a structure could coordinate union activities and prevent the decentralized delegate system from becoming too dispersed.

During the summer and fall of 1970, the metal and mechanical workers' unions took the initiative by deciding to set up councils wherever they could. Only delegates were to be council members, and the council was to be the only rank-and-file and union representative structure in the workplace. The other category unions followed the metal and mechanical workers' example over the course of the next two years. Once the new councils were in place, the old union structures such as the internal commissions finally disbanded.

The council system spread from the large workplaces of the North to medium-sized and small workplaces elsewhere in Italy (although the greatest concentration remained in the North). In 1972, Confindustria conducted a survey and found that there were factory councils in about one-third of the manufacturing workplaces in its sample.[5] Many nonindustrial workplaces also set up delegate councils. For the next several years, the total number of councils grew rapidly.

The new Italian system was an unconventional solution to the problem of union representation in the workplace. Three politically diverse and still competitive confederations shared a base structure that was made up of nonunion as well as union members. This differed from the typical shop-steward system in an open-shop situation because in the latter only union members voted for the stewards. In the Italian system, the support of the workers for their councils depended on the level of rank-and-file unity and involvement in the workplace. The situation was less fixed than in other systems.

For the unions, the main disadvantage of the new councils was that not all the delegates were union members. This meant less direct union control. The advantage, however, was a strong link to the rank-and-file base. During the early 1970s, the unions saw the rank-and-file movement as a source of strength for themselves after so many years of frustration. For the rank and file, some kind of permanent workplace structure recognized by management was necessary in order to consolidate the workers' new power and to implement gains made on paper. The councils were also a means for a new generation of activists to preserve their leadership role during times of relative calm. Until then, the rank and file had never responded enthusiastically to union efforts to set up locals. But many workers regarded the delegate and council system as more of their own making. They expected it to be more directly responsive to their needs.

Consolidation of the Councils and the "New Union"

By 1972, the workers' movement had reached its peak. The struggles continued, but they centered more often on specific contract provisions or contract renewals. They lost much of the innovative, explosive quality of earlier stages of the movement. The unions were more firmly in control, and the tenor of the times had changed. The years 1968-72 had been marked by a sometimes chaotic but consistently creative energy. There was a desire to experiment and an almost constant state of mobilization. By 1972, the delegates, councils, and unions were focusing much attention on implementing contracts. They wanted to consolidate their positions. The unions also began to alter the procedures for electing delegates in some workplaces. They enlarged the electoral units to include an entire department or several assembly lines rather than a small, homoge-

A workers' assembly in the main courtyard at Fiat Mirafiori.

neous work group. Each worker voted for several delegates-at-large rather than for a single representative. The delegates each represented 70 to 80 workers rather than 50 or 60. In order to win an election, a candidate had to receive a certain percentage of the votes. Previously, the highest vote-getter became the delegate no matter what percentage he or she received.

In those workplaces where they were instituted, the new procedures favored the unions. With larger electoral units, an organized group, such as a union faction, could determine the election of several delegates. The unions were able to place more of their own people on the councils. These structures then became smaller, more cohesive, and more homogeneous. The unions justified the new procedures by arguing that some work groups might have no competent activist leaders whereas other groups might have several. Under the new rules, several activists from the same work group could all become delegates. The unions also maintained that it was preferable that workers with very few votes (and therefore little support) not be elected and that the councils be a less unwieldy size. The overall result was to make some delegates less representative of a particular work group. Some workers felt they had lost "their own" delegate. Women in particular became more severely underrepresented in the councils. The work groups where they were concentrated often fell in with male-dominated groups to make larger electoral units.

Once the high point of the movement had passed, interest and participation in the councils declined in many workplaces. There were individuals who found the delegate's job too taxing or frustrating. In addition to the long hours required to represent a large number of workers, the delegates had to balance the specific and sometimes narrow concerns of one department with a strategy for the entire workplace. A number of delegates who had become active during the early stages of the movement but did not have a great deal of political experience dropped out of the councils. Members of most of the New Left political groups, however, continued to participate in the elections. Nonunion activists still won posts as delegates although the councils were made up primarily of union members or workers close to the unions. There was also a higher turnover among the nonunion delegates, so that over time union activists made up the most stable segment of the councils.

The councils underwent further changes in 1972 and 1973. They set up their own committees to deal with questions such as the organization of labor, press relations, and transportation. Once the councils took on these additional concerns, it became necessary to divide up tasks among the delegates. Many delegates became specialized, and a hierarchy of power and prestige developed based on the various responsibilities and competencies. Some of the committee members left their work groups to do union work full time. This was a significant change because the 1969 movement had been very critical of the previous practice of having full-time internal commission members. The egalitarianism of the late 1960s had explicitly rejected any structure in which the workers' representatives distanced themselves from or were more privileged than the groups they represented.

Another important change involved the role of the executive committee of a council. In theory, the council was to set policy for the workplace, and the executive committee was to carry out that policy. In practice, the roles were soon reversed. The executive committee took responsibility to call council meetings, establish the agenda, and deliver the initial and concluding presentations. The executive committee also had the power to postpone or cancel meetings. These responsibilities enabled the committee to influence both the content and direction of debate. In addition, there was strong antipathy to voting on issues at council meetings because the delegates considered the procedure divisive and too reminiscent of bourgeois parliamentary process. Instead of voting, the councils often made an effort to arrive at consensus, but the result was that many discussions were inconclusive. Critics felt that this system increased the executive committee's power even further. Since an executive committee was in touch with delegates from every department, it had greater access to information than any other group in a workplace. It also became the sole body empowered to negotiate with management. By 1972, many large companies had given the councils informal or de facto recognition because management generally wanted a stable and authoritative body to deal with. When the FIM suggested that the executive committees in metal and mechanical plants rotate members in order to avoid an entrenchment of power, the employers blocked the proposal.

The system of delegates and councils in Italy did meet the two sets of needs mentioned earlier. The rank and file developed a permanent structure to use as the base for an ongoing movement during periods of relative calm as well as struggle. The unions established a solid presence in the workplace and gained the support of the working class. The unions also managed to centralize the council structure and reinforce their hold on it. They did this at the expense of some degree of autonomy and control on the part of the rank and file. Yet this is not to say that the new delegate and council system in Italy was undemocratic or nonparticipatory or highly bureaucratized in the early 1970s. On the contrary, relative to union structures in many advanced capitalist countries, the Italian councils were unusually autonomous and open rank-and-file organizations. Although they had moved away from the original model to some extent, they had by no means completely abandoned the fundamental conception.

Some transformation of the council system was probably inevitable as the workers' movement dropped back from its high point of activity. The new workplace structures had to serve in periods of consolidation and even retrenchment as well as during phases of mass mobilization and intense struggle. In order for the confederations to operate effectively and in the interests of the working class at the national level, they had to build a base within the rank and file. That base required a certain degree of centralization to coordinate workplace activity with the larger, national strategy of the unions. In addition, the need to confront employers with a credible and experienced interlocutor at the company level made some consolidation of council leadership necessary.

Balancing the interests of the national unions, the immediate needs of the rank and file as a whole, and the specific demands of a single shop or department was problematic. The process inevitably generated tensions and contradictions. One fundamental question was how much centralization and union control were necessary for the adequate coordination of the workers' movement. A related question was how much control could the unions exercise over the council structure before the latter became bureaucratized and unresponsive to the needs of the rank and file. In 1973, it remained to be seen whether the "new union" as it was called would be able to promote the growth of the workers' movement and further its most politically advanced objectives.

Results of the Workers' Movement

The late 1960s were a time of more widespread labor conflict and heightened protest movements in many advanced capitalist countries. But the workers' movement in Italy set itself apart from movements in other nations. It sustained a more generalized and more intense level of activity over a longer period of time. Ultimately it had a more profound impact on society. It was the workers' movement—rather than the student or antiwar movements—that produced the greatest challenge to existing political forces in Italy. The struggles that began on the shop floor also undermined traditional capitalist relations of production for a time and further exposed the problems of a structurally weak economy.

One of the immediate effects of the movement was a change in the daily work lives of most semiskilled and unskilled employees. Work rhythms, schedules, environment, and salaries improved somewhat, and the shift in power relations created the possibility of further progress. This was the basis for the workers' continued support of the movement. The supervisors no longer ruled the shop floor. Until then, they had held discretionary power over promotions and merit wage increases. They had also been free to punish workers and to implement management's general policy of political repression. Beginning in 1969, the new labor contracts limited the supervisors' authority by establishing clear-cut procedures for promotions, salary increases, and suspensions. With less power over jobs and wages, the supervisors could no longer intimidate the labor force as effectively. The changes were less dramatic for some of the skilled workers and technicians who already had more autonomy on the job; their positions had been less subservient to supervisors to begin with.

One sign that the workers felt more secure was the rise in the absentee rate in the early 1970s. Before the movement, absenteeism was relatively low in Italian factories. For example, the rate was just 5 or 6 percent at Fiat until 1965. Workers often reported to the factory when they were sick, for fear of losing their jobs or any part of a dismally low wage. After 1969, absenteeism rose. At Fiat, the rate reached 12.5 percent in 1970.[6] Underlying the higher absentee rates were frustrations with boring and dangerous jobs. Absenteeism was also a protest against insufficient services such as public transportation, day care, and health care. Working women with children suffered especially from the lack of social services.

Another result of the movement was the stronger organizational presence of the unions within the working class. After the first few years of struggles, the unions gained in credibility. Total membership for the three confederations rose from about 4.5 million in 1968 to about 6 million in 1973. Yet only a minority of employees in industry (about 40 percent according to some estimates) and in the economy as a whole (about 36 percent) carried union cards.[7] In the metal and mechanical industries where unionization increased more rapidly, union membership included 28.9 percent of all employees in 1968 and 46.3 percent in 1972.[8]

The movement also transformed the structure of collective bargaining in Italy. National category contracts no longer restricted what could happen on the company level. Instead, national contracts established minimum conditions and protected workers who were in a weak bargaining position in their particular plants. Those in a stronger position could more easily negotiate company-level agreements that improved upon the national contract. In industry, the number of company-level contracts rose from 3,870 in 1968 to 7,567 in 1971.[9] The local agreements varied widely from company to company. Continuous bargaining became common because contracts did not include the no-strike clause. Nothing prevented the workers from challenging features of an agreement after it was signed. The factory councils regularly raised issues with management and insisted on renegotiating specific contract provisions.

The workers found support and protection for their newly won victories in the Workers' Rights Statute of May 1970 (*Statuto dei diritti dei lavoratori*). This was the first significant piece of labor relations (trade union) legislation passed in Italy since the ratification of the Constitution in 1948. The law applied to all private-sector workers in companies with more than 15 employees and in agricultural enterprises with more than five workers. Article 39 of the Constitution guaranteed the right to form trade unions and to enter into collective labor contracts. Yet in order to implement this article of the Constitution, enabling legislation was needed, and Parliament had avoided passing such laws for 22 years. The Workers' Statute of 1970 not only reconfirmed basic political and religious liberties and the right to form unions, it facilitated union organizing activities in the workplace and secured the unions' presence at the company level. The statute did this by generalizing many of the gains won in specific labor contracts. It established the legal right to post union bulletins and to hold meetings in the workplace on company time for up to 10 hours each year; it guaranteed union representatives a certain number of paid hours in which to carry out their union duties; and it confirmed the right to dues check-off. Most importantly, the Workers' Statute asserted that unions could take employers to court for unfair labor practices, dismissals without just cause, and antiunion behavior. After Parliament approved the legislation, the unions brought hundreds of cases against employers. The resulting body of legal interpretation—much of which was in labor's favor—created a new legal basis for industrial relations in Italy.

The Attempt to Reunite the Labor Movement

Another consequence of the workers' movement was the impetus to reunite the labor organizations. The unity of action that developed at the rank-and-file level and among many category federations put pressure on the CGIL, CISL, and UIL to increase their cooperation. On May Day 1970, the Italian labor movement held its first unitary celebrations in more than two decades. The following October, the national leadership bodies of the three confederations met to discuss the possibility of reunification. But the commitment to unity was not at all consistent throughout the organizations. Some factions opposed reunification, and others differed over how and when it should take place. A few category unions, including the metal and mechanical workers, wanted to proceed more quickly than the confederations. The meeting ended with a generic call for unity.

Feeling pressured by the developing trend, the forces opposing unity began to coalesce. They included the Republicans and Social Democrats in the UIL and the right wing of the CISL. Ostensibly, there were three obstacles to unity. The first was the old "incompatibility" issue. The

CISL, the UIL, and the Socialists within the CGIL wanted a more complete separation of the unions from political parties. This meant that the
Communist leaders of the CGIL would have to agree to give up their
party leadership posts. Second, the CISL insisted that peasants with
small property holdings be able to join the unitary organizations. The
CGIL argued for limiting membership in agricultural unions to wage-
earning farm workers. Third, the confederations had to resolve the question of international affiliation. The CISL and the UIL belonged to the
anticommunist International Confederation of Free Trade Unions, organized in 1949 with major funding from the United States. The CGIL belonged to the pro-Soviet World Federation of Trade Unions.

In reality, these three issues were only manifestations of deeper and
more intractable reluctances. By belonging to a smaller but autonomous
confederation, the Social Democrats and Republicans of the UIL exerted
greater influence in the labor movement than their actual numbers war-
ranted. They were afraid of losing their power in a unitary labor confederation where the larger political forces would dominate. Another
strong sentiment motivating many of the factions opposing unity was dif-
fidence toward the Communists. These groups were still wary of associat-
ing and collaborating—let alone merging—with a union confederation
much of whose leadership was in the PCI. In 1971, the CGIL agreed that
propertied peasants would be able to belong to any unitary organization.
The confederation also accepted the rule that union posts would be in-
compatible with all party positions as well as elected offices. All three
confederations indicated that they would be willing in time to withdraw
from their respective international organizations. But still the opposition
rejected the idea of what was called organic unity—the fusion of the existing confederations into a single body.

By 1972, the delays and continued bickering at the confederal level
had become a liability. The confederations began to lose credibility with
the rank and file and with outsiders who were sympathetic to labor. The
divisions affected struggles and contract negotiations. So in May 1972,
Luciano Lama, secretary of the CGIL, re-presented an earlier proposal
that the CISL, UIL, and CGIL form a loose federation in which the three
organizations would remain autonomous and intact. The new federation
would provide the three leaderships with a structure for regular deliberation and for the formulation of joint policy. Lama was essentially proposing formalized unity of action and a mechanism for policy making. The
groups opposing unity consented to the plan only on the condition that
there be no binding timetable for organic unity.

On July 24, 1972, the *Federazione* CGIL-CISL-UIL was born. The
accord stipulated that there would be equal representation for the three

component confederations although they differed considerably in size. The unionists and political forces in favor of organic unity had serious reservations about the new federation. They feared that the situation would be stabilized at this much lower level of unity. In the future, therefore, it might be more difficult if not impossible to achieve organic unity. They argued that the pro-unity groups should have pursued their objective more aggressively. Circumstances, including pressure from the rank and file, might have weakened the opposition. In the short run, however, the antiunity forces had enough weight to scuttle any project they found threatening.

The agreement between the CGIL, CISL, and UIL stifled the unitary aspirations of some category federations. They were prohibited from proceeding on their own with organic unification. In the case of the metal and mechanical workers, however, the desire for unity carried more weight than the confederal prohibition. The FIOM, FIM, and UILM merged their headquarters and leadership bodies into the Federation of Metal and Mechanical Workers (FLM). In order to remain within the limits of the regulations, the FLM also kept the three separate acronyms. Workers had the choice of joining the FLM directly or taking membership in one of the three subgroupings. Most workers soon opted for the FLM.

For the labor movement as a whole, the formation of the *Federazione* CGIL-CISL-UIL did not bury the old divisions. The dynamic of policy making was often contentious. At times this undermined the ability of the *Federazione* to take effective action, especially in the political arena. As critics of the compromise proposal had feared, a more organic form of unity was not reached. The three confederations remained quite distinct.

Notes to Chapter 4

1. Eugenio Guidi et al., *Movimento sindacale e contrattazione collettiva 1945-1970*, 2d ed., rev. and enl. (Milan: Franco Angeli, 1971), p. 26.

2. Ibid., p. 122.

3. Ibid., pp. 119, 127, 124.

4. Ibid., pp. 151-63.

5. Ida Regalia, "Rappresentanza operaia e sindacato: Il mutamento di un sistema di relazioni industriali," in Pizzorno et al., *Lotte operaie e sindacato: Il ciclo 1968-1972 in Italia* (Bologna: Il Mulino, 1978), p. 225.

6. Sergio Turone, *Storia del sindacato in Italia 1943-1980* (Bari: Laterza, 1981), p. 432.

7. Pietro Merli Brandini, "Italy: Creating a New Industrial Relations System from the Bottom," in *Worker Militancy and Its Consequences, 1965–75: New Directions in Western Industrial Relations*, ed. Solomon Barkin (New York: Praeger, 1975), p. 97.

8. Pizzorno et al., *Lotte operaie*, p. 295.

9. Marino Regini, *I dilemmi del sindacato: Conflitto e partecipazione negli anni settanta e ottanta* (Bologna: Il Mulino, 1981), p. 47.

5

The New Union in the 1970s

Through the middle of the decade, the workers' movement continued to make gains, but it operated in an increasingly difficult economic and political context. In the factories and in the political arena, the unions set far-reaching objectives but found themselves without the means to achieve many of their goals. As the economy went into crisis, the movement, which had previously assumed an innovative and aggressive stance, gradually fell back to a defensive position.

Italy's Economy in the 1970s

After the steady growth of the 1950s and early 1960s, the economy became locked into a pattern of slowdowns and recessions alternating with phases of expansion. The government used fiscal and monetary measures ("stop-and-go policies") in an attempt to stimulate business, counter salary gains made by the workers, and alleviate some symptoms of the deepening economic disorder such as high inflation. A combination of factors—both international and internal to Italy—aggravated the structural flaws of the system and accelerated the process of decline.

The changes brought about by the workers' movement were bound to traumatize a shaky economy. Employers were not as free to organize production at the expense of workers in order to raise productivity and profits. Labor was no longer the flexible factor it had previously been. In addition, capital accumulation had been weak from 1964 to 1969. The combined effect of these factors was a sharp increase in the cost of labor which cut into profits. Between 1969 and 1973, wage costs per unit produced rose 47.1 percent. During that same period, wage costs per unit produced went up in all industrialized countries (France, 18.7 percent; Germany, 24.2 percent; Great Britain, 36.2 percent), but the rate of increase in Italy was faster for the first time.[1] Private businesses and the government in Italy responded by hiking consumer prices, raising indirect taxes, and devaluating the lira. After 1973, Italy's annual rate of inflation regularly surpassed those of most other industrialized countries, and Italians could count on price increases of about 16 to 19 percent a year. The devaluations of the lira helped exports; companies could raise their prices, cover higher labor costs, and still maintain profits. But devaluation also boosted the price of imports, including food, energy, and raw materials. The consequence was still more inflation and less buying power for the salaried classes.

International factors played an important role in aggravating Italy's economic dislocation during the 1970s. These factors included the abandonment of the dollar-based international system of exchange (Bretton Woods) in 1970, the subsequent disruptive round of international currency devaluations, new competition from Third World industries, and heightened rivalry among the highly industrialized nations. In addition, the cost of raw materials had been rising relative to that of manufactured goods even before the oil price increases of late 1973. Inflation had become a serious problem for many capitalist economies. When the cost of oil suddenly quadrupled, it rocked an international system whose foundations were already weakened. The Western European economies slowed down and then dropped into the serious recession of 1974–75. The northern countries stopped hiring new guest workers, and before long, they were sending immigrants home. There were nearly two and one-half million Italian emigrés in Europe at the time. Looking at just the situation in West Germany, the number of Italians employed there fell during the course of 1974 from 450,000 to 370,000.[2] The wages that Italians sent home from abroad had improved the balance of payments. When the workers lost their jobs and returned to Italy, both employment prospects and the balance of payments deficit worsened.

Meanwhile some of the old structural imbalances in Italy became more severe during the 1970s. Peasants and farm workers continued to abandon the land. Since industry could not absorb all the job-seekers, both the employment situation and agriculture suffered further. The land was idle while food imports soared. Agricultural products (food, drink, tobacco) accounted for 21 percent of the monetary value of all imports in 1973. This was the costliest category of imports.[3] Another feature of the economic picture during the first half of the decade was the flight of capital from Italy. Business people and wealthy Italians in general reacted to the workers' movement and to declining economic prospects by transferring their assets abroad, often illegally. This weakened investments and further drained the balance of payments. The deteriorated financial situation in the mid-1970s forced Italy to seek massive and costly international loans from the EEC and financial institutions such as the International Monetary Fund.

Still another economic liability was the increased reliance of enterprises on external sources for investments and loans. In 1960, Italian businesses financed 44 percent of their activities with their own funds. In 1974, this figure had plummeted to 15.4 percent.[4] The expanded debt and huge sums of interest that had to be paid in the 1970s shackled the borrowers to their creditors and undermined initiative. During this same period, the number of Italian firms controlled by foreign interests grew. Much of the foreign capital came from the United States, West Germany, and Britain. As the financial picture worsened and as the workers' movement continued to apply pressure, some industrialists and financiers refused to invest in faltering enterprises. In certain cases, they shut down entire operations when the workers opposed temporary layoffs.

Confronted with the growing crisis in industry, the Italian state enlarged its holdings in the hope of stimulating economic activity and employment. By the end of the decade, about one-half of the large industries in Italy were part of the state system, which accounted for some 40 percent of Italy's GNP. Yet many state holdings operated at a loss. They often came under state control precisely because they were going bankrupt. Many were notoriously mismanaged. The government poured money into its industries but never formulated a coherent program for restructuring and developing them. As a result, the state holdings sapped rather than strengthened the vitality of the economy as a whole.

It is true that in the latter part of the decade, there were temporary improvements in one aspect or another of the economy—a dip in inflation, a rise in GNP, an improvement in the balance of payments. Yet, recovery was neither stable nor extensive, and the government never effectively tackled the fundamental problems. It was in this general context that the workers' movement had to maneuver in the 1970s. As the years passed, the economy proved to be an increasingly powerful impediment.

A Union Strategy for Reforms

In 1969, the three union confederations undertook a new course of action that came to be known as the "reform strategy." Acting together, they demanded that the prime minister and cabinet negotiate directly with them on a series of reform proposals. The confederations thus bypassed the mediation of the political parties and Parliament. They argued that after years of failure on the part of the center-left governments to enact serious reforms, a new force had to take the initiative. A primary motivation for the reform strategy was that the national confederations wanted to reestablish their own leadership in some area of collective action. They undertook the strategy at a time when the workers' movement was still questioning the authority of the union hierarchies and when the category federations had assumed a central role in collective bargaining. The movement itself provided another impetus for the reform strategy. Workers were not only challenging the organization of labor within the factories; they were also turning their attention to the sources of that organization in society. Their critique of the use of science and technology, for example, led them to scrutinize the educational system in Italy. They wanted improvements in the quality of their lives outside the workplace. The call for reforms elicited mass support.

The confederations' activity in the political arena did not substitute or diminish struggles in the usual domain of collective bargaining. The unions did not trade off workplace objectives for political reforms. In fact, the mobilized state of the working class was the confederations' greatest source of strength in dealing with the government. The labor leadership used movement tactics—general strikes and rallies—to pressure its interlocutor.

The confederations inaugurated the reform strategy in November 1969 with a nationwide general strike. The list of demands included improvements in housing, health care, public transportation, schooling, radio and television broadcasting, more equitable tax policies, agricultural modernization, and development of the South. Between 1969 and 1976, the confederations pursued the government with proposals, and in the process they became major participants in national policy discussions.

The unions functioned as political representatives of the working class as well. Not surprisingly, this new role generated tensions with the political parties, especially the PCI. The Communist Party's initial reaction to the reform strategy in late 1969 and early 1970 was positive because the confederations were reasserting their control over a rather unruly workers' movement. But the PCI leadership soon became openly critical of the unions, claiming that they had strayed beyond their legitimate province. The Communists argued that Parliament had to be the central forum for proposing and debating reforms. Beyond reasserting the role of Parliament, the PCI also wanted to establish itself as the leading political force in the reform campaign. The party was already contemplating Communist participation in the national government. It would not have helped the PCI's position to have the unions become the most prominent players in the reform struggle. In addition to these considerations, the PCI was generally cautious about mass mobilization if it was not party controlled. When the constant agitation of the labor movement on several fronts made the party leadership nervous, the Communists started calling on the unions to limit their activity to the more traditional labor arena.

The confederations began negotiations with the government in 1970. The talks dealt with housing, health care, transportation, and tax reform. But these issues became part of a larger vision of a "new model of development." Through government programs, the unions not only hoped to broaden the productive base in Italy and to provide jobs, they also wanted to make changes in the kind of goods produced. Production for social needs would be given priority. Vast reforms would require a reallocation of resources and a new configuration of economic and political power.

Not surprisingly, the unions' proposals met with immediate opposition in the government and in industrial and financial circles. The labor movement came under attack for attempting to subvert the economic order. For about five years, talks with the government repeatedly started up and broke down. The confederations called nationwide strikes to prod the politicians into action. In some cases Parliament passed reform legislation, but the laws remained incomplete or unimplemented. As in the past, some reforms quietly withered away in the administrative bureaucracy. (It was not uncommon for appropriated funds to remain unspent.)

The end result was quite disappointing. The new model of development never materialized. Even reforms advocated by part of the bourgeoisie to streamline the economic and social system were not realized. The ruling class in Italy was too divided by narrow self-interests to carry through substantial changes. By 1975, the economic crisis forced the unions to refocus much of their attention on layoffs, plant closings, and the defense of wages. The prospect of a new economic order receded even further. Yet in spite of its failures, the reform strategy did expand labor's role in national politics.

Collective Bargaining in the 1970s

The workers continued to win concessions from employers during the 1970s, especially during the first half of the decade. But the victories did not come easily. Most contracts required months of negotiations and repeated strikes. From the workers' point of view, the outcome was mixed. A balance sheet of gains and losses for the decade would show that the labor movement was most successful with demands focusing on the workplace (for example, issues involving the organization of labor). This was where the delegates and councils could exercise their maximum control. Issues having an impact beyond the plant walls were more prob-

lematic (for example, union supervision of investments or limits on subcontracting).

Many demands during the first half of the 1970s were innovative
and characteristic of the broad political perspective of the Italian workers'
movement. In 1973, for example, the workers won the right to take
courses on company time without losing pay. This demand grew out of
the desire to close the gap between those who enjoyed the privilege of
education and those who did not. Employers argued that education was
the responsibility of the state; a business had no obligation to finance
study that was not job related. The strategy of the unions, however, was
to step into those areas where the state had proven itself to be deficient.
In this case, the goal of the labor movement was not job training but the
general education of its members. The objective was to break down class
distinctions based on education. The workers prevailed and gained the
right to 150 hours of study time over three years with full pay for course
work in a wide range of subject areas. The courses (called *le 150 ore*) were
set up through the unions. Many of the instructors were affiliated with
the New Left, especially during the first several years when the movement
was strongest. In 1976, the number of study hours was increased for certain courses.

The organization of the labor process in the plants continued to be
a focus during the 1970s. In addition to wresting more control over the
pace of work and production schedules, the workers won improvements
in safety and health conditions such as better pollution controls. In some
company contracts, management made a commitment to develop work
processes based on less fragmented and repetitive tasks. Fiat, for example,
agreed to try out new organizational models such as the work islands that
Volvo had installed in its plants. Some large companies also consented to
make payments to local government agencies for improved social services
in the geographical areas around the factories. For the labor movement,
this was a small but symbolically important reparation for the government's long history of granting advantages to private capital.

By the mid-1970s, the standard workweek was 40 hours, and most
yearly schedules included 18 paid holidays and four weeks of vacation. In
some instances, job classifications for blue- and white-collar workers were
merged (*inquadramento unico*). This made the treatment of the two groups
more equal. As one of its most significant victories, the working class won
improved protection against inflation in 1975 under the nationwide wage
indexing system (*scala mobile*). This protection became increasingly valuable over the next several years, since Italy's inflation rate remained very
high. But the *scala mobile* also proved to be one of the greatest points of
controversy when business and the government went on the offensive in
the latter part of the decade to lower the cost of labor.

A 150 Hours course in Turin. Italian workers won the right in 1973 to study non-job-related as well as job-related material on company time.

During the early 1970s, it became clear that the workers' control over their jobs and over the quality of life outside the plants depended on their having some control over investment decisions. The question of how goods were produced could not be separated from what was produced, where it was produced, and for whom. The labor movement made productive investments in the South a central point in its program. The unions saw the South as a key to the future development of the entire country. Without alleviating the agonizing unemployment problem there or strengthening the productive base, all of Italy would be held back. By mid-decade, many company-level contracts contained provisions for specific investments in the South aimed at creating jobs. Some contracts put limits on overtime in northern plants in order to shift work to southern plants. The workers also demanded and won limits on subcontracting by individual companies to businesses whose workers were not protected by a union. The objective was to reduce the use of extremely exploitative off-the-books labor.

The new model of development proposed by the labor movement gave priority to socially useful production such as public transportation, schools, and housing. To begin directing investment toward this kind of production, the unions pressed management for the right to review company investment programs. They also wanted access to accurate information on changes in plant technology and managerial organization. Many of the larger company contracts acknowledged some of these rights by mid-decade. At that point, control over investments had become even more crucial to the labor movement because of the economic crisis. Thousands of companies were putting their workers on temporary layoff; other businesses were closing down completely. In that context, the unions saw their input into investment decisions as a way of pressuring management to save and create jobs.

The workers and the unions soon discovered, however, that they had little means of enforcing certain rights won on paper. In most cases, management did not comply with contract provisions having to do with investments. The factory councils found that they could not effectively monitor a company's activities outside a given plant. They could not even track down the data they needed. When faced with a plant closing, workers who wanted information on the financial structure of the enterprise sometimes had trouble finding out who actually owned the company. A search through labyrinths of financial arrangements could easily lead to a dead end in an account in a foreign bank. This same problem of inaccessible information came up when the factory councils and unions tried to control subcontracting. Thus some of the most politically advanced and seemingly far-reaching rights won by the workers bore little fruit in the 1970s.

As the recession deepened, the unions saw that their usual weapon, the strike, was no longer adequate for combating companies that faced stockpiles of goods and shrinking markets. Jobs became the most pressing issue. Some workers were able to win assurances against layoffs in their company-level contracts. Others were guaranteed a minimum number of paid hours each month or a minimum monthly salary. Workers who were put on short workweeks or were temporarily laid off received the benefits of a national fund called *cassa integrazione guadagni*. In 1975, the government and the confederations agreed that industrial workers who were partially employed or workers on layoff would receive 80 percent of their wages for idle time from the *cassa integrazione* (8 percent paid by the employer and 72 percent paid by the government). That year the fund took on a record number of workers.

Thus despite the economic crisis, part of the unionized working class in Italy for the time being was better able to protect its salaries and jobs than were workers in other capitalist countries. In 1974, for example, Fiat froze all hiring but also signed an agreement that guaranteed no layoffs and put a limit on overtime to preserve jobs. Meanwhile auto workers in other Western European countries were losing their positions by the tens of thousands. But for the nonunionized and the weaker sectors of Italian labor, the employment picture looked worse and worse. Very few jobs were being created, and youth unemployment soon became one of the country's most serious social as well as economic problems. By the end of the decade, the great majority of Italy's unemployed were teenagers or people in their twenties. Many had never had a job. In addition, growing numbers of Italians were doing occasional work, full-time work without job security, and illegal work in the underground economy. The division of the labor force into two segments, protected and unprotected, became more striking; the tensions between them grew more pressing. (This duality will be discussed in Chapter 9.) It was clear that one of the labor movement's most difficult tasks for the coming decade would be to devise a strategy to unify and meet the needs of both groups during a period of economic retrenchment.

In an atmosphere of growing frustration, some people resorted to illegal tactics to protest their conditions. Squatters occupied empty buildings in cities all over Italy. A few groups advocated "proletarian shopping" which meant taking goods without paying. In one case, the unions helped organize what became a mass reaction against increasing transportation costs and utility rates. When the national August vacation period ended in 1974, tens of thousands of workers in and around Turin went to take the usual commuter buses to the factories. They found that the private companies running the transportation services had doubled the fares. The unions in Turin picked up on the immediate protests by organizing a form of resistance called *autoriduzione* (self-reduction). The unions sold their own bus tickets to workers at the old rates and then turned the money over to the bus companies. *Autoriduzione* quickly spread to other Italian cities. It was used to oppose the government's increases in electricity rates as well. As a tactic, *autoriduzione* was effective in getting rates rolled back temporarily. The protest generated great enthusiasm among the New Left groups, but the Communist Party disapproved of the tactic because it bypassed legal channels.

The Workers' Movement and the New Union

Once the intensity of the workers' movement dropped back from the peak level reached in 1969–72, the unions were better able to regulate the mobilization of the workers. Strikes and other job actions had stricter time limits. They were also more focused on specific contract negotiations. The workers did reach previous high levels of involvement again, but this happened only on occasion during a long struggle. The amount of political activism also declined. There was a large nucleus of union militants, but most other workers became more passive over time. Their principal form of participation was to go out on strike. As during earlier periods, the unions began to use strike participation as their main gauge of rank-and-file support.

During negotiations, the unions' objective was to reach a successful settlement as quickly as possible. This was to the advantage of the workers. It also increased the unions' credibility as a significant force with both its membership and management. But the broader political implications of a struggle were often lost, and the further politicization of the working class was of less concern. The unions began to curb what they judged to be the excesses of the movement. They avoided certain forms of struggle, such as "putting the objective into practice" (see Chapter 4), that management found particularly aggressive. The workers saw their many demands translated into highly complex and technical contract platforms which then became the basis of negotiations. These platforms represented an effort to mediate among the various demands of different groups of workers. It was then up to a small team from the executive committee of the council and from the unions to wrest enough concessions from management to satisfy the rank and file. The willingness of the workers to strike was absolutely necessary in order for the unions to accomplish this. Labor leaders were well aware that rank-and-file support was the main source of their bargaining power. For this reason, they sought high participation and disciplined militancy during strikes. Yet the nature of that participation and militancy had changed.

Related to the issue of labor militancy was the transformation of the workplace councils. These structures lost much of their vitality during the 1970s. In retrospect, many workers and unionists have said that too much political power and too many decision-making responsibilities were given to the delegates. Yet it is equally true that most workers wanted neither the responsibilities nor the long hours of work. A delegate often spent 12 hours a day on workplace duties that ranged from getting an incorrect paycheck adjusted to insisting that a malfunctioning machine be repaired. Making sure that management lived up to all the contract provisions comprised the bulk of most delegates' activities.

As mentioned earlier, the vast amount of work to be done necessitated a division of tasks. This in turn set up a hierarchy of prestige and privilege among the delegates. Increasingly, it was party and union activists who were willing to undertake the job of delegate, and they tended to carry the political perspectives of their organizations with them into the councils and assemblies. As a result, partisan disputes among the delegates became more pronounced, disenchanting many workers and undermining rank-and-file unity. The workers' assemblies began to sound more and more like parliamentary debates. Attendance quickly dropped off, and very few of those who were present actually spoke. The same workers and delegates tended to monopolize the discussions. In addition, the inability of the three confederations to unite weighed upon the rank and file. This was still another centrifugal force.

Some observers criticized the unions for not instituting more formal mechanisms to insure representative democracy. For example, critics argued that the unions did not survey rank-and-file sentiment on a regular basis; workers rarely took formal votes on whether or not to strike or on other major policy questions; decisions taken at assemblies did not always reflect the actual opinions of the workers; and the base of the unions had little or no input into the selection of union officials beyond the council level. (Internal political dynamics and personality considerations determined who acquired and kept union posts. Leadership bodies simply ratified predetermined choices.) As a result of these factors, the gulf between delegates and workers on the one hand and between union hierarchy and rank and file on the other continued to grow. By 1978, the bureaucratization of the councils and the disaffection of the rank and file had become frequent topics of debate within the labor movement and the left.

In the period after the unions gained control of the workers' movement, the political positions of the union moderates became dominant. The left-wing unionists continued to put forward their own policies, but they usually accounted for only 10 or 15 percent of the leadership. Some of the extraunion forces that had been active during the early years of the

movement and had been critical of the unions disappeared; others became part of the left-wing minority in the councils.

Much of the left wing argued for making the labor movement an
autonomous political force in Italy. These cadres wanted the councils to
become political organizations that would set social goals and generalize
struggles. Some leftist groups and parties including PSIUP pushed this
idea farther. They saw the councils as the seeds of an alternative form of
state power. *Il Manifesto*, a New Left organization whose leadership had
come out of the Communist Party, theorized a "council road to socialism" in the early part of the decade.

Meanwhile part of the union left suggested expanding the factory
council system by organizing zone councils (*consigli di zona*). These would
bring together all the people who lived or worked in a limited geographical area in order to coordinate popular participation and to pressure local
government. The idea of zone councils came up soon after the first factory councils appeared. The underlying concept was to extend the
workers' movement outside the factories and into neighborhoods where
it could catalyze a broader social movement. This broader movement
would coordinate the transformation of the workplace with struggles to
improve the quality of daily life—housing, health care, schools, transportation, and cultural life. According to this conception, the working class
and the labor movement could not play their roles fully unless they
stepped beyond the confines of the workplace. The zone councils never
got off the ground, but some labor leaders continued to propose the idea
throughout the decade and into the 1980s. They saw the councils as a
way to revitalize the labor movement by overcoming the limits of a workplace perspective.

Despite the more radical suggestions and aspirations, moderation
prevailed. By mid-decade, the essence of the moderate position was that
the unions had to find responses to the workers' demands that were
"compatible" with the existing economic order, at least for the foresee-
able future. Compatibility became a constant issue as the crisis deepened.
Any demand that might further dislocate the rickety system (an incom-
patible demand) had to be modified. The labor movement's new model of
economic development was deferred to an indeterminate future although
it still had a place in union rhetoric.

The "new union" created an ambiguous identity for itself during the
1970s. It set many radical objectives which implied substantial changes in
the economic system (for example, working-class control over investments). It phrased its overall perspective in left rhetoric. At the same
time, it urged moderation and compromise. The unions raised expectations among the workers for social reforms as well as for economic power,
but those expectations were disappointed. The ambiguous identity of the

new union was due to several factors: the conflicting political perspectives that competed within the organizations at all levels; the desire of the leadership to maintain the allegiance of the more radical tendencies within the movement; and the growing pressures of the economic crisis. Although the government and business leaders castigated the labor movement for preaching class warfare and for creating economic chaos, the new union in fact lacked the necessary political leverage to win significant structural change. As the decade progressed, it became evident that the labor movement needed strong political allies and the active involvement of a left or left-leaning government in order to implement its proposals.

Notes to Chapter 5

1. Michele Salvati, "Politica economica e relazioni industriali dal 'miracolo' economico a oggi," in *Problemi del movimento sindacale in Italia 1943–1973*, Annali, no. 16, ed. Aris Accornero (Milan: Feltrinelli, 1976), p. 723.

2. Sergio Turone, *Storia del sindacato in Italia 1943–1980* (Bari: Laterza, 1981), p. 487.

3. Organization for Economic Co-operation and Development, *Italy*, *OECD Economic Surveys* (Paris: OECD, June 1981), p. 66.

4. Ruggero Spesso, *L'economia italiana dal dopoguerra a oggi* (Rome: Riuniti, 1980), p. 100.

6

Terrorism and the Italian Labor Movement

By the early 1970s, the workers' movement had become both the target of right-wing terrorists and the obsessive hope of left-wing terrorists. The rightists designed their violence to provoke a political reaction that would repress and ultimately destroy the independent labor movement in Italy. The extremists who came out of the left assumed they could stimulate the formation of a revolutionary, armed sector within the working class by means of terrorist acts. After more than a decade, neither side succeeded in reaching its goals, but the years of violence strained the democratic state in Italy and set up new obstacles for the labor movement.

Terrorism of the Extreme Right

Right-wing or "black" terrorism spread in 1969 as a direct response to the workers' mobilization. For the next several years, there were almost daily incidents of street violence instigated by neofascist gangs. There were bombings and arson attacks against every expression of the organized working class and the left: local party headquarters, union halls, recreation centers and schools where leftists were active, bookstores, newspaper offices, union and left rallies. Individual activists were beaten, sometimes murdered, in the streets. In addition, the extreme right sponsored several abortive attempts to organize a coup d'état.

The characteristic tactic of the far right was (and still is) setting off bombs in crowded public places. Bombings in April and August 1969 wounded about two dozen people. This was just the beginning. The device set off the following December in a bank in Milan's Piazza Fontana left 16 dead and 90 wounded; nine died and 94 were injured during a union rally in Brescia in May 1974; 12 lost their lives and 48 were wounded just outside Bologna in the Italicus train bombing of August 1974; and the toll of the Bologna train station explosion in August 1980 was 85 dead and 200 injured. Those who carried out the bombings and participated directly in the street violence were often neofascist "foot soldiers," many of them young and in the service of powerful networks of rightists. Every serious investigation of black terrorism implicated powerful organizations and high-ranking officials who helped to finance, plan, or cover up the terror. They included industrialists, officials in the armed forces, police, secret services, and government, magistrates, and international terrorist and paramilitary groups.

The purpose of black terrorism was to destabilize political and social life. The perpetrators hoped to create a climate of fear that would push Italians to accept an authoritarian regime. In the 1970s, this plan was often referred to as the "strategy of tension." An authoritarian regime would clamp down on the workers' movement; it would stifle all other forms of autonomous political activity and protest. The scenario was an extension of the philosophy and violence of fascism which was never rooted out after the Second World War. Many Fascists not only went unpunished, they retained their positions in the private sector and within the new state. Covert support for the post-1969 upsurge in right-wing terrorism came from upper- and middle-class strata whose interests were threatened by a strong labor movement and by the left. The neofascist party, MSI, operated in flagrant violation of the 1948 Constitution which outlaws the reorganization of fascist parties. (Although its fascist ideology and the corresponding cultural and political identification of its membership are common knowledge, MSI has answered accusations simply by asserting that the party is far right and not explicitly fascist.)

In the early 1970s, labor and the left responded to the escalation of right-wing terrorism with mass protests. These included a national general strike that brought the country to a standstill in April 1975. The New Left groups led a campaign to outlaw MSI, but they never generated enough pressure to force the other parties to act. At the same time, the workers' movement and the left refused to be drawn into illegal reprisals which would have raised the level of violence and played into the hands of the right.

The moderate and conservative political forces as well as the judiciary were scandalously reluctant to prosecute those involved in right-wing terrorism. In fact, authorities tried to blame right-wing violence on the left. For example, the police arrested an anarchist named Pietro Valpreda and charged him with the Piazza Fontana bombing. Valpreda was held in jail on practically no evidence for several years until the judiciary could no longer ignore public pressure and the evidence implicating the far right. An anarchist railway worker held by police in the same case mysteriously fell to his death from the sixth-floor window of a police station.

At the time of the 1980 bombing of the Bologna train station, the government's antifascist terrorist squad counted just six agents for all of Italy.[1] There was not even a data bank on right-wing terrorism.[2] This sorry state of preparation and weak commitment to the struggle against black terror must be compared to the full mobilization of the Italian state—Parliament and the entire law-and-order apparatus—against "red" terrorism. The very few magistrates who pursued investigations into the activities of the extreme right battled the obstructionism of their own colleagues and superiors. They continued to work at the risk of losing their lives. Mario Amato, the only Rome magistrate conducting such inquiries between 1977 and 1980, was assassinated, shot in the head by neofascists in June 1980. His predecessor had died under machine-gun fire in the streets of Rome.[3] The police periodically arrested neofascists, but they released most after questioning. When trials took place, they often dragged on for five or ten years and then ended without convictions for a supposed lack of evidence.

Authoritarianism was a standard threat used against the Italian workers' movement. Business leaders and conservative officials often hinted at the possibility of authoritarian solutions when they judged labor demands to be exorbitant or levels of militancy to be too high. There may have been more fear mongering than substance behind the threats, but the significant point is that limits on democracy were commonly presented to the public as possible reactions to working-class mobilization. This threw the unions on the defensive and stimulated popular sentiment against the labor movement.

Terrorism of the Extreme Left

Red terrorism goes back to the early 1970s when some of the first practitioners abandoned New Left groups, the student movement, and the Catholic left in favor of clandestine organizations and illegal tactics. From the start, frustration with the policies of the traditional left and the labor unions characterized the position of the terrorists. During the first few years, they focused their attention on the factories and on those whom they judged to be the direct oppressors of the working class—foremen, managers, and rightist workers. They set cars on fire, slashed tires, and carried out day-long kidnappings of individuals whom the workers especially disliked. The early left terrorists projected something of a

Robin Hood spirit in their campaign against injustice on behalf of the exploited. In 1973, for example, they kidnapped an activist in the neofascist union at Fiat and then deposited him in chains in front of the Mirafiori plant. There was little public outcry against these acts, and the terrorists elicited some sympathy among workers by harassing people who were particularly unpopular.

Within several years, however, the violence escalated, and the assassinations and brutal wounding of victims began. The targets of the terrorists multiplied to include politicians, judges, police, doctors, journalists, professors, and prison officials as well as industrialists and managerial personnel. The terrorists formed centralized organizations made up of small numbers of highly disciplined cadres. The objects of their attack were the state and all those who upheld or legitimized it. The strategy of the largest terrorist group—the Red Brigades—was to force the traditional left to unite with the right in a law-and-order crusade that would then push the working class into an autonomous, oppositional position. The Red Brigades theorized that their destabilizing actions would reveal the bankruptcy of the reformist left. At the same time, they would unmask the true nature of the bourgeois state controlled by the multinationals. At that point, part of the working class would arm itself and become the phalanx of proletarian combatants who would constitute an alternative to the old state power.

In the late 1970s, the number of terrorist actions soared. At Fiat alone, some 20 managers, security officers, and supervisors were killed or wounded. With the support of most of the political parties, the police and secret services undertook a massive, nationwide, antiterrorist campaign. The result was the arrest of hundreds upon hundreds who were accused of belonging to armed groups. The police eventually released many for lack of evidence, but in 1982, there were still over 1,000 charged with terrorist activity and waiting in jail for further legal proceedings. (Because of inefficient procedures and the widespread use of preventive detention, well over one-half of Italy's entire prison population has never been tried.) Although the police periodically claimed to have decapitated the left-wing terrorist organizations, there were inevitably new eruptions of violence and reports about new recruits and the rebuilding of terrorist cells. Still many known terrorists and their leaders were captured, and the number of actions dropped in the early 1980s. More than 250 of those in prison decided to testify for authorities in exchange for reduced sentences. They gave detailed information on how operations were carried out and by whom. In March 1982, Parliament passed a law to encourage these confessions. At about that time, several of the accused claimed that the police had systematically tortured them in jail to obtain information.

Consequences for the Left and the Labor Movement

Red terrorism damaged both the Italian left and the labor movement. The population was shaken by the brutality and bloodshed, and
most people rallied behind the antiterrorist campaign. It was in the interests of the moderate and conservative political forces to focus public concern on the organized violence. This shifted attention away from the
30-odd years of government mismanagement under the Christian Democrats. The DC used the issue of red terrorism effectively to attack the
Communists. They presented their own party as the guardian of law and
order. Christian Democrats claimed repeatedly that the true origin of red
terrorism was the ideology of the PCI. Even if the Communists denounced terrorism, went the argument, they were ultimately responsible.
The antiterrorist drive became an excuse for the police, secret services,
and the magistracy to harass the entire left. This was especially the case
for organizations and activists of the New Left and supporters of a political tendency called Workers' Autonomy, which became highly visible in
1977.* There were police dragnets, thousands of apartment searches, in-
terrogations, and arrests without specific charges. The authorities also
closed down radio stations and banned publications.

In 1978 and early in 1980, Parliament passed special antiterrorist
laws which curtailed civil liberties in Italy. According to these measures,
police could hold suspects with little or no evidence, detain them for 48
hours without arrest, and interrogate them without the presence of a lawyer. The police also acquired expanded rights to enter offices and private
residences and to shut down political headquarters on the mere suspicion
of either support for terrorists or the presence of weapons. The laws eased
restrictions on telephone tapping and on sweeping searches through entire blocks of buildings (a technique many remembered from Mussolini's
days). It also became possible to hold untried suspects in preventive detention for more than ten years. Prison terms for political criminals and
their supporters were lengthened.

The government's approach to left terrorism came down to a nationwide hunt for the perpetrators. There was no serious effort to get at
what were generally accepted to be the causes of the increased violence—

---

*Most New Left groups (meaning those that grew up in the late 1960s and early
1970s) condemned violence. But Workers' Autonomy argued for mass illegality and violence diffused throughout society. The objective was to counter the exploitation of the
system and catalyze dissent. Officially, Workers' Autonomy opposed acts of terrorism
carried out by small clandestine groups isolated from the population. In practice, some
but by no means all *autonomi* sympathized with terrorism. The terrorist organizations
were able to recruit some individuals from local collectives of Workers' Autonomy.

unemployment, deteriorated urban conditions, inadequate social infra-structure, corruption in public life, and a deep malaise among young peo-ple. Like the conservative political forces, both the Communists and the Socialists adopted the notion that tough law-and-order measures would be effective in combating terrorism.

In order to demonstrate its firm opposition to the violence, the PCI took the initiative for organizing local drives to ferret out terrorists and sympathizers. The unions too began vigilance campaigns. Workers and party members in some locales were asked to fill out questionnaires and to report any suspicious behavior they observed among co-workers and neighbors. The proposal created a great deal of controversy, with critics objecting to the notion of spying and secret reporting. Many also felt that the questionnaires heightened the atmosphere of tension.

Several incidents revealed the complex and diverse attitudes of workers toward the antiterrorist campaign. In autumn 1977, a bar was set on fire during a demonstration in Turin, and a young man who happened by chance to be inside lost his life in the blaze. After much debate, the unions decided on a limited response. There would be no strike, and only factory council members would attend the funeral. But on the following Monday morning, thousands of workers spontaneously walked off the job to join the funeral march. They were protesting the death of an inno-cent victim of violence. A few weeks later in Turin, left terrorists shot Carlo Casalegno, vice-director of *La Stampa*, one of Italy's major news-papers and a Fiat subsidiary. In response, the unions immediately called a protest strike which failed in almost all the workplaces in Turin. When interviewed, the greatest number of workers explained the lack of sup-port for the strike in class terms. They argued that no one made a compa-rable fuss when a worker was killed on the job. Those who were older recalled how *La Stampa* and Casalegno had played a role in the anti-worker and antiunion repression of earlier years.[4]

In 1978 when the Red Brigades kidnapped the prominent politician and president of the DC, Aldo Moro, all the parties of the government majority linked the struggle against terrorism with loyalty to the state. The unions and parties called on their constituencies to strike in support of the state. But once again, many workers responded with mixed feel-ings, and some opposed the idea of a strike. For years they had perceived state authorities as hostile forces. They remembered workers shot down during peaceful rallies, police harassment of unions, blacklisted workers, unpunished right-wing terror, government corruption, and coups plotted within the military. Many felt that the decision to strike had been im-posed on them by party and union leaderships.

In the meantime, employers began using terrorism as the basis for another attack against the labor movement. They accused the workers and unions of stimulating the terror with labor unrest. According to their reasoning, constant agitation in the workplace inured the working class to violence, and, by extension, to terrorism. Strong arm tactics, for example, picketing and blocking entrances, reinforced attitudes of lawlessness. Fiat was one of the most active proponents of this analysis. The labor movement was again thrown on the defensive. What sometimes resembled a witch-hunt began to generate tensions and suspicions inside many workplaces. The Communists offered the working class little protection during the late 1970s because they too were pressing for labor moderation as well as for an end to terrorism.

For many years, observers agreed that left-wing terrorists typically came from the educated middle classes. But terrorist groups also had some presence in the factories, judging from their ability to operate there (the appearance of leaflets, graffiti, written threats, and so on). As frustration with the economic and political situation mounted in the late 1970s, the clandestine organizations found more recruits among workers and the unemployed, most of them young people. By 1981, labor leaders admitted that terrorists had probably infiltrated the unions just as they had infiltrated all other institutions. But it should be emphasized that the number of terrorists and sympathizers among Italian workers was small (just as the number was small in the population as a whole). Many more workers may have known something about terrorist activity or had suspicions. For example, they may have noticed someone leaving off leaflets in a plant or writing graffiti on a wall. But they were generally reluctant to speak out for several reasons: a justifiable fear of reprisals, aversion to spying, ambivalence about the role of management and the state in the antiterrorist crusade, and even the feeling that while the terrorists might be completely wrong, the bosses and government were just as bad.

The assassination of a worker by left terrorists in 1979 demonstrated how difficult the situation had become. Guido Rossa, PCI member and unionist with the FLM in Genoa, had agreed to testify about terrorist activities in the factory. In revenge, the Red Brigades gunned him down. Most people were shocked at the news that the terrorists had turned their violence against a worker and rank-and-file activist. But there was an equal amount of self-recrimination among Rossa's co-workers and among factory council and union members. They believed that he should never have been left to shoulder the burden of testifying alone. The factory council or union should have assumed that responsibility collectively. The unions expected their members to help carry out the antiterrorist drive but had not considered how to protect them adequately.

By the early 1980s, there was no doubt that the red terrorist organizations had failed in their project to win over a portion of the working class to their side. No phalanx of proletarian combatants had emerged. It was also clear that both terrorism and its manipulation by the ruling class had helped to sap the energy of the workers' movement. The organized violence constricted the space in which labor could maneuver.

Notes to Chapter 6

1. Sam Pizzigati, "In Bologna, the 'Black Terror' Returns," *Italy and Us* 2, no. 1 (October, 1980):3.

2. Thomas Sheehan, "Italy: Terror on the Right," *The New York Review*, January 22, 1981, p. 23.

3. Ibid., pp. 23–24.

4. Renzo Gianotti, *Trent'anni di lotte alla Fiat (1948–1978): Dalla ricostruzione al nuovo modo di fare l'auto* (Bari: De Donato, 1979), pp. 236–37.

7

Labor and the Communists' Historic Compromise

The fortunes of the labor movement during the 1970s were bound up with the policy decisions and experiences of the Italian Communist Party. Labor needed an effective political vehicle to take up the reform strategy and to further the political aspirations of the workers' movement. The unions alone had not been successful in pressuring DC-dominated governments to redirect investments or to enact social legislation. During the same period, the Communist Party was making its bid for active participation in the national government. The PCI claimed a dual role. It presented itself as the legitimate and effective representative of working-class interests and as the political force capable of carrying through a reform program to benefit the entire country. Once the Communist Party acquired the political mandate of the labor movement, the fate of the movement and the party were tightly linked.

A More Favorable Political Climate for the Left

In the early 1970s, the political climate in Italy encouraged the PCI's hopes for greater power. After 25 years of unmet promises for reform, government corruption, scandals, and feuds, some Italians were ready to abandon the parties that had maintained the regime. The social movements—student, labor, antiwar, and feminist—created a greater political openness and helped to shift segments of the population to the left. It was a time of social tension and unrest. There were kidnappings, murders, blackmail cases, and neofascist bombings. But the general reaction was not to call for a law-and-order crackdown. Instead, there was a growing demand for a democratic renewal. This was not a mass movement for revolution but rather a vocal frustration with the political status quo. The result was a willingness to try something new.

Many of the hopes for reform were pinned on the Communist Party which pointed to its record of efficient and enlightened administration on the local level as concrete proof of the party's abilities. Bologna, where the Communists had led the government since the war, had the reputation of being the best-run city in Europe. The PCI used Bologna as an illustration of what honest and progressive government might be like in Italy. At the same time, the Italian Communists were distancing themselves from the Soviet Union. The party had condemned the 1968 invasion of Czechoslovakia, and the leadership regularly reaffirmed its autonomy in foreign as well as domestic affairs. Along with the French and Spanish Communist Parties, the PCI developed the analysis of national roads to socialism based on political pluralism, the electoral process, and democracy. This was the essence of Eurocommunism, a phenomenon that received a great deal of international media coverage through the 1970s.

Meanwhile, the reputation of the Christian Democrats was sliding to a new low. The very foundations of the DC's power system, the vast networks of patronage and the state bureaucracy, had clearly become impediments to the revitalization of political life in Italy. In many cities and towns, the Christian Democrats' local electoral base of power was beginning to erode, and the party's anticommunist ideology had less hold on Italians.

The first significant test of the new political climate was the national referendum on divorce in May 1974. The electorate was to vote on a proposition to repeal the 1970 law legalizing divorce. The referendum was also seen as a national political poll evaluating the relative strengths of the DC and the left. The campaign leading up to the vote was a revealing picture of party positions and political maneuvering. The Christian Democrats, of course, supported the repeal of divorce. They were counting on a reaffirmation of Catholic and conservative sentiment. The Communist and Socialist Parties supported the prodivorce position, but they campaigned cautiously and did not throw their full weight into the debate. The labor movement was divided. The Socialists and Communists in the CGIL shadowed their respective parties, but the confederation itself did not take an official position. The UIL, with its strong lay tradition, worked actively for the prodivorce position. Some CISL leaders also campaigned vigorously to retain the divorce law although the confederation endorsed neither side.

The referendum results were something of a shock. Practically no one anticipated the extent of prodivorce opinion. Some 59 percent of the electorate voted to retain the law; 41 percent voted to repeal. The referendum unmasked a populace that was much less tied to the Church and much less traditional than had been assumed. During the campaign, the "old left" (PCI and PSI) and part of the labor movement had feared moving too far from where they thought the population stood. The vote demonstrated that they had underestimated the changes taking place in Italy. But this was not the only explanation for the PCI's somewhat cautious behavior during the divorce campaign. The party also did not want to aggravate hostilities with the DC. In fact, the nature of that relationship had become a primary preoccupation of the Communists.

A New Approach: The Historic Compromise

To move the PCI out of the parliamentary opposition after 25 years, the Communist leadership undertook a significant shift in policy. Until then, the party's strategy, "the Italian road to socialism," envisioned a broad grassroots alliance of Communists, Socialists, and Catholics that would create a "progressive democracy." That in turn was to be the basis for the socialist transformation of the country. In governmental terms, the strategy assumed that the PCI would go into the parliamentary majority and cabinet once the largely conservative, antireformist Christian Democratic Party was either subordinated, split, or fundamentally transformed. In this way, progressive Communist policies could prevail. During the early 1970s, however, the new national secretary of the PCI, Enrico Berlinguer, proposed that the Communists enter into a government coalition with the DC in the near future. The broad grassroots alliance did not exist, and the DC had not been subordinated, split, or transformed.

The thinking of the Communist leadership was that a socialist transformation was not possible in Italy in that period; any radical changes would isolate the left and the working class, creating the conditions for a rightist reaction and perhaps even the resurgence of fascism. As an alternative, Berlinguer proposed the broadest possible government alliances among nonfascist parties, including the PCI and DC. This arrangement was supposed to preclude a center-right coalition and gradually win over the majority of Christian Democrats to "more democratic" positions. Another objective of the alliance with the DC was to buy time until progressive forces could attract a vast majority of the Italian electorate. Berlinguer argued that winning a mere 51 percent of the vote was inadequate for the left. The resulting governmental instability would put Italy's fragile democracy in peril.

The Communists' new tactic responded to a series of growing concerns of the party leadership. In addition to the Italian rightist reaction, the PCI feared the international response to the increasing strength of Italy's left. NATO and the U.S. military had a massive presence in Italy. The country played a key role in the Mediterranean and Middle Eastern strategies of the Atlantic Alliance. The United States and its allies could easily use economic sabotage (capital flight, investment strikes, denial of international loans, trade boycotts) to create havoc in Italy. Furthermore, the military coup in Chile that overthrew the democratically elected government of Salvador Allende Gossens was a traumatic event for the Italian left. The PCI's evaluation of events in Chile was that Allende had moved too quickly, alienating the middle classes and the Chilean Christian Democrats. It was, in fact, at the conclusion of an article written soon after the coup that Berlinguer gave a name to the new coalition formula for Italy: the historic compromise.* The advantage of the historic compromise was that the PCI could have a say over Italy's future without bearing full responsibility for solving her awesome social and economic problems. The capitalist class and the middle strata would not become disaffected because the government would represent their interests as well. In addition, the PCI hoped that collaboration with the DC would minimize the negative international reaction to Communist participation in the government.

As a tactical solution, the Communist approach assumed an alliance between the PCI, progressive capitalists, the working class, and the middle classes. This assumption grew out of the Communists' economic analysis. For the time being, party leaders accepted the imperatives of capitalist production, including the maximization of private profits. They argued that Italy's economic woes were due in large part to the parasitic, inefficient, and speculative nature of Italian capitalism. Whereas the PCI had formerly seen the multinationals and monopolies as a primary source of the problem, the new policy presupposed an accord with all productive sectors—monopolistic and competitive.

The Communists' basic economic program was to rationalize the existing export model with a two-phase plan. First create the conditions

---

*Some confusion has developed over the use of the term *historic compromise*. Early on, PCI leaders insisted that the historic compromise was a tactic, limited in its duration and political implications. But as the approach looked less and less successful, the party leadership tended to shift the definition to make the historic compromise synonymous with the long-term alliance strategy that would bring Communists, Socialists, and Catholics together in a movement to transform Italian society. The government coalition tactic of the mid-1970s to ally all parties except the neofascists was then called "national unity." Some PCI leaders claimed that the historic compromise had always been conceived of as a long-term strategic approach. But this assertion was in part an effort to minimize the failure of the coalition policy with the Christian Democrats.

for a new cycle of investment and expanded competitive production by increasing labor productivity, holding down wages, and eliminating inefficient and parasitic enterprises; second, undertake needed social reforms and development of the South using the surplus generated by the streamlined system. The PCI saw itself as the political representative of the working class, but the party was also critical of what it felt to be the excesses of the labor movement during a time of economic difficulty: continuous conflict, sizable wage demands, and constraints on the use of labor. In terms of reining in the workers' movement and passing basic reforms, the PCI's economic strategy was in harmony with the preferred policies of certain progressive business and finance leaders who were interested in modernizing Italian capitalism. But many other groups within Italy's divided ruling class opposed the PCI's calls for economic, social, and bureaucratic reforms.

Left critics, in the unions, New Left organizations, and some within the PCI, were quick to point out the flaws of the historic compromise proposal. Any serious program of structural reforms was bound to undermine the power base of the DC in the state ministries, agencies, industrial holdings, and banks. To promise clean government was in itself to declare war on the Christian Democrats. In addition and perhaps more importantly, the DC had nothing to gain and everything to lose from the rehabilitation of its major opponent. The 25-year ostracism of the Communists had enabled the DC to maintain its regime. The historic compromise would legitimate the PCI and undermine the Christian Democrats' most basic interests as a party. For these reasons, most of the DC vehemently opposed the historic compromise when it was first proposed. For critics on the left, it seemed clear that the Communists were putting themselves into an untenable position. On the one hand, they would have to make concessions to the DC (and to the Church, NATO, and big business) just to establish the coalition. If they then pressed hard for reforms, the DC could scuttle the accord. On the other hand, if no significant reforms were forthcoming, the PCI would undercut its own base of support.

The contradiction was equally sharp with respect to the labor movement. The aversion of the capitalist class to the Communists was generally quite strong. The bourgeoisie had no interest in giving power to the Communists unless the PCI would restrain the workers' movement. There was some sense that PCI participation in the government might be a temporary, necessary concession to obtain labor peace and increased productivity. But it was obvious that if the Communists did not play the desired role or if they were no longer needed, the business elites would use their substantial influence to exclude the PCI again. Thus the Communists were useful to the bourgeoisie in that a primary source of the party's strength was its ties to the working class. The contradiction was that in pressing for moderation and sacrifice without delivering substantial reforms or at least some new advantages for labor, the PCI risked losing the support of the workers.

In spite of these manifest contradictions, the Communist Party leadership believed it could devise policies to meet the needs of capital, labor, and the middle classes in alliance with the Christian Democrats. The proposal created confusion within the PCI's membership base since the Communists had for years portrayed the DC as a source of Italy's problems. At the same time, PCI members wanted their party to govern Italy, and so they supported a move out of the parliamentary opposition.

Within the unions, the reaction to the proposal split along party lines. The UIL was skeptical, fearing that an alliance between the DC and the PCI would squeeze out the small lay parties and reduce the UIL's influence. Many Socialists in the CGIL shared the concerns of the UIL. The right wing of the CISL saw the PCI proposal as too radical. The left CISL unionists and the left wing of the CGIL believed the new policy would undercut the dynamism of the labor movement by imposing a line that was too moderate. Despite the divisions and confusion, the *Federazione* CGIL-CISL-UIL ended up giving low-key support to the PCI's effort to enter the government. This support was always stated obliquely so as not to upset the uneasy unity of the three confederations. Both labor's lack of success with its reform strategy and the deepening economic crisis made many unionists and rank-and-filers willing to support the Communist Party's proposal. The labor movement hoped the PCI would make greater progress in winning policies favorable to the workers.

The Government of the Abstentions

The June 1975 regional and local elections and the June 1976 parliamentary elections marked the high point of Communist popularity. This was also the moment of greatest political optimism. The Communists won 32.4 percent of the regional and provincial vote in 1975, a tremendous advance of 5.2 percent over the 1972 parliamentary elections (Chamber of Deputies), in a country where a 2 percent change was considered a major shift. The DC dropped from 38.7 percent in 1972 to 35.5 percent in 1975. The PSI climbed from 9.6 percent to 12.1 percent. In addition, left coalitions achieved majorities in six of the 20 regions, almost half the provinces, most major cities, and a large number of smaller municipalities. In 1976, the Communists took 34.4 percent of the national parliamentary vote (Chamber of Deputies). The Socialists dropped back to 9.6 percent, while the Christian Democrats regained their previous level of 38.7 percent.

The PCI campaigned in 1976 with the slogan "a party of struggle; a government party." But after the elections, the DC blocked Communist participation in the government. The United States publicly announced its opposition to the PCI. West Germany threatened to cut off loans to a financially strapped Italy if the Communists were granted cabinet posts. At the same time, the DC could not pull together enough votes with the remaining parties to sustain a center-right or a center-left coalition. The result was a stalemate, broken finally by the PCI's willingness not to vote against a new DC minority government. This meant that the Communists abstained when Parliament voted on the government. For the first time since 1947, the PCI moved out of the parliamentary opposition. Four other parties, the PSI, PSDI, PRI, and PLI, also abstained. The PCI made this concession (which permitted the Christian Democrats to govern) in exchange for negotiations on a program acceptable to a broad coalition including the PCI. Thus the Communists were willing to approach government participation step by step: first by leaving the opposition, and next by playing a role in determining the government's program. The PCI also took over seven committee chairs in Parliament and the presidency of the Chamber of Deputies.

What followed was a year of "dialogue" between the DC and PCI under the so-called government of the abstentions. Given the Communists' great electoral successes and substantial political leverage, PCI supporters expected the party to pressure the DC for structural reforms. But instead the PCI took a conciliatory stance. The party agreed to or abstained on measures favored by the Christian Democrats and did not substantially inhibit the DC's usual mode of operation. The Communist leadership undertook this course in the hope of maintaining its dialogue with the DC.

The government proceeded to raise indirect taxes, utility rates, and prices for many basic consumer goods and for public transportation. It also transformed what was supposed to have been an industrial conversion program into state subsidies to various industries, with no controls over how the money was spent. Parliament voted additional sums to cover huge deficits revealed by the state holdings without investigating the operations of those companies. From the point of view of many workers, these economic measures were regressive, placing a heavier burden on lower-income people. Furthermore, there was no evidence that the DC was willing to alter its way of dealing with the state-owned industries. The Communists made additional concessions to the DC on nuclear energy, the new national police union, and agricultural programs. The regional and local branches of the PCI echoed national policy. They made an effort to compromise with the Christian Democrats even in those places where the left held a majority.

It was not long before the PCI's conciliatory policies generated bewilderment and objections. The workers, sometimes independently of the unions, protested tax and price increases and changes made in the wage indexing system. They became impatient with the slow progress on reforms. The labor confederations found themselves trapped. On the one side were rank-and-file demands and the unions' own program; on the other side was the commitment to support the PCI–DC negotiations for lack of a better political alternative. Over the course of the next several years, the unions were involved with the parties in trying to work out legislation on youth employment, job placement, industrial conversion, and pensions. Parliament passed some useful measures (and many ineffectual laws), but the usual array of conflicting interests made it impossible to deal adequately with major systemic problems. The unions' position became increasingly uncomfortable.

Leftist critics of the PCI claimed that the party was mismanaging the political situation. According to this view, the PCI should have put much less emphasis on going into the government. It should not have bargained away its moral initiative and reputation as a decisive reform party in exchange for permission to move closer to official government status. Handling the bargaining as they did, the Communists gave the political initiative back to the Christian Democrats. PCI policy also focused international attention on the controversial question of government participation.

Critics believed there was an alternative course. The PCI could have made better use of its moral status and popularity to win wider support for concrete reform proposals in a variety of areas. In all likelihood, the Communists could have enlisted the backing of the Socialists for these measures. Since the PSI was afraid of being squeezed out by the historic compromise, it was not closed to the idea of a left programmatic alliance of Communists and Socialists. The New Left, the labor movement, the growing women's movement, and students would also have rallied behind well-defined proposals. Then by focusing its political energies on attacking the DC for corruption and unwillingness to undertake reforms and at the same time carefully uniting a constituency behind a serious program, the PCI could have consolidated its base and gradually broadened its support.

This process could have been started from outside the parliamentary majority. Entry into the government or even clarification of the PCI's government status was less important than the consolidation of its base around a coherent program. The solution to the status question could have evolved as the situation changed (which was what happened in any case). This was especially true since Italian parties are ingenious at devising flexible and ambiguous formulations to define political relationships. With this approach, critics argued, it might have been possible to keep the DC on the defensive and win some tangible victories. This in turn would have increased the credibility of the PCI and, over time, strengthened its alliances.

The critique of Berlinguer's positions was not centered on the PCI's abstention in the parliamentary vote of confidence. Nor were there objections to the notion of negotiating with other parties. Instead the criticism was aimed at three aspects of Communist policy. First, the PCI was overly conciliatory and defensive when dealing with the Christian Democrats. The PCI's stance grew out of the assumption (or wishful thinking) that it was possible to persuade the DC to accept the Communists as an equal partner on a reform program. Critics pointed out that the Socialists had made a similar assumption in the 1960s during the time of the center-left governments. The PSI ended up playing a subordinate role and damaging its own image. It shored up the Christian Democratic regime while producing few reforms. More than a decade later, the PCI was attempting an alliance that looked analogous.

Second, the Communists in fact did not have a credible program of well-developed reform proposals. The party pointed out the areas where reforms were needed but was consistently vague when it came to describing what should be done. Even PCI documents that set out to define solutions were notoriously abstract. In the area of economic policy especially, the lack of a clear-cut program became a greater and greater liability for the Communists.

Third, critics believed that the PCI searched too exclusively among the centrist parties for political alliances. The Communists neglected the potential of political forces on the left (such as the PSI) and social forces (especially women and young people).

Those who held these views predicted that the PCI's policies would eventually lead to a defeat of the labor movement and the left. Even within the PCI leadership, there were those who questioned Berlinguer's policies. By late 1976, they were calling for a harder stand against the Christian Democrats and more emphasis on mass struggles.

In early 1977, angry protests against government policies developed among what were called the "emerging movements" or the "marginalized" strata: unemployed young people, students, counter-cultural activists, and women. They formed a loose movement, often referred to simply as the 1977 movement, which had no formal program or strategy. Some students and young workers were affiliated with Workers' Autonomy (see Chapter 6). The bleak employment situation spurred the protests. The characteristic sentiment was bitter disappointment after hopes for change had been raised in 1975 and 1976. The movement condemned all the political parties, but the PCI and the trade unions came under particularly heavy fire. They were accused of betraying their longtime constituencies. There were marches and rallies in many cities and at the universities. A small number of participants began to carry weapons, and the government responded by sending fully armed police to meet the protesters. Demonstrations often ended in violence. In February 1977, Luciano Lama, secretary of the CGIL, tried to speak at the University of Rome. Demonstrators shouted him down, and some tried to storm the podium.

The unions denounced this and similar incidents but also acknowledged that the source lay in the malaise of young Italians, their fears for the future. Many unionists contended that the labor movement had to reach out to the marginalized strata, making their concerns part of labor's program. But practically nothing concrete was done. The rightist and centrist parties not only condemned the disorder, they regularly accused the Communist Party of being the fountainhead of all left-wing violence. The Communists reacted by taking a law-and-order stance that was sometimes more harsh than that of the Christian Democrats. The PCI leadership accused the protesters of being hoodlums who encouraged terrorism. The condemnation at times became so sweeping that it seemed to take in even legitimate forms of opposition to the government and criticism of the PCI's strategy. The result, of course, was to antagonize young people further. Unlike the late 1960s, 1977 produced no alliance between employed workers and students. On the contrary, what had once been a fruitful relationship was now hostile and distrustful. Differences in experience, political outlook, and style created a gulf between unionized workers who seemed to have a degree of security and low-income students who had few prospects for decent, stable employment.

By July 1977, six political parties (PCI, DC, PSI, PSDI, PRI, and PLI) had agreed on a program that was supposed to be the basis for their further cooperation in Parliament. The Communists did not enter the parliamentary majority at that time, but they were to have a say on all important policy questions. The Christian Democrats managed to limit the number of issues included in the program. They also shaped the content. The final document added to the worst fears of left critics of the PCI. It included many of the antiterrorist measures described in the previous chapter (permission for police to hold suspects with little or no evidence, to detain them for 48 hours without arrest, to interrogate them without the presence of a lawyer, to enter offices and private homes, and to shut down political headquarters on the suspicion of support for terrorists or possession of weapons). In addition, the program mandated fewer restrictions on telephone tapping, a freeze on hiring in the public sector, and obligatory payment for most medications that were previously free under the health insurance program. The economic section of the accord reaffirmed the government's respect for the loan conditions imposed on Italy by the International Monetary Fund. The program also included a long overdue reform. The six parties set in motion the transfer of specific government powers from the national to the regional level.

Later that same summer, the Communist Party published an intermediate-term economic program (*Proposta di progetto a medio termine*). The party was responding to frequent questions about its economic strategy from its own cadres, other political forces, and the media. The document described Italy's economic and social ills in every area from agriculture to public transportation to health care. It then outlined general goals in each area. But the program did not provide a concrete strategy for implementing the objectives. The reaction to the PCI's presentation was quite negative. Even party members were disappointed at how vague the program was. In terms of actual policies, the Communist leadership continued to press for austerity, labor peace, lower wages, less absenteeism, and a more flexible use of labor in the workplace. In opposition to union policy, the PCI also supported what was called external labor mobility. In effect, this meant putting large numbers of workers on temporary layoff with some form of compensation until they could be productively employed elsewhere.

EUR: The Labor Movement's Compromise Strategy

During the long period of party negotiations, the PCI leadership persuaded much of its own base and most of the labor confederation hierarchies that no issue could be completely resolved and no substantial reforms passed until the Communists went into the government. Thus a possible change in the PCI's status remained the center of attention. The unions kept up their advisory role in policy making. They had a voice in various government agencies and committees. But there was a sense of marking time while the Communist question remained open. Finally an exasperated FLM called on its members to protest the stalemate. On December 2, 1977, 250,000 metal and mechanical workers marched on Rome. On January 16, 1978, the government fell.

While the negotiations for a new coalition dragged on, the union leadership took another step to help move the Communist Party into the government. The three confederations held a national conference in the

EUR convention hall in Rome at the end of January.* More than 1,400 delegates and union cadres attended the conference to adopt a new policy for the labor movement. The contents of the platform were known ahead of time, and the outcome of the vote was a foregone conclusion. Nonetheless, the meeting at EUR was seen as a turning point for Italian labor. The delegates voted on a platform that accepted wage containment, a more flexible use of labor inside the workplace, and labor mobility between workplaces in exchange for a government-coordinated investment program aimed at creating jobs. The platform envisioned a radical shift in economic priorities for Italy, to be implemented by the investment program.

The ratified document targeted the following problems: youth unemployment, the South, agriculture, housing, energy, transportation, state finance, companies in crisis, and the tax system. These were the unions' usual areas of concern. So the novelty of the platform was not its investment or reform proposals but the explicit exchange being offered. The unions were trading shop-floor contractual concessions for a coherent program of investment and reforms. The working class would make sacrifices to stimulate a new phase of capitalist accumulation; in return, the workers' representatives would have a say in economic policy. It was a formalized shift away from a highly adversarial relationship toward one of greater cooperation.

The successful implementation of the platform clearly depended on the PCI playing a full role in the national government. Thus the EUR strategy, as it came to be called, was an endorsement of the Communists' position: A government including the PCI would take primary responsibility for fashioning the economic model while the unions, in a more subordinate role, would keep the workers' movement within compatible limits. The EUR strategy also responded to the confederations' concern about the growing number of unorganized and "marginal" workers. The unions believed that government action to create jobs through investment programs would best serve the needs of these groups.

Although the theme of EUR was sacrifices with compensation, some rank-and-file workers feared that the compensation end of the bargain would never materialize. The left wing of the labor leadership opposed the EUR strategy arguing that it remained within the logic of the old capitalist model. According to this view, the unions were mistakenly abandoning the course they had adopted in 1969 when they set out to develop their own model. The intermediate level of unionists was more

---

*EUR stands for *Esposizione Universale Roma*, a section of Rome built for the 1939 World's Fair, which never took place.

heavily represented at the conference than rank-and-file workers among whom disagreement with the platform was somewhat stronger. In the end, about 1,300 conference delegates voted in favor of the strategy. There were 12 *no* votes and about 100 abstentions.[1]

A Government of National Unity

Pressure to admit the PCI into the government was at a high point in January 1978 when the Carter administration in the United States issued a strong public declaration against this choice. The U.S. government had kept up its active opposition to the Communists during the 1970s. Through the CIA, the Nixon administration funneled $10 million to Christian Democrats and other political candidates in the 1972 election campaign. President Gerald Ford had the CIA spend another $6 million to bolster the noncommunist parties in 1976.[2] As mentioned earlier, shortly after the June elections, the United States and West Germany threatened Italy with reprisals if the PCI went into the government. As a presidential candidate, Jimmy Carter expressed a more flexible and noninterventionist attitude, but once in office, he shifted back to the hard-line stance.

Although the U.S. government's position reinforced those in the DC and in other parties who objected to Communist participation, a compromise solution still seemed possible. The PCI could join the parliamentary majority without formally entering the government and taking over ministries. Aldo Moro, president of the Christian Democrats and a former prime minister, took responsibility for convincing his party to accept this solution. Parliament was set to consider the new government formula on March 16, 1978. That morning, on his way to the Chamber of Deputies, Moro was kidnapped by terrorists of the Red Brigade. In the atmosphere of national crisis that immediately developed, Parliament voted the Communists into the majority for the first time since 1947. The government acted quickly to pass, by decree, a series of antiterrorist measures based on the six-party accord of the previous summer. In May, Parliament voted the special decrees into law.

The Moro kidnapping and murder 54 days later, the antiterrorist measures, police dragnets and searches, and the overall atmosphere of tension set the tone for the "national unity government" (or "national emergency government" as it was sometimes called). The political parties called on the citizenry to defend the state and to support the struggle against terror. That single issue, the government claimed, took precedence over all others. Once again, there was no room at the top of the government's agenda for a comprehensive economic program. The political climate was hostile to all protests and demands. The Communist Party, representative of working class interests to the government, called on labor to act responsibly and in the national interest.

The confederation leaders, who had thrown their lot in with the government and with the PCI, soon faced a restive and angry rank and file. The investment program proposed in the EUR strategy seemed ever more illusory. In fact, it turned out to be difficult even to pin down the exact meaning of the EUR platform. The confederations had purposely left the wording of the document vague in order to minimize conflict. In the months following the conference, union leaders of various political tendencies gave their own interpretations of the program. This aggravated their disputes and made them less able to formulate productive policies.

The labor movement was losing both its sense of direction and its cohesiveness. The interests of single sectors or workplaces or work teams began to take precedence over a classwide perspective. By fall 1978, rank-and-filers, as groups and as individuals in scattered cities and towns, were in open defiance of the unions. The employees of the major hospitals in Florence, for example, walked off the job in October, and by the end of the month wildcat strikes had spread to hospitals all over Italy. When the PCI and PSI accused the health workers of not being union members or of belonging to autonomous unions (non-CGIL, CISL, or UIL), the newspapers published photographs of the strikers holding up their confederation membership cards. There were frequent reports of factory council delegates resigning their posts. In the late October factory council election at Alfa Romeo, the workers voted out many of the delegates closely linked to the political parties, especially the PCI. Some of the workers explained that they wanted delegates who were more responsive to the rank and file and less tied to party and confederation positions. The strength of autonomous unions began to grow, especially among public employees. These workers had joined the confederation unions during the early 1970s and had been a new source of strength. The shift to autonomous unions in the late 1970s was a clear sign of the mounting dissatisfaction with CGIL, CISL, and UIL policies.

The situation had become intolerable. At its November 1978 General Council meeting, the leaders of the CGIL were frankly self-critical. Secretary Lama, who had led the campaign for salary containment and labor mobility, admitted to having pushed the line of working class sacrifice too far. Most CGIL leaders agreed that the EUR program was too vague, and they proposed, as a minimum, a militantly pro-working-class interpretation of it. The left wing argued for scuttling the platform altogether. The CGIL leadership also acknowledged that it had lost touch with its base; bureaucratic ways of operating were shackling the union.

But in spite of self-critical statements, neither the CGIL nor the CISL nor the UIL was able to devise a unitary policy alternative. When major contracts came up for renewal in late 1978, the unions made rather ritualistic references to the EUR platform but pressed for at least part of what their various constituencies demanded. The employers claimed that the unions' bargaining positions were unacceptable and that the EUR platform was therefore a dead letter.

Like the union hierarchy, the Communist leadership was aware of the growing restlessness and discontent within its membership base and electorate. In May 1978, Italians voted in scattered municipal elections. The PCI dropped an average of 9.1 percent below what it had won in 1976. The DC increased its share of the vote by 3.6 percent, and the PSI by 4.1 percent.[3] By the following fall, it was not unusual to hear local Communist activists grumble that the party should go back into the opposition. PCI leaders became more vocal about their frustrations with the government. Its measures were fragmented and inadequate, and Communist input into policy making was insufficient. In January 1979, the PCI pulled out of the parliamentary majority, precipitating a long governmental crisis and another round of early national elections.

As expected, the Communists suffered a significant defeat in the June 1979 vote. They dropped from 34.4 percent to 30.4 percent in the Chamber of Deputies. After having received a mandate in 1976, they had clearly disappointed their electorate, especially their new supporters. The small Radical Party (PR), which had been extremely critical of the PCI, made the largest gains of any group (from 1.1 to 3.4 percent) and won a following among young Italians. The Christian Democrats sustained a slight loss (from 38.7 to 38.3 percent), and the Socialists registered a very modest gain (from 9.6 to 9.8 percent). Observers generally agreed that the voting indicated disaffection and hostility toward the entire political system. For the first time since the war, less than 90 percent of the voters turned out, and the number of blank and spoiled ballots increased.

In 1975 and 1976, the electoral victories of the left had opened the way for a possible, albeit gradual, political renewal in Italy. Yet the tactics chosen by the PCI (historic compromise–national unity government) ended up undermining that possibility. The Communist leadership propped up the Christian Democrats at precisely the moment when the DC's position was weakest. By accommodating its policies to the DC, the Communist Party disoriented and discouraged its supporters. It also badly damaged its image as a decisive reform party. The Christian Democrats quickly regained the initiative and then blocked any attempt to alter the status quo. The decade ended with the PCI back in the opposition, having no clear strategic direction, its leadership divided. The labor movement was left without any promising policies. The EUR strategy

Striking workers (one with the Communist Party newspaper) outside the main gate at Fiat Mirafiori in 1979.

had never gotten off the ground, and there was little hope that future DC-dominated governments would undertake far-reaching reforms. With more economic troubles on the way, the stage was set for a renewed offensive against the labor movement.

Notes to Chapter 7

1. Sergio Turone, *Storia del sindacato in Italia 1943–1980* (Rome: Laterza, 1981), pp. 499–500.

2. Michael J. Harrington, "The U.S. in Italian Democracy," *The Nation*, July 3, 1976, p. 16.

3. Joseph LaPalombara, "Two Steps Forward, One Step Back: The PCI's Struggle for Legitimacy," in *Italy at the Polls, 1979: A Study of the Parliamentary Elections*, ed. Howard R. Penniman (Washington, D.C.: American Enterprise Institute for Public Policy Research, 1981), p. 127.

8

Feminism, Working-Class Women, and the Unions

While the political parties and labor confederations maneuvered in the national political arena, a significant social change was taking place. Feminism was challenging deep-rooted assumptions and demonstrating its capacity to stimulate new thinking in an ongoing way. Although the feminist movement began among women who were for the most part young and middle class, it had a notable impact on working-class women and the labor movement. In order to analyze that impact, the first sections of this chapter provide an overview of the genesis and evolution of the feminist movement in Italy. The following sections explore the influence of feminism on working-class women and the unions.

The Genesis of the Feminist Movement

The origins of the new feminism in Italy date back to the late 1960s when the mass political movements were taking shape at the universities. Enrollment was rapidly expanding, and more of the incoming students were women. By 1967–68, the female portion of the university population was about 36 percent, a sizable jump from less than 29 percent in 1962–63.[1] Many young women had their first political experiences in the student movement and in left organizations, especially the New Left parties. They acquired skills in political analysis and in organizing. But they also found themselves frustrated by the subordinate position they occupied in relation to men. There was a pervasive indifference to their particular interests and needs as women. They were "angels of the mimeograph machine" (angeli del ciclostile), doing behind-the-scenes support work for those (mostly men) who had a public presence as leaders, speakers, and writers. For the women involved, it was not much of an improvement over the traditional female role as angel of the hearth. They also objected to the rigid hierarchies of power in the New Left parties. They criticized the "old-style," undemocratic ways of doing politics.

Over the course of several years, a large proportion of these women activists came to see themselves as feminists. They eventually concluded that the sexually mixed organizations stifled the politics they wanted to develop. They resigned from the parties to form loosely structured, local collectives and consciousness-raising groups where they could couple radical ideology with new organizational forms.

The mid-1970s were a time of enthusiastic exploration and theoretical growth for the feminists. They published journals and newspapers, set up cooperatives and archives, ran bookstores, theatres, and women's centers. Among their most important efforts were the women's health counseling services (*consultori*) which they organized in many cities and towns. Through the *consultori*, the feminists provided information on birth control, abortion, mothering, and health problems. They saw this alternative health service as part of the struggle for self-determination and women's control over their own bodies. In all their activities, the feminists took up themes that the left and the labor movement had largely ignored. They criticized the sexual division of labor in society; they explored the relationship of class oppression to sexual oppression and the autonomous nature of the latter; they assigned reproductive rights a preeminent place in the struggle for women's liberation. The movement was anticapitalist. According to adherents, feminism was revolutionary in its potential to transform economic, political, and cultural norms.

The feminists criticized the older women's groups, especially the PCI-dominated Union of Italian Women (UDI, see Chapter 1), for adopting tightly structured and hierarchical forms of organization. According to the feminists, these groups had not seriously considered the need for separatism and financial independence from male-dominated institutions; they had maintained a false division between what were considered personal questions (such as sexuality and the family) and political issues. For the feminists, UDI's conception of women's emancipation was too narrowly focused on formal equalities. They also argued that UDI fell short in its approach to issues such as divorce, abortion, and birth control for fear of alienating traditional Catholic forces.

Conscious of being small and homogeneous, the feminist movement did not want to remain an isolated ghetto of young, educated leftists. Since they were particularly interested in reaching out to working-class women, feminists began doing grass-roots organizing. They set up health counseling services in working-class neighborhoods. They put together educational slide shows and took them into small towns and outlying communities. They began publishing material that would have a wider appeal. The grass-roots efforts increased their contact with other women and produced a useful exchange of ideas in some locales.

Many working-class women reacted negatively to feminism at first. The politics of sexuality, separatism, and consciousness-raising were new to them. They felt confused, afraid, even offended. UDI members responded in much the same way. They were often antagonistic and competitive. The PCI was especially wary because the feminists confronted topics that were highly controversial among Catholics and conservatives. The party at that time was trying to minimize its conflicts with the Christian Democrats. Some New Left groups embraced feminism on a theoretical level, although many male members reacted hostilely to the notion of separatism. Men from one of the groups (*Lotta Continua*) stormed a separatist march in Rome in 1975, but the other organizations respected the decision to organize events and projects for women only.

The Abortion Campaign

The divorce referendum in 1974 gave feminists a new opportunity. They were able to raise the issues of women's dependency and the roles of the Church, marriage, and family in the context of a national debate. But it was the abortion controversy that made feminism a significant social force in Italy. The struggle for abortion rights convinced large numbers of women to adopt a feminist perspective. It also brought the various political factions within the women's movement—feminists, UDI, libertarians—into a productive, although often combative, relationship.

The campaign began in the early part of the decade as pressure grew to repeal the Fascist regulations which were still the law of the land. According to this code, abortion was permitted only in cases of rape or incest. For religious, cultural, and political reasons, there had been no effort to educate extensively about birth control or to make contraceptives easily available. In fact, until 1971, another surviving Fascist law forbade the advertising and sale of contraceptives. The result was recourse to illegal abortions. It was estimated that 1.5 to 2 million illegal abortions were performed in Italy each year.[2]

In the mid-1970s, some feminist groups became involved in providing abortion services for women. They helped run an illegal clinic in Florence and arranged flights to Britain where abortion was allowed. They worked on these projects with the Movement for Liberation of the Woman (MLD), a women's organization linked to the small Radical Party. Both MLD and the PR were influential in catalyzing the divorce and abortion campaigns. Their ideological position was libertarian, and they devoted most of their energies to single-issue struggles. MLD, whose membership was sexually mixed, viewed women's liberation primarily in terms of civil rights. This outlook put MLD at odds with the feminists on many points, but tactical alliances were still possible.

Responding to the pressure to legalize abortion, the Christian Democrats supported a new and very limited law rather than have all restrictions on abortion abolished. The other parties put forward proposals, none of which was acceptable to the feminists. So on December 6, 1975, 50,000 women marched in Rome to demand full abortion rights. It was the first appearance of a mass feminist movement in Italy. The separatist event (in which UDI refused to participate) captured the attention of the media. It forced the left, especially the PCI, to begin to take feminism somewhat more seriously. By April 1976, the number of women marching in Rome had grown to 100,000 and included UDI. The impact was strong enough to bring down the government.

After the June 1976 election, Parliament continued working on abortion legislation that most activist women regarded as inadequate. But the various political groupings within the women's movement could not agree on an alternative proposal of their own. Women holding a libertarian position argued for simply repealing the Fascist laws. This would have legalized abortion. The majority, however, maintained that the legal right alone was not sufficient. They wanted a law providing for completely state-financed abortions on demand so that poor women would have the same rights in practice as wealthier women. Emphasizing the right to self-determination, the feminists argued that the decision to have an abortion should belong to the woman alone and not to doctors or judges. Furthermore, they wanted abortion to be just one part of a comprehensive health care and welfare system that not only met women's needs but was also controlled by women.

For the next two years, the abortion legislation was entangled in the complex negotiations over Communist participation in the government. The Christian Democrats proposed one provision after another to weaken the draft law, and the Communists went along with some of the limitations. During the spring of 1978, feminists and UDI members joined together in demonstrations outside Parliament to protest the PCI's compromises. This was one indication of how UDI had become more autonomous of the PCI during the abortion struggle. The organization had also begun to adopt an increasingly feminist viewpoint.

In June, Parliament finally passed one of the more progressive abortion laws in Europe. It provided for state-financed abortions within the first 90 days of pregnancy for any woman over 18 years of age. The reasons for seeking an abortion could be health related, economic, social, or familial. A doctor or recognized health facility issued the permission for an abortion after examining the woman and discussing alternatives with her. The women's movement considered the law only a partial victory because certain provisions fell short of desired goals. For example, formal authorization for an abortion still rested with the medical establishment; the lawmakers also raised the age for abortions without parental consent from 16 to 18 years; they stipulated that doctors had to perform all abortions in hospitals and specially authorized clinics.

The Evolution of the Movement

In just a few short years, the abortion campaign had become a powerful force that involved tens of thousands of women directly and touched many others. It also gave many women their first contact with feminism. The mass media greatly amplified this exposure. There were feature reports on feminism in newspapers and magazines and debates on television and radio. The result was that a new and more critical consciousness of the condition of women in Italy filtered through society, influencing how women saw themselves and their lives. This did not mean that millions joined the feminist movement as activists, but it did mean that many women identified or agreed in large part with feminism.

In the meantime, the movement ran into theoretical and organizational difficulties. There was an ongoing debate in the collectives and groups on these unresolved issues: the autonomy of the feminist movement and its relationship to state and political institutions such as Parliament and the parties; an adequate organizational structure that would provide coherence but not reproduce old hierarchies; the relationship between individual needs, private life, and activism in the movement; the focus of future activity. At first, many feminists turned their energies to the serious problem of implementing the new abortion law. About two-thirds of the doctors in state institutions and entire staffs of Catholic hospitals declared themselves conscientious objectors and refused to perform abortions. (Some of them, it was found out, were still doing clandestine abortions for high fees.) Feminists organized sit-ins in hospitals to protest the situation. They also helped set up the neighborhood family planning and health centers which had been promised by law. But they found that the local political powers and party cadres often dominated the process and absorbed the new health facilities into the existing institutional framework. Because of their informal organization, the feminists were at a disadvantage when dealing with the bureaucracies.

By the end of the 1970s, many of the early consciousness-raising groups, collectives, and coordinating committees had disbanded. Others

were operating at a lower level of activity. There was less attention focused on the movement as a national phenomenon. Feminism had developed during a time of general political mobilization. This environment
had provided ideological stimulation, organizing opportunities, political
interlocutors, and recruits. Once the mobilization had ebbed and the left
had suffered defeats, the feminists had to adjust to a less dynamic context. Many of them spoke of a serious crisis, but others insisted that, despite difficulties, the movement was still very much alive at the local level.
There was evidence that it had spread to provinces and small towns
where feminism had never before been present. Women there were responding to their immediate needs. They came together because they
were concerned about specific problems or shared an interest or simply
wanted to be with other women. The impact of feminism had not ceased,
but new women were finding different ways to incorporate and use it.

As in other Western countries, the great significance of feminism in
Italy was to awaken new attitudes and perceptions. The change in consciousness continued to transform social relations even when the movement itself was less visible. There were two striking examples of this in the
early 1980s. The first was the national referendum on abortion. The
Christian Democratic Party, the Vatican, and the Italian Movement for
Life were unwilling to let the abortion law stand. Assuming that the more
conservative political climate and the disarray of the left would give them
an advantage, the Catholic forces threw themselves into a campaign to
repeal the 1978 law. The neofascist party, MSI, also supported repeal. But
the referendum held in May 1981 showed that most Italians endorsed the
important reform. The vote was 68 percent in favor of the law and only
32 percent against. The sentiment in 1981 affirming a woman's right to
choose motherhood was even stronger than approval for divorce had
been in the 1974 referendum. Moreover, the pro-abortion vote was
equally heavy in southern, northern, and central Italy. The Alto Aldige,
a German-speaking alpine region, registered the only majority in favor of
repeal.

The second example involved the women's organization, UDI. At
its national convention in May 1982, the participants confronted the issues of delegated democracy and UDI's hierarchical structure. Adopting
a radical alternative, they essentially dissolved UDI as a centralized national organization. There would be no more full-time functionaries, no
unified political line, and no privileged relationship with any of the left
parties. A national office would still be open, but it would be staffed on a
rotating basis. There would be open general assemblies called by members rather than meetings of delegates scheduled by leaders. In addition,
UDI would no longer accept financing from the left parties.

The decisions were the result of an analysis in which UDI's leaders acknowledged they were losing members. The organization was having difficulty attracting young women and feminists. At the same time, UDI's leaders recognized the existence of a dispersed and largely unseen feminist movement which, they believed, did not identify with any national organization. By decentralizing itself, UDI hoped to link up with that movement. It also decided to make one of its publications an open magazine which could be used as a voice for the entire feminist movement.[3]

The convention decisions were risky as well as radical, and not everyone supported them. But many UDI members had changed during the course of the 1970s, arriving at a point where they wanted to abandon what they saw as traditional and hierarchical forms. In addition, they no longer wanted a close affiliation with male-dominated parties. It was a perspective not unlike that of the New Left women who had founded the first feminist groups. At that time, UDI had been one of the political forces that criticized, fought with, and distanced itself from the feminists. A decade later, the oldest women's organization in Italy undertook a sweeping self-transformation based on an understanding of and commitment to feminism.

Working-Class Women: An Overview of the Labor Market

Just as UDI underwent a process of change during the years of feminist mobilization, the perceptions that working-class women had of themselves and of their position in society were altered by feminism. The change in consciousness took place at a time when more women were entering the labor market. They were grappling with the problems of discrimination in hiring procedures and sexism in the daily routines of the workplace. Many were wives and mothers carrying the double burden of work outside and inside the home. Some were looking for jobs after being absent from the labor force for years.

To understand the context in which feminism gained acceptance, an overview of women in the Italian labor market during the 1970s will be useful. Early in the decade, female participation in the labor force fell to a low point. Then the trend reversed itself, and the participation rate for women slowly climbed back to where it had been 20 years earlier. By 1980, it had reached 26 percent.[4] Yet this was still quite low compared to other industrialized countries in the West. (In the United States, for example, 52.7 percent of the female population was in the labor force in 1982.)[5] In the meantime, the participation rate for Italian men continued to drop (see Table 8.1).

The bolting department at Fiat (Dante Boulevard, Turin) in 1917.

A worker at Fiat Mirafiori.

TABLE 8.1: Labor Force Participation Rates* for the Female, Male, and Total Populations in Italy, 1960–78

Group	1960	1965	1970	1975	1978
Female population	26.4	22.8	21.8	22.4	24.5
Male population	62.5	59.3	56.6	54.6	54.1
Total population	44.0	40.5	38.7	38.1	38.9

*Labor force as a percentage of population.

Source: Donald C. Templeman, *The Italian Economy* (New York: Praeger, 1981), p. 338.

In 1977, Parliament passed an equal treatment law (*legge di parità*) to promote the hiring of women and to expand the choice of jobs available to them. The law forbade discrimination based on sex in access to jobs, in wages, promotions, skills, training, and dismissals. It also equalized the treatment of women with respect to pensions, family allowances, and retirement age. The possibility of taking childcare leaves was extended to fathers (if the mother worked outside the home and did not take the leave herself). Feminists criticized the law because it did not establish any mechanisms for training women in new skills. It therefore tended to reinforce the existing sexual division of the labor market. In addition, there was no widespread effort to implement the provisions for equal treatment on the job and in hiring. Many women did not know their new rights, and neither the unions nor the government made enforcement a primary concern.

Despite serious problems, the law did have a positive effect on women's employment in some instances. One of these had to do with the local government job placement offices. Before the passage of the equal treatment law, employers hiring new workers were supposed to go through the job placement offices. In practice, most employers ignored the offices and hired on their own. But when they took on large numbers of workers, employers had more difficulty bypassing official channels. Even in this case, women were at a disadvantage because the job placement offices kept separate lists of unemployed men and unemployed women. The men's lists were regularly used when jobs traditionally held by males became available. Once the equal treatment law was passed, male and female lists were combined, and women were given an equal opportunity for at least some jobs. In Turin, for example, the combining of the sex-segregated placement lists in 1978 coincided with Fiat's decision to hire thousands of employees. Over the course of the next two years, about 17,000 new workers entered Fiat in Piedmont, and about half of them were women. A number of other industries also hired more women during this period.

TABLE 8.2: Unemployment Rates for Women and Men in Italy, 1977–80

	1977	1978	1979	1980
Women	12.5	12.6	13.3	13.1
Men	4.6	4.7	4.9	4.8

Source: "Raccolta dati sulla forza lavoro femminile" (Document prepared for the conference Produrre e riprodurre, Turin, Italy, April 23–25, 1983), mimeographed, p. 19.

The total number of Italian women employed in industry increased slightly during the 1970s although most women found work in the service sector. (The number of men with industrial jobs actually fell toward the end of the decade.) Of all employed women in 1979, 17.5 percent worked in agriculture, 27.9 percent in industry, and 54.6 percent in the service sector.[6] In general, more women found work than men. Between 1977 and 1981, the number of employed people in Italy increased by 690,000; of them, 472,000 were women.[7] But not all women who entered the labor market found jobs. The high female unemployment rate continued to mount during the 1970s and was consistently much greater than the rate for men (see Table 8.2). Thus the overall picture for the decade was one of more women working in Italy and many women wanting employment but unable to find it in an economy that was not generating enough new jobs.

The Impact of Feminism

Once feminism gained visibility, its themes gradually found a responsive audience among some working-class women and women unionists. The feminist approach to health care and the abortion campaign drew new supporters. Issues such as the sexual division of labor, power relations, economic independence, and the impact of work conditions were reformulated to relate directly to the daily experiences of women.

After discussing these topics informally, some women unionists and workers set up women's courses in the 150 Hours program. The enrollment of these courses was unusual. In addition to rank-and-file workers and unionists, they attracted housewives, women doing home labor, students, and feminist intellectuals. The presence of feminist "outsiders" was an important stimulus because they functioned as a link to the ongoing feminist debate. The subject of the courses ranged from the history of the family to women's health care to work environments to women in politics. The course structure was also innovative. Often the formal teacher–student distinction dissolved. The classes became more like consciousness-raising sessions, and the participants adopted the language of the feminist movement. The first courses were held in the large industrial centers, but the phenomenon soon spread to smaller cities and towns. Some classes were so popular that the participants continued to meet together after the courses had formally ended.

The emphasis of the 150 Hours classes was not on how women could attain equal status with men or how they could win a larger share of the economic pie. Instead the discussions explored how women were different from men and how these differences could be a source of strength. Differences were investigated as the possible basis for alternative values, alternative working arrangements, and new life styles. For many women, the experience of the 150 Hours courses was a turning point. It marked a profound change in attitudes, a new self-knowledge, and, for some, the inspiration to alter their circumstances. There were, of course, many working women who did not take the courses. Moreover, working-class women did not become activists in the feminist movement in large numbers. But few remained completely indifferent to the basic perceptions. Once the mass media focused attention on the women's movement, feminism and women's liberation were common topics of conversation. In subtle as well as explicit ways, the new notions were a source of strength to a growing number of women, giving them a way to evaluate their experiences and to validate their choices.

The relationship between the subordination of women at home and exploitation in the labor market was one aspect of feminist analysis to which many working-class women responded. In April 1981, a group of agricultural workers attended a CGIL national conference for women activists. When they described their situation in the countryside, they used categories and terms that were typical of a feminist perspective. They emphasized sexual roles and how subjugation and violence at home were a part of daily life for women. Until these were changed, they argued, women could make no headway in improving agricultural and work conditions or their position in the labor market.[8]

Similarly, many women at Fiat in the late 1970s maintained that liberation at home was necessary in order to feel autonomous and strong enough to struggle inside the factory. (Interviews with some of these Fiat women appear in Part II of this volume.) Of the women between 30 and 40 years of age, some had been in the factory for eight or ten years. Others had found jobs in the recent wave of hiring. They were back on the assembly line after a long period devoted to parenting and housework. Few were active in the women's movement. Yet they often considered themselves feminists or identified with aspects of feminism. Many working women of this age group felt they had struggled at home and at work to achieve a degree of independence and political consciousness as women. They saw younger female workers as more fortunate because that generation had grown up with the feminist movement and had absorbed it "by osmosis."

Unlike the "older" workers at Fiat, women in their late teens and early twenties had often completed one or two years of senior high school. Many had participated in student strikes and demonstrations. An antiauthoritarian attitude and a greater self-awareness were part of their identity as women. The feminist ideas being debated in Italy during that time helped shape their perceptions, although most young women workers, like the older generation, did not become activists in the movement.

Feminism in the Unions

Women not only entered the labor force in greater numbers, they also joined unions, participated in strikes, and attended workplace assemblies. But they rarely played leadership roles within the rank and file, and they spoke infrequently at meetings. There were few female delegates in the councils compared to the number in the workplaces. For example, the various Fiat plants in the area of Turin employed a total of 147,000 workers in early 1980; 30,000 of them were women (about 20 percent). But of 1,600 delegates, only 111 were women (about 7 percent).[9] Female council delegates were among the first to bring up women's concerns in the workplace, but they were handicapped by their small numbers. The unions employed women on a full-time basis, but most of them did secretarial work and the more menial technical tasks. Few played a political role. The higher the level of leadership in the unions, the rarer the presence of women became. The local and provincial FLM in Turin employed a total of 131 people in 1980, and 33 of them were women. Just six of the 33 had political functions. All the other women were secretaries or had technical jobs. Of the 98 male employees, three had technical jobs.[10]

The scarce representation of women and the disregard for their leadership potential were not at all new in the Italian labor movement. But in the context of the feminist mobilization, more women began to assert their specific needs. They spoke out against the indifference and paternalism of the labor organizations. They also started to discuss issues raised by the feminist movement and the 150 Hours courses within the union context. At first, female delegates, union members, and functionaries got together informally after meetings or after work. Then they organized local networks of union women belonging to the different labor categories and to the three confederations. These networks were called *intercategoriali donne* (women's intercategories) or *coordinamenti donne* or *coordinamenti femminili* (women's coordinating groups). The hope was to overcome divisions by plant, industry, and union and to give priority to questions affecting all women workers. Coordinating committees were established within some of the single labor categories as well.

The goal of the women was not to struggle for more power or higher union positions, but rather they were trying to create a new way of being women within the unions. Instead of relegating their interest in personal relationships, maternity, and sexual roles to "private life," they wanted to build an alternative culture within the unions around feminist themes. They argued that in order to do this, they needed autonomous structures and a group identity.

The entire project violated the traditional boundaries of union politics. It challenged the accepted style of operation. The initial reaction of most union leaders was vehement opposition. Many of them could not tolerate the idea of separatist, autonomous structures within the unions. They argued that it would undermine the unity of the working class. They also saw most feminist concerns as irrelevant to the labor movement. Their attitude changed, however, as feminism gained more acceptance within the population at large and within the PCI and UDI. Union leaders also saw that the desire for autonomous women's groups was spreading from the major cities to smaller cities and towns. Over the course of several years, the unions learned to accommodate feminist themes and a certain amount of autonomous activity. Indicative of this acceptance were the separate women's contingents marching under their own banners at huge labor demonstrations. By 1980, unions in Milan were even holding factorywide assemblies during working hours to discuss legislation on sexual violence in the broader context of women's subordination, sexual needs, and matrimonial duties.[11]

The women's networks also directed their attention to work conditions and to the particular problems confronted by women on the job. In most factories, the environment was still as alienating and uncomfortable for women as ever: no dressing rooms, dirty bathrooms, an insufficient number of toilets, and machinery built for the average male height and weight. With little skills training or seniority, women were often saddled with heavy or noxious tasks. (Women made up just 13.8 percent of Italy's total skilled labor force in 1972.)[12] They also did the most fragmented and repetitive jobs, having been stereotyped as patient and precise. Since they were in the lowest skill categories and since the tasks they regularly carried out were valued less, women earned lower wages. In 1978, blue-collar industrial jobs gave Italian women just 74.1 percent of what men were earning.[13] Day-care facilities were still very inadequate, and women received little help at home to relieve the double work burden.

The women's networks responded to these problems by trying to devise demands that would become part of the union platforms. Their proposals included courses and work-study programs for skill development, the recombination of assembly-line tasks to raise skill levels, the reduction of time spent in a job category before a worker was automatically promoted, better safety and health conditions, 40 hours per year of paid child-care leave for women and men, a 35-hour workweek, the option to work part time, better social services, and the scheduling of social services to make them more available to workers. Many of these positions required extensive debate but were still not completely settled. For example, some women felt that making part-time work a legal option (it was very limited in Italy) would ghettoize women and undermine equality. Others believed that a more flexible schedule would meet women's needs.

The debate on objectives was further complicated by the difficulty of translating emotional and domestic concerns into specific contract demands. Some women maintained that not nearly enough had been accomplished in this area. They were also frustrated by what they saw as the unions' reluctance to press hard enough for women's demands during contract negotiations. Although there was a more open attitude toward feminism among male unionists, most women believed that the labor organizations were still operating in the old bureaucratic, sexist, and top-down ways. The unions had changed neither the content of their policies nor their methods.

Another unresolved question was the structure of the women's networks and committees. Some argued for a very loose format in order to avoid hierarchies and undemocratic practices. Others thought that a somewhat more formal organization was needed in order to represent women workers systematically and to operate more effectively within the unions. As was the case in the feminist movement, the debate on structure for union women was ongoing.

After five or six years of intense activity in the women's networks, many of the original unionists felt they had to withdraw. The strain of working in the networks while trying to operate within the unions had fatigued them. Some were discouraged with the results. Not as many rank-and-file women were actively involved as they had hoped, and the unions sometimes seemed impervious to change. Moreover, after years of self-examination, they were in touch with new needs as individuals. Many wanted to explore other kinds of work. But the departure of some of the first generation of union feminists in the late 1970s and early 1980s did not mean that the women's committees and networks disappeared. New women were coming into the unions, and there were also experienced feminists who stayed on.

Union women confronted an extremely unfavorable economic and political situation in the early 1980s. The labor movement as a whole had suffered serious defeats after 1978 and was on the defensive; the confederations were divided and without a coherent strategy; large numbers of workers, many of them women, were being laid off; and the conservative political forces were determined to win concessions from labor. It was difficult for women to make gains, and yet the networks did not passively accept what they called "the crisis." They did not give the traditional male leadership complete freedom to analyze and define the situation. Women examined the crisis from the standpoint of their own interests. They continued to educate themselves and to build a sense of solidarity.

Just one example of this was the large international conference on women and work in industrialized countries held in Turin in April 1983. The meeting brought together feminists, women scholars, and worker-activists from Italy, other European countries, and America. Significantly, the conference was organized as a joint effort by three components of the Italian women's movement: autonomous feminist groups, UDI, and the *Intercategoriale Donne* CGIL-CISL-UIL. The conference represented an impressive level of collaboration achieved by three different traditions. It was also a reminder that despite setbacks and periods of discouragement, the feminist experience had forged a new and stronger collective voice for women in Italy.

Notes to Chapter 8

1. Yasmine Ergas, "1968–79—Feminism and the Italian Party System: Women's Politics in a Decade of Turmoil," *Comparative Politics* 14, no. 3 (April 1982):276.

2. Lesley Caldwell, "Church, State, and Family: The Women's Movement in Italy," in *Feminism and Materialism: Women and Modes of Production*, ed. Annette Kuhn and AnnMarie Wolpe (London and Boston: Routledge and Kegan Paul, 1978), p. 84.

3. Ritanna Armeni, "Una femminista che vince," *Pace e Guerra*, March 31, 1983, pp. 34–35.

4. Milan Women's Collectives, "La Crisi" (Document prepared for the conference *Produrre e riprodurre*, Turin, Italy, April 23–25, 1983), mimeographed, p. 8.

5. U.S. Department of Labor and Bureau of Labor Statistics, *Employment and Earnings* 30, no. 9 (September 1983):7.

6. "Lavoro donna, donna lavoro," *Il Manifesto* (Rome, June 1980), p. 2.

7. Nicoletta Giorda, "Donne a confronto con la crisi economica," *Bollettino delle Donne* 2, no. 2 (March 1983):3.

8. Ritanna Armeni, "Lavoratrici o donne che lavorano? Un problema in più per il sindacato," *Il Manifesto*, April 8, 1981.

9. *Il sindacato di Eva: Documenti 1978–81* (Turin: CGIL-CISL-UIL Piemonte, 1981), pp. 56, 59.

10. Ibid., p. 59.

11. Lynn Frogett and Antonia Torchi, "Feminism and the Italian Trade Unions," *Feminist Review*, no. 8 (Summer 1981):40.

12. Commission of the European Communities, Directorate-General Information, *Women in Statistics*, *Women of Europe*, suppl. 10 (Brussels, 1982), p. 26.

13. Ibid., p 22.

9

The Legacy of the 1970s

The renewed offensive against the labor movement in the early 1980s was aimed at lowering the cost of labor and increasing management's control over its use in the workplace. This offensive took place in a rapidly changing context. Computer-controlled machines were eliminating jobs in factories and offices. Many of the jobs that remained were being radically transformed. The industrial working class employed in large and medium-sized plants, the traditional heart of the Italian workers' movement, was shrinking. Employers were decentralizing production to small shops and into private homes. Jobs and workers were disappearing into the underground economy. In the meantime, a new generation of workers had entered the labor market. They were women who had been touched in some way by the feminist movement, and they were young people whose attitudes toward work and the labor movement differed from those of the Hot Autumn generation.

These far-reaching changes began in the 1970s. They were, in fact, the critical legacy of the decade. They shaped the context in which the labor movement subsequently had to operate.

Restructuring the Economy: New Technology

By 1974, economists and political commentators were reporting on a new effort by private industry to restructure the productive base in Italy. Realizing that it might be difficult in the short run to take back what workers had won during the 1969–72 mobilization, many businesses began planning for a more long-term shift in industrial relations. In addition, international markets were rapidly changing. In order to compete effectively, Italian capital needed to produce new goods more efficiently and cheaply. Industrialists began using two major tactics to achieve their goals: the introduction of computerized technology and the decentralization of production. The result of this restructuring process has been more unemployment, an increasingly divided labor market, and new dilemmas for the labor movement.

The development of the microprocessor, a computer "brain" no larger than a fingernail and costing just a few dollars, set off a revolution in manufacturing and office technology which has been transforming production and clerical work in most industrialized nations. The potential of labor-saving robots and computer-coordinated production systems has made experts in manufacturing claim that the transformation will be as significant as the introduction of the assembly line or even the industrial revolution of the nineteenth century.

In the auto industry worldwide, robots do a large proportion of the welding and painting. Automatic machinery has replaced half the workers on the presses in many plants. But these jobs are just a start. The trend is to produce robots that can take over more and more tasks in all industrial sectors. The new generations of "smart" robots will be able to "see," "feel," "hear," and make decisions. Rather than being limited to fixed sequences and to precisely set positions, smart robots can respond flexibly to changing stimuli. They can undertake long and varied processes. Manufacturers have created entire production complexes by hooking individually computerized machines into central computers (often referred to as direct numerical control), into multilevel systems of computers (computer-integrated manufacturing), and into computer-controlled transport networks (flexible manufacturing systems). Computers also play an important role in the designing of machine parts and in translating those designs into actual pieces. This kind of operation replaces skilled machinists. Aside from supervisory and repair personnel, entire production departments in some plants function without humans. Engineers have tested prototypes of the so-called unmanned factory. The costs of computerized machinery have been dropping steadily, so that smaller businesses can also acquire the new technology. Coordinated production systems are proving to be particularly efficient for varied, small-batch production.

In offices, the use of computers, video display terminals, data banks, and printers has revamped the entire field of information processing. Systems designers have completely restructured traditional tasks such as filing, typing, correspondence, and scheduling. Clerical workers now record, retrieve, and manipulate data of every kind with the new machines. The overwhelming majority of these workers are women.

In Italy, basic research and development have never received adequate support from private capital or from the state. As a result, Italian industry has depended heavily on foreign technology. The stronger companies have modernized and stayed competitive by adopting new technology as it becomes available. A few companies, such as Fiat, have used imported technology to develop their own capital goods production for export as well as for domestic markets. Their success depends on copying or modifying foreign equipment and incorporating it into innovative production systems.

From the point of view of management, the new programmable technology has a long list of advantages. It is more versatile. One machine can be set to produce a combination of different models or parts, allowing a company to respond more quickly to shifting market demand. Much of the technology can also be reprogrammed when old products are dropped and new ones introduced. This saves on expensive retooling. Production is uniform and of high quality, and costs are lower. In the U.S. auto industry, for example, the average hourly cost of a robot was about $6 in the early 1980s; a human worker earned about $20 an hour, including all benefits. The increase in productivity is also great. Unlike their flesh-and-blood colleagues, robots can work three shifts a day, every day of the year. They do not take coffee breaks and never go out on strike. Employers can also use the new technology to reduce conflict inside the plants. The departments where work is particularly strenuous, dirty, or hazardous tend to have higher levels of conflict and more strikes. When machines take over the worst jobs, the level of contention falls.

In addition to all these advantages, there is still another which is probably most important: control over the labor force and the process of production. Centralized computer-run systems do not simply displace workers. They can monitor the movements of every remaining human. Management can use computerized machinery to set rigid production times, to regularize rhythms, and to eliminate almost all flexibility. Even the limited autonomy and control over the labor process that Italian workers achieved is often lost when management restructures using the new technology.

The reaction of workers in Italy to the computerized machinery and production systems has been mixed. Some employees feel positive because their manufacturing jobs are less taxing and dangerous. Their work environments have more space, more light, and less noise. In some cases, the new systems recombine tasks or string together a series of tasks so that each operation may require three or four minutes rather than 45 seconds. This reduces boredom and fatigue. In other instances, however, the technology fragments the labor process further. It can increase monotony even to the point of producing severe psychological problems. The workers on these jobs feel that their activity has been debased as never before and that they have lost even the minimal control they once had over the labor process. When robots are stationed among humans on an assembly line, many workers resent seeing a machine perform exactly the same task just a few paces away.

Many clerical workers operating computers and video displays feel that their jobs are much more monotonous than before. Each task has been broken down into components that a worker repeats over and over. Instead of performing a variety of functions, an office worker often does just one part of a task. Many sit in front of display screens and key in data all day. Eye strain, back problems, and nervous disorders have become hazards of the job.

The process of restructuring within Italian plants and offices can divide the work force and create dissension. The new machinery appears in a factory piecemeal and over the course of many years. Employers modernize some assembly lines or departments but not others. The most up-to-date equipment can stand next to machinery that dates back to the early postwar period. Workers doing the same kind of job may have completely different work conditions. At Fiat, for example, the one computerized system for installing mechanical parts into a car body produced the 131 model. Workers carrying out the same tasks on other models used the old methods and equipment, and consequently their jobs were much more strenuous. This generated resentment and competition.

The attitude of workers toward the new technology also depends on whether or not they perceive their jobs to be threatened. In companies that are expanding enough to relocate or retrain displaced workers, the technology is less menacing. Between 1975 and 1979, Fiat workers accepted new machinery with relative calm because the company had agreed not to dismiss workers and even hired thousands during a brief period of expansion. But these circumstances turned out to be an anomaly. The grim employment picture at Fiat, in Italy, and all over Europe in the 1980s makes jobs and control over the work process the two key issues raised by the new technology.

The predictions of technology-related job elimination for the remainder of this century have been dramatic. A 1979 British study contended that microelectronics would cut overall employment in the United Kingdom 23 percent by 2000 A.D. The researchers expected a 25 percent decline in wholesale and retail trade employment and a 31 percent drop in banking, insurance, and finance jobs by 1995. A study completed for the French government anticipated that new technology would shrink the work force in French banking and insurance 30 percent by 1990.[1] In 1980, a Fiat engineer stated that the use of smart robots could eliminate 90 percent of the Italian company's work force, leaving just a core of white-collar computer technicians. Such a factory, he pointed out, would be feasible by 1990.[2]

These predictions may well exaggerate the speed of job elimination. During the deep recession of the early 1980s, companies invested in new technology at a slower rate than had been assumed. But even if the process is much less rapid, current trends point to significant job destruction in the coming decades. The increase in productivity, the rate of job elimination so far, and the lack of new employment possibilities support this interpretation. An Olivetti mechanical typewriter required 14 hours of production time in 1976, and a mechanical telex required 80 hours. In 1982, an electronic typewriter produced with new automated machinery required just 5 hours of production time and an electronic telex just 20 hours. Olivetti was able to slash employment from 29,000 in 1978 to 18,000 in 1982. Necchi, a company which makes refrigerator compressors among other things, undertook a program of automation and robotization in the mid-1970s. By 1985, Necchi will produce about twice as many compressors with half the number of workers once needed. At Alfa Romeo, the number of hours required to complete a car dropped from 170 in 1976 to 118 in 1982.[3]

When evaluating job elimination due to computer technology, it is important to keep in mind that the countries of the EEC produced no net new employment during the 1970s.[4] Moreover, it was estimated that while job growth remained static through the mid-1980s, 5 million new job seekers would enter the labor market.[5]

The more optimistic analysts and business people maintain that after a period of dislocation, there will be new jobs in design, programming, and machine maintenance. They direct this claim at those who most fear mass unemployment—workers, labor unions, and government officials. The reasoning ignores the fact that one central purpose of the new technology is to replace human workers. The new jobs created will most likely be few in number compared to those lost. When promoting their products to prospective buyers, robot manufacturers rarely fail to emphasize their labor-saving potential. Even the argument that workers will find jobs making the new machinery is not very persuasive. Automated factories can manufacture more automation, and there are already robot-producing robots. Company directors also argue that without automating and cutting labor costs, their products will be uncompetitive and they will have to close down their businesses. This is no doubt true, and it underscores the difficulty of the problem. In both cases, when enterprises are antiquated and uncompetitive or when they automate rapidly with new computer technology, hundreds of thousands of workers may lose their jobs.

The unions in Italy were slow to respond to employers' initiatives using the new technology. In their present weak position, the unions' influence over the process is minimal. During most of the 1970s, they saw robots and other innovations as improvements in work conditions which reinforced the labor movement's strategy of transforming the work process. The FLM, for example, asked Fiat to install computerized systems for motor assembly and for bolting mechanical parts in all its plants.

Critics of union policy did not dispute the argument that the new machinery often improved workplace conditions. But they insisted that the crucial issue was control over the use of technology. It was not long before the labor confederations acknowledged this, but they never devised specific programs or emphasized tactics to gain more control. By the end of the decade, the union leadership admitted that it had not acted in time and that management clearly had the upper hand. Labor's only concrete proposal in terms of jobs was to generate openings with a shorter workweek, longer vacations, and early retirement. These defensive measures might slow down the rate of layoffs somewhat. But they do not address the questions of new job opportunities and job retraining. Equally important, they do not deal with the problem of control. Whoever decides what technology will be developed, where and when it will be installed, and what information its computers will collect will also dominate the process of production. So far, employers in Italy are holding on to that control.

The Decentralization of Production

In the overall process of economic restructuring in Italy, businesses have been decentralizing production as well as introducing new technology. Since Italian industry has a high proportion of small plants relative to other advanced capitalist countries, decentralization has been an expedient and important approach in the restructuring process. It is a direct response to the workers' movement that began in the late 1960s. As the labor force gained more control over how work was done, employers began shipping some of that work out of plants and into smaller shops and the home. While decentralization of some jobs such as foundry work started in the early 1960s, the significant increase in decentralization has taken place since 1969. The result is the spread of the "diffused factory" (la fabbrica diffusa)—minifactories, tiny shops, new forms of artisanry, and put-out work in the home. Part of the decentralized activity is legal, but part uses unrecorded "black labor" (lavoro nero). This illegal work is the substance of Italy's growing underground economy.

Using *lavoro nero* offers great advantages to employers. Workers in the underground economy are not unionized. This means low—often abysmally low—wages, no benefits or pension payments, and no taxes. (Social insurance contributions add an average of about 38 percent to labor costs in Italy.) In addition, there are no controls over health and safety conditions and no labor protests or strikes. In some industries, home labor operations save 60 to 75 percent of the usual factory production costs.[6] The workers must often buy their own tools and machines and pay their own utility bills. Thus capital investment and operating costs for the employer are minimized.

Minifactories that are legally recorded also offer advantages. The Workers' Statute does not cover shops with fewer than 15 employees. The unions are usually absent or extremely weak. Most forms of decentralized production give management much greater flexibility to change products and quantities produced in order to meet market needs. When a large company decentralizes even part of its production cycle, it weakens the unions in the main plants because their strikes have less impact.

The substantial advantages of black labor for employers are at the same time disadvantages for workers. Labor conditions often rival those of nineteenth-century sweatshops. The 16-hour workday is common, and payment by the piece encourages grueling production rates. There is no job stability. Some work is only seasonal or part time. Years of black labor mean a reduced pension even if a worker eventually finds a legal position. The underground economy draws on the social groups traditionally pushed out of the regular labor market: women, older people, the young, unskilled Southerners, students, undocumented immigrants, as well as laid-off workers. In the South, especially around Naples, the underground economy pulls in many children. As for undocumented foreigners, no one knows for sure how many are living in Italy. In the early 1980s, economists estimated that there were 700,000 to 800,000. Many come from North Africa, Yugoslavia, and the Far East. A large proportion have settled in the industrial centers and around Rome. Some are unemployed, and the others take the least desirable jobs as dishwashers, porters, and domestics. So far there has been no racist reaction against the immigrants, but it is hard to predict what will happen if their numbers increase and the job situation continues to deteriorate.

It should be pointed out that some Italians use the underground economy to supplement their incomes. There are families in which one member has a legal job that provides benefits to the rest of the family. Other members add to the collective income by doing black labor. Moonlighting (*doppio lavoro*) is also part of the underground economy since many labor contracts forbid holding second jobs. Most moonlighters are men in the northern industries or in low-paying, public-sector positions with short workdays. They receive wages and benefits from one job and a second salary without deductions.

Decentralization, legal and illegal, is a national phenomenon, but its magnitude and exact form vary from industry to industry and from region to region. Much of the work is labor intensive, but some involves advanced technology. The kinds of jobs most often eliminated from large plants include tasks performed by one to three workers on a single machine, dangerous and noxious tasks (employers can thus eliminate conflict and bypass union controls), highly skilled work such as machine repair (management often rehires dismissed workers on a free-lance basis for less pay), tasks not requiring machines (for example, tile decoration), and small assembly-line production using 10 or 12 workers.

As the decentralized economy absorbed more jobs during the 1970s, the scope of home labor in Italy also broadened. In addition to the traditional work in textiles, clothing, toys, and shoes, home laborers began to do metal and electronics work such as assembling appliances, auto parts, and computer or even housing components. Companies also started to put out clerical tasks to workers with computer terminals in their homes.

Contrary to what most economists once thought, Italy's large underground economy is more widespread in the North than in the South, except for a few areas like Naples. The technological level is generally higher in the North, whereas illegal work in the South is more consistently labor intensive. Two regions where the underground economy grew noticeably in recent years are Emilia-Romagna, where the Communists are the dominant political force, and the Veneto, which is Christian Democratic.[7] The extent of Italy's underground economy is unknown, although it is proportionately larger than those of other Western industrialized nations. Economists believe Italy's true GNP may be 15 to 30 percent higher than the official figures because of the underground economy. The magnitude of unrecorded work is one explanation for the country's exceptionally low official rate of labor force participation. As much as one-third of the actual active population may do black labor or have temporary or precarious jobs.[8]

The media in Italy and abroad often portray the decentralization of the Italian economy as a sign of new vitality and reanimated entrepreneurship. Thriving small businesses are compared to sluggish large industries (especially the state holdings) plagued by labor unrest, absenteeism, low productivity, and red tape. But in fact, decentralization often has little to do with a revived business spirit because many small shops depend directly or indirectly on existing large industries. In Emilia, for example, most medium-sized and small foundries supply the Fiat plants in the region. When the large firms get into trouble, their satellites suffer as well.

To base future economic development on the kind of decentralization described here would mean creating an increasingly exploitative system. In addition, some companies decentralize by shipping phases of their
production cycles out of Italy altogether. They set up plants in countries
where labor costs are much lower. This forces unprotected Italian
workers in the underground economy to compete with exploited Third
World laborers. Playing on the Communist Party theme "the Italian road
to socialism," some economists and unionists refer to decentralization
based on the growth of the underground economy as "the Italian road to
underdevelopment."

Because of decentralization, the Italian economy is taking on still
another dual characteristic in addition to the North–South and private–
public dualities. One part of the economy is centralized, with concentrated industries often using advanced technology. Italians call the employees of these more capital-intensive enterprises "guaranteed" workers.
They are unionized, better paid, and have some small degree of job protection. The other part of the economy is decentralized, much of it unreported and labor intensive. Its workers are the unorganized, superex-
ploited, "nonguaranteed." This increasingly pronounced duality is an
ominous trend for Italian labor unions. The proportion of workers in
organized, stable situations is shrinking relative to the active population.
Unreported workers are hard to track down and hard to unionize. They
do illegal work to survive. They fear losing their jobs or seeing their employers, who depend on cheap labor, go out of business. Yet in order to
rebuild its strength, the labor movement in Italy will have to find a way to
incorporate the expanding ranks of the nonguaranteed.

A New Generation of Workers

For much of the public as well as for the unions and the political
parties, there was a typical Italian worker during the 1970s. He or she was
25 to 40 years old, on the assembly line, an immigrant from a nonurban
area to an industrial center, veteran of the 1969–72 mobilization, militant
even if sometimes critical of union policy, educated politically in the
workplace, and strongly identified with the factory. Even if the workers
fitting this description did not make up a majority of the labor force, they
did dominate the labor movement culturally and politically. Then toward the end of the decade, a new generation began entering the labor
market. Its members no longer conformed to the model. Their assumptions, experiences, and expectations were different. The phenomenon
was widespread, and it presented still another challenge to the labor
unions for the 1980s.

Young workers at a discotheque in Turin.

The new generation of workers had grown up in an "automotive" and more highly industrialized Italy where television and superhighways were among the most powerful forces unifying the country. Unlike the previous generation of industrial workers who entered the plants at the age of 12 or 13, many working-class youths by the late 1970s stayed in school until 16 or 18. This meant they were socialized for several years in what Italians called the *mondo dei giovani* (young people's world), a

world of music, discos, drugs, and "hanging out" which did not exist in
Italy before the 1970s. Many young people also had their first political
experiences in high school where they observed or participated in school
strikes and assemblies.

All this took place during the period of debate around the historic
compromise and the national unity government. It was a time when frustration and disillusionment with the political system grew especially
strong among the young. Unlike many older workers, much of the new
generation no longer looked to the PCI or to the New Left for a solution.
They were less interested in organized politics; many were cynical about
it. Most institutions in Italy, including the state, political parties, and
trade unions, elicited suspicion or rancor. Antiauthoritarianism was pervasive. At the same time, young people tended to have a greater sense of
their individual self-worth. Many had high-school diplomas or technical
degrees. They wanted fulfilling jobs, some security, and also time for
themselves and their own projects. They evaluated work in terms of
whether it was intrinsically worth the time spent on it.

These young working-class people were entering the labor market at
precisely a time when the economy offered little satisfying work or security. Many of them spent months unemployed and finally went into the
underground economy to do part-time or seasonal work. Some took full-
time industrial jobs after having vowed they would not end up on the
assembly lines. They had seen their fathers and mothers grow old and ill
inside the plants. Despite the great victories they had always heard of, the
new generation found industrial work environments noisy, dark, smelly,
and dangerous. They had less tolerance for monotonous tasks and were
less willing to observe existing rules. More generally and perhaps more
importantly, they did not share the older workers' commitment to staying in the factory in order to change it. For the young, the workplace was
no longer the center of existence or the focus of concern as it had been for
the activist workers of the 1969 generation.* Many young people did not
even define themselves as workers in the way that had been common
until then. The older politicized workers saw themselves primarily as
members of a class. They defined their relationship to society in terms of
that class identity and solidarity. The younger people saw themselves
more in terms of their interests, aspirations, and lives outside the workplace. Most hoped to get out of the jobs they hated as soon as possible.
Even with the difficult employment situation, they maintained that their
current work situations were only temporary.

---

*Many of those who had participated in the 1969–72 mobilization were in their
late twenties to late thirties by 1979.

Nowhere was the contrast between the two generations of workers highlighted in a more striking fashion than at Fiat. The reason for this was fairly simple. Suffering the worst financial crisis of its history, Fiat closed its gates to new workers in 1974. When the company ended the freeze in 1978, about 17,000 employees were hired within the brief span of two years. In the meantime, the new generation had entered the labor market. Since Fiat was obliged to select its workers through the government placement offices, most of the recruits were young (between 18 and 23 years of age) and many were young women. The result was a starkly divided work force.

Inside the plants, the new generation rejected the assumptions of the older workers. They challenged the policies of the factory councils and the unions. The young people complained that they were always hearing lectures about the workers' movement of the late 1960s. They were irritated by what they felt were moralistic attitudes. Many were unimpressed with the changes won during the previous decade. Some took it upon themselves to change work rules in order to make their jobs more tolerable. For example, they switched tasks with one another to break the monotony.

Most young workers at Fiat joined the FLM soon after being hired. But among those who joined, some did not believe the union was doing much; others thought union policies were selling out the workers; and still others were simply not very interested. They did not question the necessity of a union. They joined spontaneously and went out on strike. But many would take off with friends rather than participate in rallies and marches. This too was different from the experiences of older workers. Members of previous generations had often risked their jobs to join a union or to strike. In other cases, they had affiliated with a union as part of a larger process of politicization.

Many older workers at Fiat were perplexed and rankled by the attitudes of the young, characterizing them as lazy, irresponsible, or unappreciative. One common complaint was "they don't want to work." Yet other veterans of the struggles at Fiat believed the new generation could be won over to the labor movement, where they had the potential to become militant and politically committed. These workers urged the labor organizations to reach out to young people. Unionists often agreed with this perspective in theory, but in practice, the unions did little to attract young workers or to address their particular needs.

The Italian labor movement built its strength in the postwar period on the organized, politicized, and activist workers of the industrial sector. But the weight of this group was declining in the late 1970s as the economy was restructured and as a new generation of workers and more women entered the labor market. The transformations generated diverse needs and aspirations within a working class that was increasingly divided. At a time when the labor movement was hard pressed just to protect past gains, the unions were not yet able to develop new policies and strategies to respond to the changing context.

Notes to Chapter 9

1. "The Speedup in Automation," *Business Week*, August 3, 1981, p. 66.

2. "Robots Join the Labor Force," *Business Week*, June 9, 1980, p. 76.

3. Leo Sisti, "Dopo la Fiat l'Alfa, dopo l'Alfa . . .," *L'Espresso*, February 6, 1983, pp. 109–10.

4. George Gilder, "Built Upon Bankrupt Theories," *New York Times*, July 24, 1983.

5. "The Speedup in Automation," p. 66.

6. Philip Mattera, "Small is Not Beautiful: Decentralized Production and the Underground Economy in Italy," *Radical America* 14, no. 5 (September–October 1980):69.

7. Ibid., p. 73.

8. Ruggero Spesso, *L'economia italiana dal dopoguerra a oggi* (Rome: Riuniti, 1980), p. 117.

10

Labor in the Early 1980s

The period of the early 1980s in Italy was bounded by two national elections, the June 1979 and the June 1983 parliamentary contests. The first of the two delivered a serious blow to the Communist Party and isolated the left. With the country's economic troubles unresolved, both political and economic conditions favored a successful assault against the labor movement. The conservative political parties attempted to redistribute income at the expense of the working class, and employers reasserted their authority inside the workplaces. The unions had neither the strength nor the political leverage to stop initiatives that undermined the workers' interests. As a result, the major employers' organizations and the government took bold steps that would have been unthinkable eight or ten years earlier. The period ended with a substantial electoral defeat for the Christian Democrats. But even this would not improve the position of the labor movement in the short term.

Political Realignments after National Unity

The June 1979 parliamentary elections failed to produce a stable majority. The Christian Democrats and the small center and center-right parties (PRI, PSDI, PLI) claimed less than 50 percent of the vote. The dominant sentiment among them was to avoid PCI collaboration in another national unity experiment. This left the Socialist Party with the power to make or break a majority. The PSI wielded political leverage that went far beyond its modest standing (9.8 percent of the vote in the Chamber of Deputies). The party found it could use its leverage in one of two ways. It could press for an opening for the left as a whole, including

161

the Communists. This option presupposed at least tactical programmatic agreements with the PCI. Or it could isolate the Communists, offer itself as a solitary partner for the center, and bargain for as much influence and as many political plums as possible.

The Socialists chose the latter course. Bettino Craxi, secretary of the party since 1976, was determined to diminish the weight of the Communists and to make the PSI into a modern social democratic force, modeled after the northern European parties. He also made it clear that he wanted to become prime minister as soon as possible. In order to shift power away from the Christian Democrats, the Socialists had to convince major industrialists and financiers that the PSI was the most likely architect of a modernized and efficient capitalist system. The party did not have great success, however, because the leadership spent more energy on political maneuvering than on developing credible economic programs. The Socialists' position was vacillating and ambiguous. The result was a great deal of rhetoric criticizing the Christian Democrats but little in the way of alternative proposals other than a PSI-led government.

Meanwhile the Christian Democrats were worried about the deterioration of their base. The party still appealed to many practicing Catholics, but the proportion of these in the population as a whole was declining. The DC claimed it wanted to cut public spending, increase tax revenues, and improve the balance of payments, but the party was fettered by the conflicting interests of its heterogeneous constituency and by its dependence on the support generated by the patronage system. In addition, the divisive factions that traditionally plagued the DC inevitably reasserted themselves despite regular calls for party reform.

Hoping to improve their status, the Christian Democrats agreed in 1982 on a new party secretary, Ciriaco De Mita, who was supposed to unify and invigorate the DC and take a harder line with the Socialists. Rather than juggle competing interests in the usual way, De Mita set about fashioning a new image for the DC as rigorous, modern, secular, and committed to putting Italy's economic house in order. He allied with those factions of Confindustria that were most adamantly determined to win major concessions from the labor movement.

The leadership of the Communist Party came out of the 1979 elections divided and uncertain. Many high officials agreed that the PCI had made serious errors during the national unity period. But the critique of those policies did not quickly lead the Communists to a positive alternative. The party remained immobile and segregated in the parliamentary opposition. Meanwhile an internal debate centered on the nature of the party, its future role in national government, and its evaluation of the Soviet Union and Eastern European countries.

In 1980, Secretary Berlinguer abruptly shifted positions. He began to support workers' struggles in order to rebuild the party's credibility within the working class. In late 1981, he called for a "new party," a re-founding of the PCI based on a revitalized relationship with mass constit-uencies. According to this proposition, the party would direct its atten-tion to women, young people, new cultural forces, and the growing peace movement. Berlinguer argued that the PCI could no longer judge its po-litical success primarily in terms of votes won or cadres placed into office. Nor could the party limit its concerns to economic questions and labor struggles. In a new economic policy statement, the Communists called for economic planning based on European integration, a 35-hour workweek in Europe, and a national labor service that would guarantee a minimum wage to the unemployed. The statement was a departure from past calls for austerity and working-class restraint. The policy maintained that the working class was under attack. It stated that structural problems, and not primarily the cost of labor, were the source of inflation.

Although these stands oriented the rhetoric of some of the leader-ship in a new direction, the proposals remained vague or applicable only in an indefinite future. On other occasions, party leaders had made simi-lar declarations of new intentions which did not result in concrete poli-cies. Moreover, it was unclear if the PCI's more militantly pro-working-class stands would continue if the Communists tried to enter the parliamentary majority again. In the meantime, the PCI was losing strength among young people. The membership of the party's youth or-ganization dropped from 120,000 in 1978 to 60,000 in 1981.[1] About 50 percent of the PCI's members were over 60 years of age in 1982, and 80 percent were over 40.[2]

The Communist leadership condemned in unequivocal terms both the Soviet invasion of Afghanistan in 1979 and the declaration of martial law in Poland in 1981. Berlinguer went on to criticize the economic and political failures of the Eastern-bloc countries. Coining a phrase which immediately became an important theme, he asserted that the phase of socialist development which began with the Russian Revolution of 1917 had "exhausted its driving force." These positions precipitated a rupture with the Soviet Union, but it was clear that the party leadership had long prepared for and approved of the break. What remained uncertain at the time was how much pro-Soviet sentiment existed within the base of the party. The PCI's sixteenth congress in March 1983 seemed to answer the question once and for all. In precongress local assemblies all over Italy, the party's rank and file had an opportunity to debate a policy amendment put forward by a small pro-Soviet group. The amendment won almost no support (less than 5 percent) among party members. The issue was formally laid to rest at the congress.

What turned out to be the true concern of the PCI membership was the question of internal democracy. Almost two decades earlier, the mi-nority left wing, led by Pietro Ingrao, had begun arguing for more open debate within the party. But the dominant leadership groups clung to a rigid form of democratic centralism. The debates of the most important bodies were closed to observers. Dissenting positions were not made public, and every leader abided by the majority's decisions. In 1983, Ingrao proposed once again to make information on the debates and on minority positions within the powerful party directorate available to the central committee and to the party press. Secretary Berlinguer initially opposed the idea. But when the local party assemblies showed how strongly the membership favored the reform, he and his group dropped their opposition. The change won overwhelming support at the congress. Small as the reform was, most observers judged it to be a first important step toward a more complete and open confrontation of differing positions.

By the time of the 1983 congress, the PCI leadership was less divided over a general conception of political alliances for the coming period. A proposal called the "democratic alternative," understood as a coalition *not* dominated by the DC, had replaced the historic compromise proposal. The new formulation was more appealing to the party's base and to its working-class constituency. The problem, of course, was that the PCI needed the Socialists in order to make the democratic alternative a concrete proposition that could be implemented. But the PSI preferred keeping the Communists in the opposition while trying to win more support at their expense and at the expense of the Christian Democrats.

As a result of party antagonisms, constant political maneuvering, and the defense of special interests, Italians saw six governments fall between 1979 and 1983. The Socialists brought down three governments in the eight months between August 1982 and April 1983. Needless to say, not one of the six governments carried through a coherent program. They did, however, enact scattered economic measures in the name of austerity, measures encouraged by the International Monetary Fund. In January 1983, the last of the six governments completed an important agreement on the cost of labor (which will be discussed in the next section). The austerity measures raised taxes, electricity and telephone rates, and train and plane fares. The lira was devalued, and workers' benefits were cut. The burden of austerity fell most heavily on dependent workers and the poor. The governments made no effort, for example, to stop the tax evasion of the wealthy.

The steps taken were fragmentary and inadequate for dealing with Italy's woes. As a consequence, the overall picture had not improved by mid-1983, and Italy's economic profile looked worse than those of other advanced capitalist countries. Inflation was running at about 17 percent (more than twice the average rate for other EEC countries); the budget deficit was about 17 percent of the GNP (in other European countries, deficits were usually 2 or 3 percent); unemployment was over 9 percent and still rising; and interest rates were well above 20 percent.[3] In 1982, the total number of jobs in the economy actually declined in absolute numbers for the first time since the Second World War.[4] One significant political change was that Italy had a non-Christian Democratic prime minister for the first time since 1945. Giovanni Spadolini of the Republican Party headed two short-lived governments in 1981 and 1982.

Hoping to raise their political standing, the Socialists pressed for parliamentary elections in June 1983, a year ahead of schedule. The campaign did not arouse much political passion in the population, but the results were something of a surprise. Contrary to the predictions of all the polls, the Christian Democrats tumbled 5.4 percent in the Chamber of Deputies and ended up with just a three-point edge over the Communists. The Socialists fell far short of their declared goal of a 4 percent increase. The biggest winner was the Republican Party (see Table 10.1).

From the perspective of the labor movement, the election results were mixed. The DC's anti-working-class stance had not impressed voters. But at the same time, the Republican Party, which was supported by big business leaders including Fiat's Giovanni Agnelli, won a substantial victory. The PCI, which had given active support to working-class struggles, held its own. The votes it lost probably went farther to the left. One of the most significant outcomes was that the Christian Democrats could no longer realistically claim that they held a relative majority. The possibility of forming a government without the DC seemed less remote, and the long tradition of voting Christian Democratic simply to contain the Communists had been broken. PSI Secretary Craxi continued to pursue the position of prime minister. Five weeks after the election, he became Italy's first Socialist head of government.

Although the noteworthy results of the 1983 election opened the way for new possibilities in the future, the chances for political stability and greater support for labor in the short run were small. Craxi headed the same unstable five-party coalition (DC, PSI, PRI, PSDI, PLI) in which the center and center-right forces still dominated. Thus despite the electorate's protest against politics as usual, it seemed that Italians would get more of the same.

TABLE 10.1: Percentage of Total Votes Won by Parties in the 1979 and 1983 Elections for the Chamber of Deputies

Year	DC	PCI	PSI	PRI	PLI	PSDI	PR	DP*	MSI
1979	38.3	30.4	9.8	3.0	1.9	3.8	3.5	0.8	5.3
1983	32.9	29.9	11.4	5.1	2.9	4.1	2.2	1.5	6.8

*Proletarian Democracy, a party to the left of the PCI.

Source: Compiled by the author from official statistics reported in the press.

Labor Relations at the Start of the Decade:
The Longest Strike

On September 10, 1980, Fiat announced that it was firing more than 14,000 workers. Plans to relaunch the automobile division had faltered, and the company was heading toward a sizable operating loss. The announcement came like a declaration of war. When faced with a serious financial crisis just six years earlier, management had negotiated with the work force and had agreed to a no-layoffs policy. The unilateral decision in 1980 indicated that Fiat judged the labor movement's position to be weak. In addition to 14,000 jobs, the balance of power between labor and management was at stake. The unions responded by calling an open-ended strike which lasted 35 days. It was the longest strike in a major Italian industry since liberation.

The situation at Fiat at once became an event of national importance. The government fell in late September, and the president of the republic did not approve a new cabinet until the strike was settled. But beyond its immediate political impact and the consequences in Turin where almost all the jobs were to be eliminated, the strike took on a wider meaning for the labor movement. It reemphasized in a dramatic way the union's lack of policy alternatives in a time of economic retrenchment. The strike also demonstrated the significance of labor's inability to influence investment and production choices. For years to come, the long strike at Fiat will probably be seen as a watershed event marking a trend in labor relations in the early 1980s. For this reason, it is worthwhile to examine in some detail what happened.

The strike came at a time when tensions were already high between the political parties and the unions, between the FLM and the confederations, and between the rank and file and the union leadership. In terms of support and cohesion, the initial stages of the strike went well. PCI Secretary Berlinguer went to speak to the workers at the factory gates. He declared that if they decided to occupy the plants, he would stand by them morally and materially. Workers and unionists from other cities joined the picket lines. Strike funds were collected. The students held a general strike in support of the Fiat workers. There was also a general strike in Piedmont and a national strike of metal and mechanical workers. In the meantime, the company took out large newspaper ads to explain its position and began court proceedings against the union for blocking gates.

On October 14, just four days after a successful general strike, another "first" for the postwar period took place. Between 30,000 and 40,000 Fiat supervisors, guards, technicians, and office workers marched silently through downtown Turin under a banner claiming that the FLM did not represent them. They demanded the right to go back to their

Workers at Fiat Mirafiori demand 8 hcurs of national strikes to speed up labor negotiations in September 1980.

jobs. Several hundred production workers and some strikebreakers joined in. That night, the union settled with Fiat. According to the agreement, the company would lay off 23,000 workers who would receive 93 percent of their pay from the *cassa integrazione*. Fiat would consider rehiring them in July 1983. The company would also freeze all new hiring and encourage voluntary resignations and early retirement.

The union leadership, including some of the highest-ranking confederation and category officials, immediately met with council delegates and workers to discuss the agreement. The reaction was violent. Workers not only shouted down union leaders, they threw rocks and stormed podiums. Pierre Carniti, secretary of the CISL, barely escaped to his car shielded by several other unionists. Giorgio Benvenuto, secretary of the UIL, needed a police escort to leave an assembly. The unions summarily called for a vote by show of hands at the various plants and declared that a majority had approved the agreement. Some workers protested that a majority had voted *no*; others said the count was illegal because supervisors and strikebreakers had voted. At a few later assemblies, the workers clearly rejected the pact. Back in Rome, the union leaders maintained that they had based their decision to sign the agreement on a realistic assessment of the workers' strength. According to the unionists, the workers could not have kept up the strike much longer. Fewer and fewer were on the picket lines, and the disaffection was growing every day. There were outside observers who argued that the decisive factor was the back-to-work march organized by the supervisors. The unions panicked seeing so large a force that was antiunion and antiworker in the streets of Turin. Furthermore, the unions worried about their relationship to technicians and other white-collar workers who were becoming a larger segment of the labor force.

Many commentators concluded that the essence of the confrontation at Fiat was political, not economic. If it had been simply a matter of reducing the labor force, Fiat could have accepted one union proposal for rotating layoffs. Added to the normal yearly attrition of 12,000 workers, this would have sufficed to reduce the payroll. But Fiat wanted to alter the balance of power in the factory. The objective was to reassert its control over the labor force and the process of production. For their part, the workers were trying to hold on to the prerogatives they had won during the previous decade. They needed to break out of the defensive position that offered them just two alternatives, dismissals or long-term layoffs. On this fundamental issue, the agreement was a clear defeat for the workers. The labor movement was unable to impose a substitute policy. The real origin of the defeat was not in the nature or conduct of the strike but in the difficulty of finding a strategy to protect the interests of labor during a period of economic crisis. This was related to the inability of the

labor movement to win some control over Fiat's investment and marketing policies in the 1970s. The company's production decisions within the
national and international auto markets had determined in part the financial crisis of 1980.

Fiat used its victory effectively. Since there was no seniority rule
(i.e., the last hired is first fired), the company decided unilaterally who
would be laid off. Among the 23,000 expelled, Fiat included many activist workers, women, young people, and disabled workers. (The obligation
of employers to find suitable jobs in the plants for their disabled workers
had been won in a previous contract.) For those who kept their jobs, the
atmosphere inside the plants changed radically. The supervisors began to
reassert the authority they had lost during the 1969 movement. The level
of conflict plummeted. Fiat lost only one million worker hours to strikes
in 1981 compared to 13.5 million worker-hours in 1980.[5] There was growing apprehension among the workers and even fear—fear of being laid off
and fear of the supervisors. Management gained more of the labor mobility it wanted and transferred workers around the plants. The company
was also better able to impose its own interpretation of the contract.

Striking figures on absenteeism and productivity demonstrate the
changes at Fiat. Before the 35-day strike, the company had an absentee
rate of 14 to 18 percent, depending on the plant. After the strike, absenteeism dropped to an all-time low of 3 to 5 percent.[6] (The average absentee rate in U.S. auto factories is 11.8 percent, and in Japan, the average
rate is 8.3 percent.)[7] Productivity at Fiat jumped 20 percent in 1981, and
the company ended the year with a modest profit.[8] In the first 18 months
after the strike, Fiat closed several plants and continued to lay off
workers, often 40,000 or 50,000 at a time, for short periods. The company
also made plans to invest almost $5 billion on automation and moderni-
zation over three years with the probable outcome of eliminating still
more jobs.[9] In negotiations with the FLM in 1982, the company refused
to say whether it would readmit any of the 23,000 laid off in 1980. This
aggravated the divisions between the employed and the various categories of unemployed and underemployed. When the July 1983 date for rehiring arrived, Fiat announced that it was taking no one back until the
auto market improved.

The march of the supervisors made the union leadership more willing to abandon some of the egalitarian practices that had survived from
the 1970s. The FLM platform in 1982, for example, proposed two new
"super" job classifications for technicians and other highly skilled
workers. They were to receive higher pay but remain within the unified
classification system along with production workers and other white-collar workers. The union leaders reasoned that unless they supported the
interests and material demands of the highly skilled, these groups would

form autonomous, competing unions. Many rank-and-file production workers opposed the change in philosophy. They did not believe it would win support for the confederation unions.

The Labor Movement on the Defensive

The effects of the 35-day strike reached beyond Fiat. Rank-and-filers everywhere, unionists, and outside observers acknowledged that the Italian labor movement was in crisis. The alarmist view held that the entire system of factory councils and the "new union" built during the 1969–72 period were falling apart. While this was probably an exaggerated conclusion at the time, there were unionists who seriously questioned the viability of the councils. They wanted to see more centralization under the three confederations.

The defeat at Fiat added to the already considerable strains on confederation unity. A source of this tension was government policy and the relationship of unionists to the political parties. The government wanted to hold down the cost of labor, cut spending on social services, and lay off workers in state-controlled industries. The unionists who supported parties in the cabinet had a more conciliatory approach to government policy than did the Communists or the unionists from the far left and the independent left. The decision to call a general strike, for example, depended on a union's relationship to the government. Such decisions often set off fierce polemics within the *Federazione* CGIL-CISL-UIL. Beyond the complex relationships to the government and parties was a deeper source of division within the unions. Once again this was the lack of a strategy for dealing with the attack against labor in the context of a faltering economy, the restructuring of the productive base, and changing international markets.

During this period, the rank and file became increasingly discontented. The nature of labor struggles had changed; the battles were all defensive. It was no longer a question of gaining more control in the factory. The concerns were plant closings, layoffs, and the ability to keep up with inflation. Organizational problems persisted—ossified councils, bureaucratized unions, and lack of rapport between leaders and the rank and file. The disunity of the political factions added to the frustration. It was not unusual for workers to jeer union leaders at assemblies or to reject contracts negotiated by the unions. Rank-and-filers often refused to participate in strikes or dropped their union membership. In March 1982, 300,000 metal and mechanical workers demonstrating in Rome shouted down UIL Secretary Giorgio Benvenuto and created something of a national scandal. They were angry that Socialist leaders of the confederations had blocked a general strike in order to avoid protests against the government. Prime Minister Spadolini called the demonstrators' behavior "the work of authentic fascism." In the ensuing tempest, both the unions and the left split over whether to defend the workers and whether their conduct was an acceptable way of expressing discontent.

A dramatic verification of labor's weak position and the aggressive attitude of business leaders came in June 1982. Confindustria announced that it was unilaterally canceling the 1975 national wage indexing agreement (*scala mobile*) as of January 1983. The employers' association also refused to negotiate the industrial contracts that had come due earlier in the year. These included the metal and mechanical, textile, food workers, and other category contracts. The labor movement found itself backed into a corner, unable to mount an adequate counterattack. All the confederations eventually acknowledged that there was no longer any way to avoid changing the wage structure and the *scala mobile*. But they were badly divided on how this should be done. The stalemate dragged on. The minister of labor mediated, and almost eight months after Confindustria's declaration, he managed to get the adversaries to accept a compromise program.

The cost-of-labor agreement signed on January 22, 1983 included the following provisions: protection against inflation dropped by 15 to 22 percent, depending on the interpretation of the document; a ceiling was placed on wage increases for the still unsettled contracts; company-level negotiators were barred for 18 months from increasing wages or reopening any questions already settled in confederation and category negotiations; the yearly work schedule was to be reduced by 40 hours starting in the second half of 1984; limits were placed on the use of the *cassa integrazione* fund; on an experimental basis, employers were allowed to hire whomever they wanted in the youth category (15 to 29 years of age); employers could also fill 50 percent of all non-youth vacancies with anyone of their choice. To offset the loss of protection against inflation, the government agreed to lower taxes in certain wage categories, to increase family allowances, to hold down the cost of certain public services, and to assume some of the employers' pension payments.

Confindustria, the labor confederations, and the government all claimed to be minimally satisfied with the agreement. The unions asserted that they had kept wage levels intact. The government hailed what it saw as a successful model for tripartite negotiations which could lessen labor conflict. Confindustria achieved its primary goal. It had shattered the accepted notion that the *scala mobile* was inviolable. Until then, the labor movement's slogan had been "the *scala mobile* is not to be touched" (*la scala mobile non si tocca*).

Workers had many criticisms of the cost-of-labor agreement, but there was also a sense that it could not be changed. Women were especially displeased with certain provisions. They argued that allowing employers to hire whomever they pleased would nullify the equal treatment law of 1977. Women would have more difficulty finding work, and when hired, they would be trapped in the traditional job ghettos. They also believed that the increase in family allowances favored the traditional nuclear family and ignored changing social patterns in Italy, especially the increase in single-parent households and the drop in the average number of children per family.

The employers' associations and the category unions were still unable to finalize all outstanding contracts until September 1983. This was more than a year and a half after the old contracts had expired. One stumbling block was the bitter conflict among unions over their negotiating position. A striking feature of the drawn-out struggles was the ever more diminished effectiveness of strikes and mass demonstrations. In June 1982, for example, the *Federazione* CGIL-CISL-UIL called a national general strike to protest the threat against the *scala mobile*. The strike, which the confederations claimed was the largest in the history of the Italian labor movement, stopped activity throughout the country. But it did not persuade Confindustria to withdraw its ultimatum. In June 1983, the FLM called a national strike of metal and mechanical workers to protest the delay in contract negotiations. Some 300,000 workers marched in Turin, the largest gathering in that city since 1969. Yet once again, the strike seemed to have little effect on Confindustria.

The January 1983 cost-of-labor agreement did not usher in a new phase of cooperation and compromise. In fact, just a year later, Prime Minister Craxi's government and Confindustria were calling for deeper cuts in the *scala mobile*. Top-level negotiations between government, confederations, and the private sector soon reached an impasse. The *Federazione* CGIL-CISL-UIL could not agree on a united negotiating position. The labor movement was under tremendous stress, and on February 7, 1984, the pressure became too great. Deliberations among the three confederations broke down. The leaders announced that it was useless to continue searching for a unitary position. Since the *Federazione* could no longer function effectively, each group withdrew to separate deliberations. The unity achieved 12 years earlier was shattered.

A week later, Prime Minister Craxi issued a government decree slashing the *scala mobile* by 38 percent. The UIL, the CISL, and the Socialists in the CGIL accepted Craxi's decision; only the Communists and small left groups in the CGIL opposed it. What followed were weeks of strikes, mass demonstrations, and workers' assemblies all over Italy, culminating in a rally of over 700,000 people in Rome on March 24. These actions were marked by the disunity of the labor movement. The leaders of the CISL, the UIL, and the Socialist wing of the CGIL refused to support the strikes and rallies. In many instances, they called on their followers to boycott the actions. The polemics between factions were bitter. Most rank-and-filers protested the prime minister's decree, but there was discord at every level of the movement—among workers, local unionists, and national leaders. Some observers claimed that the break was worse than the 1948 rupture. They believed that unity could be rebuilt only by refounding the entire labor movement. Others hoped that the confederations would find a way to mend the breach before long. In the midst of the turmoil, only this much was clear. The policies and vision pursued since the 1960s could no longer hold together a unified movement. The collapse of the *Federazione* CGIL-CISL-UIL symbolized the end of an era.

Notes to Chapter 10

1. Henry Tanner, "Despite Divisions and Crises, Italy Avoids Disaster," *New York Times*, February 14, 1982.

2. Diana Johnstone, "Communists Turn to a 'Third Way'," *In These Times*, March 31–April 6, 1982, p. 7.

3. Paul Lewis, "Italy's Stumbling Economy," *New York Times*, July 27, 1983.

4. Joseph LaPalombara, "Economy: Recovery Not Near," *L'Osservatore, The Italian Observer*, April 15–May 15, 1983, p. 15.

5. "Fiat Hopes to Be No. 1 in Small Cars Again," *Business Week*, March 8, 1982, p. 44.

6. John Tagliabue, "A Sharp Turnaround at Fiat," *New York Times*, January 8, 1982.

7. "Toyota Makes Cars Faster, with Fewer Workers," *New York Times*, March 21, 1982.

8. Tagliabue, "A Sharp Turnaround."

9. Ibid.

11

The Limits of Labor Strategy

A movement that once seemed to promise transformation of the economic and social order in Italy is stymied. With the livelihood of workers in most sectors of the economy threatened, it is natural to look to the unions for a solution. Some observers argue that the impasse will not be overcome until the unions make a successful bid for much greater economic and political power. How to do this, given past failures, is the problem. Others maintain that only by relinquishing autonomy in exchange for a collaborative role will the unions have any impact on Italy's economy. But who is willing to collaborate with the unions? Still others doubt that a viable strategy exists during times of economic crisis and restructuring. To understand the implications of these different perspectives, a final look at union strategies—past choices and future options—is in order.

The Struggle for Structural Transformation of the Economy

The Italian trade union confederations did not base their strategy during the 1970s on a complete rejection of the capitalist system. Instead they called for structural changes in the short run that would modify control over the economy, presumably within a capitalist framework. The confederations wanted the labor movement to assume some decision-making power over key aspects of macro- and microeconomic policy, including allocation of government resources, income distribution, input into private investment decisions, and worker control over the organization of labor. The overall strategic conception remained vague. Union rhetoric varied along with changing economic and political circum-

Workers at an assembly listen to a discussion of a proposed contract before voting on it.

stances. The extent to which organized labor planned to transform the system was unclear. Some elements of the movement were more radical than others. The confederations presented positions that functioned as common denominators. The result was that the confederations could project a developed critique of the existing economic model, but they lacked a well-formulated alternative.

The three confederations often expressed their visions in different ways. But all assumed that economic power would be won gradually. They were also open to sharing control with employers and the state. What they refused to compromise was their autonomy in the bargaining process. The confederations were prepared, if necessary, to win structural changes by means of sharp confrontations. The labor movement rejected models of management–labor codetermination in the workplace. An institutionalized collaborative relationship with employers and the state at the macroeconomic level was also refused. Such arrangements would have required the labor movement to relinquish some autonomy. The EUR program of 1978 (see Chapter 7) was a departure from the usual stance, but the experiment failed early on.

Even if the global vision of the labor movement lacked definition, there was no doubt that winning structural reforms would require significant political leverage or strong political allies. This is where the strategy failed. The labor movement had sufficient strength in the market arena to disrupt the economy, but it never exercised enough influence in the political arena to gain structural reforms. When the economy went into crisis, the labor movement was vulnerable to serious defeats precisely because the model of development had not been substantially altered. The unions could not redeploy their full strength in the market arena because this would only have aggravated the economic crisis. The dilemma is unequivocal. Labor has the ability to destabilize the economic system but still depends on the existing system and cannot change it in the near future. This constitutes the impasse of the Italian labor movement.

Alternative Strategies

Some observers propose a neocorporatist arrangement as an alternative strategy for labor in Italy. This arrangement would involve an institutionalized tripartite collaboration between labor, employers, and the state. The three major players establish macroeconomic policy and resolve major disputes in their regular deliberations. They attempt to coordinate the interests of constituencies and encourage cooperation. In theory, neocorporatism should be able to go beyond simple compromises. It should promote coherent strategies for economic stability and growth. In exchange for its inclusion, the labor movement relinquishes some of its autonomy. The confederations would no longer promote their own strategy. Instead they adopt the tripartite agenda. The unions agree to reduce the level of labor conflict at all levels.

The neocorporatist model does not question the exigencies of the capitalist system. It does not transform the system in significant ways. The three protagonists assume the responsibility of making the economy function more smoothly. The goal is to eliminate some of the dislocations caused by the business cycle and by labor conflict. Given the commitment to the smooth functioning of the existing system, labor ends up playing a subordinate role in the tripartite arrangement. This is reinforced because wage restraint is a primary concern of neocorporatism. Using West Germany as an example, many analysts conclude that neocorporatism integrates the labor movement into a centralized system dominated by a state that protects the interests of capital.

The central question is whether this arrangement, which characterizes labor relations in several northern European countries, can function in Italy. Most prognoses are negative. There are several reasons for this. First, Italian labor is not yet prepared to relinquish its autonomy in a formalized and ongoing way. The unions have been reluctant to give up full recourse to conflict in the usual arenas. They continue to identify with a class-based militancy. While the confederations may periodically accept far-reaching agreements negotiated with the government and employers' associations, there is always the sense that these agreements are time limited and conditional. They are seen as unavoidable and basically unsatisfying compromises between hostile parties. They do not grow out of an institutionalized relationship.

Second, many powerful business leaders and political forces in government are as reluctant as labor to institute neocorporatist relations. This is especially true during periods of economic difficulties. Employers believe they can confront labor in the market arena and win. A period of economic crisis offers an opportunity to roll back previous gains made by labor; a neocorporatist arrangement would probably institutionalize some of those gains.

Third, the major labor party in Italy, the PCI, has not been in the national government for nearly 40 years and has no prospects of entering a ruling coalition in the near future. This leaves the labor movement without a sympathetic or accountable political representative in the tripartite arrangement. From labor's point of view, there is little reason to believe that adequate benefits would be forthcoming. Without this belief, neocorporatism lacks sufficient credibility to survive.

The fourth reason for Italy's resistance to a neocorporatist solution involves pessimistic evaluations of the economy. A successful tripartite arrangement presupposes sustained periods of economic growth. This allows at least some needs of all three components to be met. When a national economy drops into a long and serious recession, the political parties and employers' associations inevitably call for austerity measures. Such policies are much the same as those used by conservative governments not bound by neocorporatist arrangements. In Italy, the negative prospects for sustained economic growth in the near future make neocorporatism look like just another instrument of austerity.

Unattracted by neocorporatism, some labor activists and leftists propose greater militancy in the market arena. They argue that combative struggles against employers and the government are still the best means to further working-class interests. While militancy of this kind may be an effective tactic to block specific efforts to weaken the position of labor, it does not seem to be a promising strategy for the current period. The labor movement has sufficient power to destabilize the economy, but not enough to win concessions. The unions have already suffered debilitating defeats. Furthermore, in a time of economic instability and transition, struggles to improve immediate material conditions within the current capitalist model can damage the capacity of the system to provide economic improvements and jobs in the short term.

Public opinion is another consideration. The labor movement was seen as an innovative and democratic force during the early 1970s. But over the last several years, public opinion has shifted. More Italians now blame the country's economic woes on what they judge to be an overly combative working class and intransigent unions. More conflict would intensify the antilabor sentiment. This in turn would weaken the movement's already inadequate political leverage. Given these drawbacks, it is likely that part of the rank and file would refuse to risk further defeats in the market arena.

Faced with the unlikelihood of a successful neocorporatist strategy and the limits of labor conflict, some union leaders and observers sympathetic to labor have one other proposal. It is not so much a new strategy as a re-presentation of the idea of labor control over the economy. The unions must win effective control over policy making at all levels, especially investment decisions. The rank and file must exercise control over the organization of labor in the workplace. It is argued that in the process of achieving these goals, the unions will be able to rebuild their relationship with the working class. Some believe it is the only means by which the unions can resolve the crisis of representation.

Exactly how the strategy differs from what the unions claimed to be doing, in part at least, during the 1970s is not clear. Presumably this time their tactics would be more coherent, their energies more focused, their specific goals better defined. Yet even if this were the case, the difficulties that barred success in the past are no less formidable at present. The strategy involves a radical redistribution of power and wealth. This would certainly entail political and social conflict. The unions would need a broad political consensus, strong leverage in the government, and durable alliances with social strata and movements beyond the unions' usual constituency. It is precisely these alliances, leverage, and consensus that have eluded the unions in the past. They have eluded the left in Italy as well. What would make them more feasible in the future is not apparent at this stage.

Considerations for the Future

The obstacles that continue to frustrate the elaboration of a successful labor strategy can be grouped into several categories for the purposes of this analysis. They are political consensus and alliances, the imperatives of capitalist accumulation, and the process of economic restructuring.

The labor movement in Italy cannot carry through a program of structural transformation except in alliance with the organized left and a strong prolabor party. This means that a credible labor strategy would actually be a labor–left strategy. If this alliance were made, the problem of political consensus would then become paramount.

The consensus necessary to counter a hostile economic and political reaction to radical changes in the model of development would have to be broad indeed. Expanding the traditional constituency of the labor movement to include the nonguaranteed (unemployed, underemployed, workers of the underground economy) would not be sufficient. The unions and the left would have to attract supervisors, technicians, other high-level white-collar workers, professionals, intellectuals, opinion makers, and other middle-class strata. Since their immediate material interests and their privileges would not necessarily be served by a redistribution of income and power, other potential gains would have to attract them to the labor–left program.

In the 1970s, leftists theorized that improvements in the quality of life, such as cleaner air, better schools, safer streets, more free time, cultural events, and so on, could attract large segments of the population.

The PCI promoted this vision as part of its program. But judging from electoral results, the Communists did not project a vision that was compelling enough to generate a truly broad consensus. The combined left vote rose no higher than 46.6 percent (1976). In the 1980s, the political mood seems less auspicious than before. The narrow aspirations of special interest groups have grown even more pronounced. The population seems more divided and the chances for a new consensus more remote. There is an increased scepticism about the feasibility and even the desirability of reform programs. Obviously this state of affairs could change dramatically. But such a shift remains only a possibility and not a tactical opportunity for now.

Even within the working class, the tendency toward a fragmentation of interests is strong. While workers share certain interests as a class, many issues divide them by economic sector, industry, geographical region, age, sex, and seniority. During an economic transition or downswing, the competition among workers increases. Once again, the chances of creating consensus diminish.

The imperatives of capitalist accumulation—or profit making—are a second consideration. A labor–left strategy must operate within the current capitalist model in order to change that model. Not only does the labor–left coalition maneuver within the system, it must promote accumulation. An economic breakdown would quickly destroy any consensus for a program of structural reforms. Political stability would become impossible in the midst of economic chaos. This consideration is not limited to a scenario of rapid, radical change. It can apply to partial programs of structural reform as well. Any threat to the status quo can provoke a cutback in production levels, a decline in investment, increased unemployment, the flight of capital from the country, strains on the balance of payments, rising prices, and a boycott by international financial institutions.

There is certainly a somewhat greater margin for maneuvering during a period of strong economic growth. But Italy has produced few signs of recovery from the severe dislocation of the early 1980s. In other countries, the recovery is slow and shallow. This makes it necessary to devise a labor–left strategy for a period of long-term stagnation or decline, punctuated perhaps by short upswings. During downswings, left parties or coalitions typically fall back to austerity policies that are very much the same as those espoused by conservative forces. The general thrust of these policies is to hold down labor costs and to reduce government spending on social services in order to free resources for investment. The goal is to protect and relaunch the capitalist process of accumulation. This was the Italian Communist Party's economic orientation when it pursued government participation in the mid-1970s. It is the approach of left governments in France and Spain in the 1980s. Workers and the poor suffer under austerity, even when the left tries to soften the blow. The middle classes become disaffected.

The question for the labor movement in Italy and in other capitalist countries is whether any strategy could avoid the usual measures to stimulate private accumulation. Is there any program that could alter the fundamental logic of the system without precipitating an economic breakdown or a loss of consensus? No labor movement or left coalition so far has successfully tested an alternative approach. Until there is one, the process of capitalist accumulation will inevitably dictate limits for labor. When the economy is expanding, the working class's share will increase in size. But when the economy goes into a downswing, that share will shrink. If there is no alternative, the labor movement is chained to the business cycle and to the long-term trends of capital.

In addition to the problems of political consensus and capitalist accumulation, labor movements must confront extensive economic restructuring at the international level and within national boundaries. The restructuring of the Italian economy, involving computer technology, decentralization, and the growth of the underground economy, has been described at length (see Chapter 9). At the international level, the process is equally significant. First, the division of labor among the capitalist countries is changing. This means there will be shifts—often dramatic shifts—in what is produced by each country and for whom. Second, the internationalization of capital is increasing. Transnational corporations are expanding operations. Corporations based in different countries are collaborating on production projects. Components for single products—for example, one manufacturer's automobiles—are being produced in several countries and assembled in still others. Third, rapid technological changes, especially computer-related developments, are altering international markets and the relations among the various national labor forces.

As general categories, the dilemmas of political consensus, capitalist accumulation, and economic restructuring are not new. Indeed, they have thwarted working-class movements throughout the twentieth century, although the specific problems change in every period as economic, political, and social conditions change. Recent years, however, have added new obstacles that contradict even long-held assumptions. The preceding chapters describe these changes. Many traditional tactics no longer work. For example, given new technology, the internationalization of capital, merger policies, and so on, it may no longer be true that working-class concessions to increase profit levels during a downswing will protect jobs. Or to mention one critical factor again, the traditional core constituency of many labor movements, the industrial working class, is dwindling. Any strategy that does not take this into account is already outmoded. Looking at the overall situation of labor, it is as if players, rules, and even playing fields were changing simultaneously.

The *caso Italiano*—the Italian case—still has its national characteristics. But the long crisis has ravaged many of the striking and innovative features of the previous decade. This may turn out to be only a temporary setback. The workers' movement could reemerge as the focal point and inspiration of a broader movement for social change. But it is also possible that labor will not be able to reassume the leading role. The coming years might then see new protagonists emerge and new visions of emancipation take form.

II

Conversations in Turin

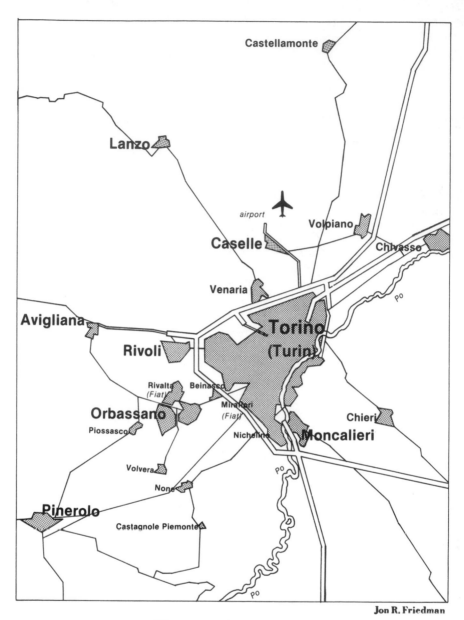

Turin and Vicinity

Jon R. Friedman

Introduction: Fiat and Turin in Profile

In Part II, protagonists of the history presented in the previous chapters speak for themselves. They are Fiat workers and others connected in some way to Fiat. To say that they are protagonists is not to imply that these individuals played leading roles in the labor movement. Nor are they examples of the "typical Italian worker." No such standard exists in a highly diverse and fragmented labor force. Rather, these persons are protagonists because they participated in or lived through many of the events described in this book. They are its primary subject—women and men, old and young, pessimists and optimists, activists and observers. Their viewpoints and opinions vary, but what they share is the experience of a factory and a city that have been strongly identified with the workers' movement.

Fiat

If Fiat has been a center of the Italian workers' movement throughout the twentieth century, it is not because the workers at Fiat have always been the most militant or because the level of unionization has been high. There have been serious defeats and periods of repression and resignation at Fiat. At other times, the workers there have provided innovative leadership for the entire movement. But whatever the particular circumstances, Fiat has functioned as a kind of barometer of changing conditions affecting Italian labor: the organization of the work process, new technology, patterns of investment, the social composition of the work force, its political consciousness, the relationship of unions to the rank and file, and the balance of power between management and labor.

Major events at Fiat inevitably move beyond the factory gates to affect the workers' movement in direct and indirect ways.

Fiat came into being in 1899 when a group of Turin's affluent citizens put up the capital for a new incorporated business called the *Società Anonima Fabbrica Italiana di Automobili*. They adopted the initials *Fiat* (the *t* is for *Torino*—Turin in English) as a label for their products. From the start, the founders had every intention of diversifying production to include vehicles and vessels "of any size or system." The company competed with dozens of small motor plants until the 1907 recession drove many out of business. Fiat emerged in a stronger position. The labor force of 50 hired in 1899 had grown to over 2,000 by 1910.

Fiat began to use modern industrial techniques more extensively than other Italian firms, borrowing the latest ideas in labor organization from the United States. The company also started vertical integration at an early stage. Steel mills, for example, were acquired in 1917. In this way, Fiat secured its supply of intermediate products and compensated for Italy's weak industrial development. By 1935, commercial vehicles, marine engines, lubricating oil, aircraft, rolling stock, iron, steel, tractors, railway cars, and machine tools all carried the Fiat trademark. The policies of the Fascist regime, including protectionist measures and tax breaks, helped the corporation get through the 1930s and consolidate its monopoly status. Then Fiat became involved in war production for Mussolini. After 1945, the company enjoyed more favors from the republican government and moved into new areas of production: construction machinery, electronic components, nuclear energy, gas turbines, space research, and bioengineering.

Today Fiat is still Italy's largest private enterprise. In 1980, it ranked sixth in money turnover among all the world's companies, excluding the oil giants.[1] The corporation employed 265,000 in 1982, about three-quarters of them in Italy.[2] At the end of 1979, about 77 percent of the work force was blue collar, 22 percent was white collar, and executives and managers made up 1 percent of the payroll. About 41 percent of the workers belonged to unions in 1980. This included about 48 percent of the blue-collar employees and 15 percent of the white-collar group. By far, the greatest number of Fiat employees in Italy work in the metropolitan area of Turin (about 147,000 in early 1980). There were about 39,000 employed in the South, and the rest are scattered over the northern and central regions.[3]

During the 1970s, Fiat was completely reorganized to become a holding company made up of 11 operating sectors, each of which is legally autonomous and accountable for its own profitability. The sectors include automobiles, commercial and industrial vehicles, agricultural tractors, construction machinery, steel, components, machine tools and pro-

A boy doing mechanical work at Fiat's plant on Dante Boulevard, Turin, about 1900.

duction systems, civil engineering and land-use planning, energy, rail-based transportation systems, and tourism. Altogether there were 212 Fiat production plants in 1980, 162 of them in Italy.[4] Fiat's largest endeavor continues to be the automobile sector which in 1982 controlled 51.6 percent of the Italian market, took the second largest share of the European market (Renault was first), and employed 126,000 people.[5]

Turin

Once the elegant baroque capital of the House of Savoy, Turin will-fully industrialized in the last quarter of the nineteenth century. Entre-preneurs and financiers from both Italy and abroad were invited to invest in Turin. The city advertised a hard-working population that would ac-cept modest wages. By the start of the new century, the municipal leaders were successful in their bid for capital. Turin rapidly became one of Italy's great industrial centers.

The *Torinese* working class expanded in size. It grew more radical under the political leadership of the *Ordine Nuovo* (New Order) group and Antonio Gramsci, an innovative Marxist theoretician and a founder of the Italian Communist Party whose writings now have an enthusiastic international audience. In August 1919, the workers at Fiat set up a factory council. It was to be an autonomous revolutionary structure that would take control of production and constitute the embryo of a new workers' state. By October, almost all the metalworking shops in Turin had organized councils. During the period of factory occupations in 1920, Turin became the revolutionary center of Italy. Armed workers ran the plants for several weeks and defended working-class neighborhoods. But as the "red biennial" of 1919 and 1920 ended without a victory for the workers, Mussolini and his *fasci* quickly picked up strength. They were aided by the industrialists who wanted to make sure there would be no repeat of the factory occupations.

Today the ornate *palazzi* and baroque churches still line the long, straight boulevards. Venerable porticos shade the most elegant cafés. But the working-class neighborhoods make it clear how postwar economic development has ripped apart the social fabric of the city. During the mass migrations between 1951 and 1971, the population of Turin swelled by more than 62 percent. This can be compared to an average growth during that period of just 40 percent in other Italian cities with over 100,000 people.[6]

The immigrants arrived in Turin with their local dialects, food, and forms of social relations which the natives looked down on. The *Torinesi* set up what amounted to rigid racial barriers against the newcomers, especially the Southerners. One phrase in particular, used in advertising vacant apartments, came to epitomize the discrimination: *non si affitta ai meridionali*—not for rent to Southerners. The natives moved from the old center of the city to the elegant hill districts on the other side of the Po River. The immigrants were left crowded in decayed buildings which were often without heat or hot water. Later they settled in the expanding working-class ghettos to the north and south of the city. Turin's neighborhoods are now quite segregated by social class and regional origin. This is typical of cities in the United States, but it is unusual in Italy where urban neighborhoods tend to be more heterogeneous.

By the late 1970s, Turin had become the third largest "southern" city in Italy, surpassed in size only by Naples and Palermo. The contradictory significance of this is brought home by the small fact that on a clear day, it is possible to see the Alps from downtown Turin. Of the city's 1.2 million inhabitants, about 700,000 are of southern origin, 200,000 more come from the northeast Veneto region, and only 300,000 are natives of the Piedmont region. The labor force at Fiat reflects this population shift.

There are now few *Piemontesi* workers in the plants. As they left or retired over the years, immigrants and the children of immigrants replaced them.

The unmonitored growth of Turin was directly linked to the expansion of Fiat. The company dominated the city politically as well as economically. For years, the local government met Fiat's needs but did almost nothing to provide adequate housing, public transportation, schools, or even sewage systems for the swelling population. Even today, while there is one automobile for every two inhabitants, many people in Turin cannot find a decent place to live. The situation is symptomatic of Italy's rapid and unbalanced development since the war. But among Italy's urban centers, Turin represents more than dislocation and decline. It is a workers' city and a union city. Along with Fiat, Turin has had a special place in the labor history of this century.

Notes to Introduction, Part II

1. *Fiat*, edition no. 10039/81 (Turin: Fiat, 1981), brochure, p. 1.
2. *Notiziario Fiat*, January 21, 1983, company newsletter, p. 7.
3. *Fiat 80*, edition no. 10033/80 (Turin: Fiat, 1980), catalog, pp. 264, 267.
4. Ibid., p. 7.
5. *Notiziario Fiat*, pp. 7–8.
6. Guido Martinotti, "Immigration, Social Structure, and Politics in the Auto City" (Background paper for the conference *Economic Crisis and Political Response in the Auto City: Detroit and Turin*, Detroit, December 10–13, 1981) (Cambridge: Center for European Studies, Harvard University, 1982), mimeographed, pp. 3–4.

Interviews with Fiat Workers

Nazareno

The metal and mechanical workers' union (FLM) in Turin is divided into "leagues" which are the local-level unions. The fifth league (quinta lega) is the union for Fiat Mirafiori, and like the factory, it is a familiar name in Italy. Its headquarters are directly across from the plant.

The union is housed in a small building which is usually bustling with functionaries and workers, but one morning, it was deserted when I arrived. The unionists were all downtown at a conference on terrorism, the factory council delegates were across the street preparing for a two-hour strike, and one young man was left operating the switchboard. By chance, a worker named Nazareno stopped in. He asked if I was looking for someone. I explained what I was doing in Turin, and he agreed to be interviewed. Fiat workers are often reticent when speaking to journalists unless a trusted intermediary has arranged the meeting. So it was surprising that Nazareno ended up speaking so freely and at great length.

Nazareno was 42 years old, a factory council delegate, and a member of the Socialist Party. His manner was energetic and intense. When he spoke of his early years at Fiat, his hand kept passing over his forehead and eyes, trembling. Nazareno was one of the "older" activist cadres at Fiat who believed that the unions should reach out to young workers and become more responsive to their needs. It turned out that Nazareno had been on leave from Mirafiori for the previous two months because of an accident. When I inquired if it had been job related, he replied with a touch of embarrassment that he had fallen off his bicycle.

I was born in Rovigo, in the Veneto region. It's about 60 miles from Venice. There was zero in Rovigo. I always used to say that we were the poorest of the poor. We never recovered from the flood of 1951, when everything was under water. It was like Holland.

So when I was 20, I decided to emigrate. It was an adventure, like looking for gold in the West. A lot of people my age were doing it. You would go wherever you had a relative or knew someone from the same town. Entire families were leaving, but I went alone. It was 1957. I thought I'd find a job—any job—and a wife.

I ended up in the hinterland, in the little towns around Turin. For three years, I worked in construction. In those years, a lot of the immigrants had their first jobs in construction. That's where Fiat fished for its new workers. You had to show a spirit of sacrifice and a willingness to work.

It was a terrible time. Besides bad work conditions, there was the handicap of not knowing the language and not having friends. You were really lost and out of place. There was also the character of the *Torinesi*. They're closed, not very social. They don't talk much. In the Veneto region where I came from, that wasn't true. It was a poor agricultural area, but the quality of life was much better. We'd go to the bars where we knew everyone. When I came to Turin, workers got up at five in the morning, worked until half past two, did overtime, went home to sleep, and got up for work the next day. I lived like that for years.

I developed pleurisy doing construction work, so in 1960 I went back to my home town for a year. Then in 1962, I finally got a job at Fiat. When it happened, I felt like I, Nazareno, had touched heaven with my fingers! It was security and health. You were privileged if you were at Fiat. You were even treated better by the shopkeepers. But after the first euphoria, I realized it wasn't what I had expected. Then came the trauma.

Why? The work rhythms, the environmental conditions, the impact of the assembly line. After seven or eight months, you realized you were being destroyed. You saw that "heaven" was an illusion. It was like a military state inside the factory. I liked to read as a kid. When I was 12 or 13, I read about Fiat and thought it was democratic and that the relations between management and the workers were good. But once I was there, I saw that I had no liberty.

For the first four years, I worked in the paint department. When you painted a car, you had to sand the first layer of paint so that the second would adhere. We did this with a machine that ran with water. Your hands were always in water. You stood in water. It was 125° in the summer and humid. Freezing in the winter. From the time the bell rang at

6:00 AM until it rang again at noon, you couldn't stop, you couldn't sit down. The pace was killing.

The relationship between workers in those years was zero. Zero discussions, no talking at all with that policelike structure. It was worse than school. If the supervisor said you had to make 300 pieces, you made 300 whether or not there were workers absent. Fiat used a lot of overtime. Most workers did 12 hours overtime a week, 60 hours altogether. That was normal. You came from a region where there was no work. You came to Fiat, and you had a job. So you'd work like crazy, like a glutton. Someone who's starving always overeats.

I once saw a worker beg his supervisor to go to the bathroom. First the supervisor told him to wait 20 minutes, and then he claimed the worker didn't really have to go. So the worker left his place and risked getting fired. He went to the bathroom and brought the "product" out for the supervisor to see. The worker was suspended for three days.

I got two fines for reading the newspaper during my break. They had a system of vigilantes in the johns to make sure no one read newspapers there either. *Alla Fiat si viene per lavorare* [At Fiat, you come to work]—that was the slogan. The supervisors were like *carabinieri*, the military police. If they caught you with the Communist newspaper, you were fired or sent to an "exile" department. Goons would beat up union activists, slash their tires, or set their cars on fire.

One day my supervisor told me I wasn't using my tool the right way. So I said to him, "I thought this was a better way of doing it." He answered me, "You're here to work, not to think!" That's the kind of thing you remember for years. You carry it around with you, and then one day you explode.

One thing that scared me in the early years was the continual coming and going of workers. It was like ships in a port. People quit, new workers came in. They left after three or four years because they couldn't take it anymore. When you saw you were dying, you left. They found jobs in the service sector, the government, or became small merchants. Some workers were able to save money to do it.

I saw this constant turnover and asked myself what happens when people demand to stay at Fiat for 20 years. Things would change. And that's what happened. Now Fiat can't fire you if you're hurt on the job. They have to find some work for you to do. There are 6,000 disabled workers at Fiat right now.[1]

What happened in 1969 didn't come as a surprise to me. You had normal people working on the assembly lines. You would work next to the same people for years. You'd never talk because you were afraid, but you knew they were good people. Then all of a sudden, you see them rebel, throw things, and break the machines. It means that for years they had bottled up their anger.

After years of repression, is it surprising that some supervisors were beaten up and a few cars burned? In Iran, the Shah put people in jail and tortured them. Then there was a revolution. The revolution at Fiat had to come. You couldn't win it with carnations the way they did in Portugal. You have to struggle for change. The bosses don't give you gifts. Liberty isn't a gift.

But we had to go beyond that explosion of anger. We had to use diplomacy too. I didn't act out of anger. I was always considered a moderate in immediate actions.

I got married six months after I went to Fiat. I married a woman from the Veneto. You know, *moglie e buoi ai paesi tuoi* [wife and oxen from your own towns]. Oh well, I guess it's not like that anymore. My wife worked as a seamstress. Our daughter was born in 1964. The only social life was in the house with the TV on. On Sunday, it was soccer or you bought a Fiat 500 and took the family for a ride.

Even now it's like that. It hasn't changed much. Turin is still a dormitory city. There are two shifts, so half the city is always asleep while the other half works. I live in Nichelino. It's a town of 50,000, and they're building the first movie theater just now! There's still this mentality that if your car is two centimeters larger than your brother's, then you're better. You get married, rents are high, you think you have to buy a TV and a washing machine and a car. So you work like crazy. But I think among the very young, this is changing. They reject this kind of work, and that's positive.

I don't know what will happen ten years from now. The new generation of workers is mute. They're reserved. The factory council isn't being renewed. The same people have been doing the work for ten years. Our union is becoming like the old union before 1968, with political divisions and political labels. There's not enough democracy in the union.

Several months ago, there was a spontaneous strike in the paint department. I think spontaneous struggles are a good thing. The union should accept them. I took three young workers with me to the negotiations with management. One was studying philosophy part time at the university. Another had a degree in electrical engineering. They weren't involved in the union, but they ended up leading the negotiations. They had tremendous abilities and an understanding of power relations in the factory.

These are the people who should be in the factory council. The union has to involve these young people. One of them is already lost. The bosses gave him a desk job and bought him off. If we don't involve the young people, either they'll become self-interested and model citizens or they'll explode. Fiat's a pot that's boiling.

Marisa

Fiat Mirafiori spreads over 1.3 million square meters on the outskirts of Turin. The company opened the main part of the plant in 1939. Yet as late as the 1950s, the town of Mirafiori was still small, and the area surrounding the factory was open and undeveloped. Now boulevards as wide as expressways circle the entire factory complex. The district is crowded as far as the eye can see with large apartment buildings that house workers. A generation of young Italians has grown up in the shadow of the Mirafiori plant while their parents worked inside.

High concrete walls wind around and seal off the factory. At one point on Giovanni Agnelli Boulevard (named after a founding father of Fiat who later became chairman of the board), the massive, rectilinear administrative palazzo rises up. It was built during the Mussolini years and is an example of the stark imperial style. Other than the palazzo, only wide iron gates periodically break the smooth stretch of walls.

Mirafiori holds more workers within its walls than any other Fiat plant. At times, there have been as many as 56,000. Some observers argue that the size of Mirafiori was a serious mistake on the part of Fiat's management. The concentration of employees made it easier to build and coordinate a workers' movement. It also made Fiat more vulnerable to the effects of strikes and factory occupations. To counter this, management began decentralizing production in the mid-1970s. This meant using home labor, smaller workshops and factories in Italy, and shipping some parts of the production cycle out of the country.

I met Gianni, a factory council delegate, outside gate number 30 one afternoon just as the first shift was ending. He had agreed to introduce me to a few workers for interviews. Since they were on their way home and didn't want to lose too much time, we sat and talked on a patch of grass on the traffic island in the middle of the boulevard with the cars and motor scooters whizzing by on all sides. The first worker I spoke with was Marisa, 32 years old. She had black hair, olive skin, and a lively and irreverent manner.

I emigrated from the Veneto region ten years ago. Before I came to Turin, I worked as a maid for a family. I did that from the time I was 15 until I was 19. Then I did black work [*lavoro nero*], knitting sweaters for three years. But it just didn't pay. I spent more than I made. There were no factories in the Veneto then. My mother had already moved here, then my sisters. So finally I left, too.

I've been at Fiat for nine and a half years. I spent two years on the assembly line, and since then I've been doing individual work on a machine that turns out small metal pieces. I like mechanical work, and I'm good at it. But working at Fiat is terrible—monotony, repetition, alienation after a while. And it's not safe. There're no guards on some of the machines. Some of them are so old they're from the Marshall Plan. They still have plaques on them that say *dono dagli Americani agli Italiani per ricostruire l'Europa* [gift from the Americans to the Italians to rebuild Europe].

There's no way out but working at Fiat. One salary isn't enough to support a family. I'm married and have an eight-year-old son. We live in north Turin, about 40 minutes from here. I have to pay for a private school for my son. It's a Catholic school. They keep him from seven in the morning until five in the afternoon. The bosses talk about the absenteeism of women in the factory, but who can take care of your kids if they get sick?

A lot has changed in the factory. There was much more repression before. Now the union is more effective. The factory is better because of the young people too. They woke up the old ones a little. The workers who come into the factory now have things better. Some people say they have privileges, but I think that's wrong. I like these young people. The older ones, the ones who've been here 20 years, are set in their ways. When they got a little liberty, they were scared. But the young people feel lost and out of place in the factory. They've always lived with their families, and they've gone to school for years. The factory is a completely different thing for them.

There's not much Workers' Autonomy[2] at Mirafiori or at least not in my department. But there're many of them at the Rivalta plant. What they say is crazy. They're not terrorists. They just don't know what they want. They say crazy things like "Let's break the machines so that the bosses will have less to eat."

There were very few women in the factory before. But even now, the women aren't really organized. There're a few small groups, not much yet. The older women live in their own little worlds. The younger women struggle.

We have the same rights as men, but it's all on paper. The men pass from one job category into a higher one more easily than the women. I like my work, but there isn't any place for me to go. I'm at the third level out of five after ten years! Any man who had done my work the way I have would be in a higher category. If a woman gets ahead, the men go around saying she winked at the supervisor. I'm very much in agreement with feminism—a reasonable feminism, not bra burning.

Now I always participate in the marches and rallies. I don't just go home when there's a strike. A lot of workers strike because they're embarrassed to be the only ones working or they're afraid of the reaction of the other workers if they don't go out. I scabbed once when I was at another Fiat plant. I admit it. I'm not like the others who try to hide it. I didn't understand anything then. The others all went out, and I was left alone, really embarrassed.

Right now, I'm not in the union. I argued with one of the unionists last year and didn't renew my card. But next year, I'll probably renew. I'm not in a political party either. But I'm a leftist without a doubt.

I came from a patriarchal family. We were landowners in the Veneto. We came out of the Fascist era, and that influenced our ideas. But for me, there's been a gradual shift to the left. It just took me a little longer. I saw injustices, and I began to change. Now if anyone tries to get away with something, I protest.

I'm Catholic. There's no contradiction between religion and left politics. The farther you are to the left, the more you are Christian. The Church is a bigger contradiction than left Catholics. I haven't been to communion for ten years, but I base my ideas on the Gospel. If being Christian means being a Christian Democrat, then we're lost! The Christian Democratic Party kills people, marginalizes people, and steals.

I believe in an afterlife. If I thought that this life on earth was the only life we had, I'd shoot myself tomorrow, or I'd become a terrorist!

Antonella

After Marisa, I spoke with Antonella, who was 19 years old, attractive, and soft-spoken. As soon as the interview ended, she rushed off to meet friends.

I'm the youngest of five children. My parents and brothers and sisters were all born in Sardinia, but I was born in Turin. My father immigrated in 1959. He worked as a plumber. He's retired now with heart trouble.

I grew up here in Mirafiori near the factory. I finished junior high school and then studied for a year to be an administrative secretary. I quit school when I was 16. Then I spent two years unemployed or working different jobs for short periods of time. I worked as a saleswoman and a secretary.

I always said I'd rather starve than work at Fiat. But finally, it was the only way I could make a little money and get work papers.[3] I didn't have papers on any of my other jobs. I didn't come to Fiat because I wanted to.

I've been in the factory for five months. My job is to finish one of the parts for the gears on a grinder. The work isn't hard, but it's monotonous. I'm on my feet for eight hours. The machines use oil and water, so I breathe fumes all day. They're also old and dangerous, and it's easy to get your hands caught. The supervisors are always saying that they'll adjust the machines. They talk and talk, but as far as doing anything—forget it!

I really hope to find something else to do. I always say I'm just passing through Fiat. I plan to study some more to get a diploma. I'd like to find a job as a secretary. Going to work here everyday is ugly. It's the same way for all the young people. It's the environment. It's dark and smelly. I can't wait to get out every day.

There aren't any other young women in my department. So when I came in, I was something new. The men pestered me and wouldn't leave me alone. Now they're used to me.

There's been an invasion of young people in the factory, and there's a gap between the old and young. We have different ideas. It's the same way in other places too. I don't talk with the other workers. There's no possibility of a dialogue. The only person I've made friends with is the delegate. He's more my age. At first I felt very isolated in the factory, but it's a little better now.

The other women are all older. They've been at Fiat for about ten years. With the women, there's more to say, but they've been here so long that they've become like the men—vulgar. I don't want that to happen to me.

I joined the union my first week. It's useful. When you need something, you can go to the delegate. They can help you. When I first came in, I didn't know anything.

I go out on strike. The struggles are right and just. You have to improve conditions. I went on strike at school too, to improve things there.

I don't understand anything about politics. I'm not interested. I've always stayed outside. Maybe that's a mistake. The way things are now, you have to try to understand something. The struggles of the past helped those who work now, and my struggles will help those who come later. The struggles here at Fiat are politics that touch me directly, much more than party politics. The contract negotiations interest me because I'm here. They wouldn't otherwise.

Terrorism is wrong. To get to the point of killing each other, that's wrong. People are afraid now because it's become an everyday thing.

During my free time, I go around with my friends. I have a boyfriend. There's dancing and movies. There're enough things to do. But there're also a lot of drugs and people dying from drugs. It doesn't serve any purpose. They do it because they're dissatisfied. Most of all, there's this problem of work. They need something to do. For me, I just hope that Fiat will be a short experience.

Older Worker

As the interview with Antonella ended, a council delegate from another part of the factory came up to say that a fight had broken out at gate 28. We drove a half-mile or so around the plant to see what was happening. When we arrived, a truck driver and some workers were arguing. The trucker, an independent, was gesturing and shouting that he wanted to unload and get back on the road. The workers were blocking the gates as part of a strike action in connection with the contract negotiations. They were not allowing any vehicles to enter or leave the plant. The workers tried to calm the driver and explain their situation. The trucker claimed that he supported the workers but did not see why he had to suffer because of their strike. After a few more minutes, he threw up his hands in exasperation, climbed back into the truck, and drove off.

Several months later, after Fiat and the union had finally signed a contract ending the 1979 confrontation, management fired 61 workers for unlawful and violent activities during the negotiations. One of the actions Fiat most objected to was the blocking of factory gates. In its accusations, the company tried to link the 61 workers to the terrorists. The union and the workers sued Fiat, and a prolonged series of trials and verdicts followed. The courts decided in favor of the workers, but the company still tried to delay their reinstatement.

The afternoon I was at gate 28, the factory council delegates introduced me to an older worker who agreed to talk until his group of pickets was due back inside the plant. He was straightforward and quite willing to answer questions although he preferred not to give me his name. He was in his early 50s.

I was born in the city of Treviso, in the Veneto, but I immigrated to Biella near Turin in 1940, before the war. I worked in the textile industry for 14 years and then I got a job at Fiat. I've been at Fiat for 20 years.

I don't belong to a political party, but I've been in the union, the CGIL, since 1945. I've always collaborated with the union. When they call a strike, I always go along. I've never challenged union policies. The struggles are for the workers, not for the bosses. The union is for us. Maybe the union makes mistakes, but I personally haven't seen any.

The struggles changed conditions in the factory, but too much has changed. The positive part is that conditions are better. What is worse is that productivity has gone down, and there's less satisfaction in work. I

used to be satisfied with my work, but now there's an atmosphere of violence and an I-don't-give-a-damn attitude about work. I'm retiring next
year, but as far as I'm concerned, unless something really changes, the
factory can't go on like this.

There's violence even inside the factory—between workers, and between the supervisors and the workers. Before, the supervisor com-
manded, and the workers followed. Now the supervisors aren't in control. They're afraid. You can't work when it's like this. Before, the worker
was oppressed too much, and the supervisors were dictators. Now it's
switched around completely. It's gone too far. The workers got a little
freedom, and they've exploited it.

It'll be difficult to get back to normal times. There has to be a political solution. The bosses have to understand that people don't have
enough money. You can't stop workers from striking until they get more.
Now, if your wife doesn't work, you can't live.

The younger people don't want to work. They've been unemployed
too long. The system is all wrong. Young people should go to work right
away. Instead they want an easy life. We older workers accept orders—we
obey. These young people don't. There's no communication between us.

It's up to the political system to change things around. If I could, I'd
vote for the party in power, the Christian Democrats. I'd vote for them if
they would begin to change the direction of the country. But they won't.
Only the left parties will change things.

The 150 Hours Course

*Many workers still attend the 150 Hours courses although the program
has lost some of the spirit it had in the early years (see Chapter 5). The particular course I observed was for Fiat workers from the Rivalta plant. The subject
was the organization of labor in the factory. There were a few older workers in
the course, but most of the students were quite young, in their late teens and
early twenties. Many of these young workers identified with Workers' Autonomy and belonged to an autonomous political group at Rivalta. They claimed to
have 50 members in the plant.*

*Marco Revelli taught the course. Over the previous months, he and his
students had achieved a certain reknown—notoriety for some—in connection
with the campaign against terrorism. In February 1979, the police shot and
killed two young people in a bar in Turin. Prima Linea (Front Line), then one of
the principal terrorist groups, claimed that the two dead were members of the
organization. As it turned out, one was Barbara Azzaroni, wanted by the police
in connection with other terrorist actions and in hiding for several years. The*

*other was Matteo Caggegi, a 20-year-old worker at Fiat Rivalta and a student
in Marco Revelli's 150 Hours course.*

*The news of Caggegi's death sent a shock wave through the work force at
Fiat and the dormitory towns like Orbassano where Caggegi lived. He was the
first native of Turin captured or killed as a terrorist by the police in the city. All
the others had come to Turin from outside.*

*The students in the 150 Hours course were stunned and upset. Many of
them decided to attend Caggegi's funeral. According to Revelli, their attitude
was, "I could be Caggegi. I could have fallen in with those people." A few
weeks later, a member of the provincial secretariat of the Communist Party
accused Revelli of harboring terrorists in his course and teaching guerrilla warfare tactics. Most people agreed that the accusations were completely out of line.
The incident provoked a debate in the press and a lawsuit.*

*The 150 Hours course met in the union headquarters for Rivalta, a small
modern building just a few minutes' drive from the plant. There were about a
dozen worker-students sitting on chairs scattered around the room. The class
was casual. Students wandered in and out; some didn't come back; others read
newspapers and magazines.*

*During the first part of the class, the students talked about how to orga-
nize the rest of the course. Then I asked a few questions that started a discussion
involving seven of the students. There were two older workers, both men in their
mid-forties who were activists in the FLM. Revelli told me later that they often
took dissenting positions within the union, and one had been disparagingly
called an* autonomo *(someone identifying with Workers' Autonomy). The two
women who remained were 19 and 22. At first, they seemed uninvolved politically, but at the end of the session, it came out that they and all the younger men
belonged to the autonomous political group at Rivalta. The women were rather
hard and angry. As we walked out of the union building, the 19-year-old ripped
a Communist campaign sticker off the wall. There were two men in their early
twenties, both calm and self-possessed. The seventh worker was about 30 and
very talkative. He had been in and out of various factories and worked as a
political activist for years, first in the New Left and then in Workers' Autonomy.*

THIRTY-YEAR-OLD WORKER: I spent nine years at Lancia.[4] I was fired,
then rehired. I've been at Fiat Rivalta for three years. As far as the working class goes, there's a gap between the Southerners and the workers just
hired at Fiat who are educated and aren't immigrants. Now there are
drugs in the factory. Before it was alcohol.

FIRST YOUNG WOMAN: The older workers are irritating and boring.
They're always moralizing about what they've done. Then they accuse us
of not working hard enough.

FIRST YOUNG MAN: The older workers say that they went out on strike so we would be hired, but they struck for their own jobs first.

FIRST OLDER WORKER: We went through two years of struggle to get new workers. We told the bosses that if they wanted more production, they should hire more workers.

SECOND YOUNG WOMAN: I've been at Fiat for seven months, and I don't want to stay. I can't accept this kind of work. I want more free time, but this is the only job there is. I'm in an assembly shop, and it's hard work.

FIRST YOUNG WOMAN: I object to the schedule and the environment. I'd like to leave. Everyone wants to leave. At the beginning, I really felt the difference between the older and younger workers. It's less an issue now. You fight with older people outside the factory, too. And it's not just older people. It's anyone with different ideas.

At first, there was hostility between men and women in the factory. The men were curious and aggressive. Now they're more relaxed.

This is my first experience in a contract struggle. It doesn't mean much to me. I'm not against the struggles. I joined the union automatically, but it's nothing important. Someone came up to me my first day at work, and I signed up. The workers don't participate in the union. It shows that they don't care about it or that the union doesn't meet their needs.

SECOND YOUNG MAN: The union deals with management on a contractual basis. Management takes something away and gives something in return. The union makes these little exchanges with the bosses.

SECOND YOUNG WOMAN: I don't care about the union. I don't believe in it.

SECOND YOUNG MAN: Young workers have had other experiences in school. The factory is no longer the center of life the way it used to be. The union accepts the current system and the idea that the hours spent inside the factory are the center of everything. The union won't go along with any other conception. During strikes, the young workers go off to shoot up in the parks or make love rather than go to the union rallies.

The union doesn't want to make a revolution. It lets the bosses have all the power. It just makes deals over little things. Before, for ten years, the salary increases were egalitarian—the same amount for all workers no matter what their category was. Now the union is asking for increases according to category, so the more skilled workers will get even more pay. This shows the change in union policy.[5]

The workers have fewer and fewer skills. The robots are a good example. With the new technology, the machines do everything. I'm glad there's less work to do, but it also makes you a cretin. There's nothing to do now but push a button. You're more isolated.

SECOND OLDER WORKER: The workers asked for the new technology to do away with dangerous and harmful jobs. It's a victory for the workers. They complained about conditions, so they got the new technology.

SECOND YOUNG MAN: The supervisors don't have control anymore the way they used to. That's positive. But the workers are even more the slaves of capital than before, and these things are contracted by the union.

FIRST YOUNG MAN: Before the work was much harder, but now you produce a hundred times as much. You become a cretin in five years. The union kept saying that there would be a new way of making cars in capitalist society. Then there was the restructuring at Fiat. The workers struggled, and look at what they got.

SECOND YOUNG MAN: The workers didn't struggle for robots. They struggled against bad conditions. We don't want to stop technological progress, but we want to change it and control it.

THIRTY-YEAR-OLD WORKER: You can't do anything without seizing power.

SECOND YOUNG MAN: The union didn't even get us more money. Now we make more profits for the company because productivity is higher. We're more exploited than ever.

FIRST OLDER WORKER: Who's going to make the revolution? You? You go home whenever there's a strike. How could you make a revolution? You go dancing.

SECOND OLDER WORKER: There're scabs even now. There aren't so many differences between old and young. There've always been committed workers and scabs. What do you mean by revolution? If you want to use your rifle, take it and go hunt birds. You don't make a revolution during contract negotiations. You construct it little by little.

SECOND YOUNG MAN: It's not the job of the union to make the revolution. That's not what I criticize the union for. I'm critical of struggles that go in the direction opposite of what workers need, like salary increases based on categories.

The union has changed. There's no more recall of factory council delegates. We don't use write-in ballots anymore for the delegate elections.[6] The delegates aren't a direct expression of the rank and file now. They've become an arm of the union bureaucracy. The assemblies aren't democratic.

SECOND YOUNG WOMAN: I feel the same way. There has to be a revolution for things to get better. You begin in the factory, working with others. It's not a question of unions or parties. I don't believe in any of the parties. The workers should organize themselves autonomously. There aren't many autonomous struggles now, but there will be.

Maria

*I drove out to Orbassano with a young Communist Party functionary who
had set up several interviews for me. Orbassano, once a farming village with a
population under 5,000, was now a dormitory town of 18,000 for the nearby
Fiat Rivalta plant. To get to Orbassano, we drove for about a half-hour, past the
outskirts of Turin and into open country where there were cultivated fields to the
sides of the road and in the distance the silhouette of the Alps.*

*In the center of Orbassano, there were still a few cobblestone streets and
old stone buildings. The rest was modern apartments, six or seven stories tall,
parking lots, a pizzeria, and a huge new supermarket. Behind the pizza restaurant were the meeting rooms and crowded office that constituted PCI headquarters for the district. It was one of the few social gathering places in Orbassano,
and whenever I stopped by, there was a meeting going on or people standing
around talking or running off a leaflet.*

*I spoke with Maria and Sandra in the back office. Maria was a short,
robust woman of 33. She had wide-open eyes and a completely unselfconscious
and bustling manner. She had very much wanted to do the interview and talked
eagerly. At one point when another woman from the party sat down to listen to
us for a while, Maria made a few comments about her husband doing chores at
home. The party functionary told me later that Maria's husband had been skip-
ping work to go fishing and had refused to help around the house. The previous
year, Maria had threatened to leave him, but for the time being things seemed to
be going better.*

*After the interviews, Maria insisted that everyone come over to her house
for coffee.*

I was born in Palazzo San Gervasio in the South, in the region of
Basilicata. It was a town of about 10,000, but it's empty now. Everyone's
emigrated. I had two brothers, one older, one younger. We were farm
workers in the tobacco fields.

Everyone worked in the fields, even little kids. The kids worked all
day in the summer. The rest of the year, we went to school in the morning
and then out to the fields. I was born in the middle of it. Even the babies
were out in the fields because there was no one at home to take care of
them.

It was hard work, and then you accumulated debts all year long.
You waited for the one cash payment at the end of the year. Finally in
1957, my father went to Switzerland to find work, and my brother went
to Turin. He was 14.

The next year, when I was 12, I finished elementary school and left for Turin. I didn't go to work but to clean and cook for my brother who was all alone. But as soon as I got to Turin, I found a job in a sweater workshop. There were three or four workers, all young girls who sewed the sweaters together. The owners worked with us. We got 85 lire an hour [about 14 cents in 1958]. It was black labor. We sewed from 7:00 AM to 10:00 PM—15 hours a day, six and a half days a week. I stayed there for two years.

My brother made 130 lire an hour working as a welder in a small factory. He worked ten hours a day. So between us we had enough to pay the rent and buy clothes. But that was only because we were working 25 hours a day.

Then at 14, I went to work as a welder too. I made mechanical parts for trucks. I did that from 9:00 AM to 6:00 PM, and then I went to the sweater factory for another four hours. There was an internal commission in the truck parts factory. I joined the union right away. We were making 270 lire an hour, but the work conditions were horrible. It was dirty and dangerous. Sparks were flying everywhere. They gave me the heaviest jobs because I always participated in the strikes. I was the youngest in the factory.

I changed jobs two more times before I was 20. First I went to another factory where they made car pistons. The work was lighter, and there were regular shifts. I worked nine hours a day. We didn't win the forty-hour week until 1969. While I was working there, I went to a Red Cross school to get a nurse's permit. The course took three months. Then I got a job in a private clinic. The pay was bad and so were the hours. There was no union. The clinic was run by nuns. You had to work very late whenever they said. My husband made me quit.

I married someone from Basilicata, one of my brother's friends. My brother was working in a restaurant, and I met my husband there. We liked each other a lot. It wasn't one of those forced southern marriages. I was 20. He was 23 and worked in a small sheet-metal factory. We found an apartment in the town of Beinasco, but it turned out to be too expensive. So we moved here to Orbassano. After a few months, I went to work at Fiat, in the paint department in the Rivalta plant.

I'm so used to working that I can't imagine not doing it, even aside from the economic reasons. I'd work anyway. I want to develop my potential in society. I want to involve others in the union and the struggles. I don't feel frustrated at Fiat the way others do. It's up to me to change my work conditions.

My husband and I work in the same department but different shifts. We have an eight-year-old boy who's in school, and a four-year-old girl in the Fiat day-care center. Our son is alone every day during the interval after my husband leaves for work and before I get back.

We argue every day, but it's like that for everyone who has this kind of life. My husband helps me in the house, but there're certain things he doesn't want to do. He washed the floor yesterday, and then I polished it. He's a comrade. He shares my political ideas, but he's not an activist. Sometimes, when we have time, we talk about union problems together.

When I first began to do union work, he was upset. But I made him accept it. I said, "Look, you have your hobbies. You go fishing. Let me have mine." Mine aren't really hobbies though. I said, "You have your life. I have mine." I've never had that southern mentality. I made my life here.

In the South, the women worked in the fields, and the men went to the bars to drink. My grandmother was a teacher. She had a diploma, and it was seen as a disgrace. So she had to go and hoe the fields and carry a basket on her head. That wasn't a dishonor. Meanwhile my grandfather was running after other women.

I don't feel at all *Torinese*. If I had the possibility of going back to my village, I'd do it in a minute. But there's no chance of that. There's no work.

If I don't go home for the holidays, they're not holidays for me. All the old friends come back. Call it nostalgia if you like. You feel at home. Everyone speaks your dialect. You remember old things. Here in Turin, the values aren't the same. At home, they are. If you were sick, people came to help you. There was a sense of community. Life here is one of sacrifices to make ends meet at the end of the month. Among Southerners here, we help each other, but we have no ties to the *Piemontesi*.

You have to find free time somehow to do things, even if it's just a walk in the country. We do it. We have friends. We go on picnics. There's no money for anything else.

At Fiat, I do inspecting. I check to see that the paint jobs are OK. About a quarter of the workers at Rivalta are women. Many of the new ones are housewives who've never seen a strike before. All they ever thought about was a clean house and food for their husbands. Now all they care about is the pay. It doesn't matter to them if it stays the same at Fiat. But they'll learn after a while.

I always voted for the PCI, and then I joined in 1975. The PCI is a serious party. The DC isn't serious.

If I said I was satisfied with my life, I'd be talking bull. But if you live badly, you have to understand why so you can do something about it.

Tell people in the United States what it's like here. Write about us so they'll know what's happening in Italy.

Sandra

Sandra arrived at the PCI headquarters in Orbassano with her 17-month-old son, Marcello, who toddled around the office while we spoke. She was separated from her husband and, according to the PCI functionary, had recently been coming to the headquarters with a young man who belonged to the party. He was there that day, quiet, playing with Marcello, and waiting for the interview to end.

Sandra was 23 years old, pretty, with long, light-brown hair that she kept pushing out of her eyes with a slow gesture. She gradually lost her self-consciousness and spoke emphatically. At times, her eyes filled with tears.

During that period in Italy, Sandra's optimism and idealism were rare among people her age. She had none of the anger or bitterness that were so common. Even joining the PCI seemed a less qualified or ambivalent choice for her than for others.

I've been at Fiat for four and a half months, and it's really a new thing for me. Before I worked as a saleswoman. That job gave me more responsibility, and it was more interesting, but I felt excluded from a certain type of social life. When you do that kind of work, you aren't part of a class. My father, for example, worked in a factory, and he passed his experiences as a worker on to me. We were a proletarian family.

I wanted to study, but I only went through junior high school. Now I feel as though I don't have the words I need. It's hard for me to express myself. But my parents couldn't afford to let me study. So I went to work, one job after another. I couldn't find anything that gave me satisfaction.

I worked in an interior design store. Maybe if I could have been in a bigger place, it would have been OK. But this store was a small, isolated world. I felt terrible whenever I would see a political march pass by the store. I knew there were problems and injustices in my job, but I had no one to ally with. I felt impotent. No one could help me because I was alone.

I was really exploited, just the "little girl" who helped. I did some decorating work, but mostly I sold things and just helped around the store. When there were design exhibitions, I had to work until 11 at night without taking a break to eat, and I wasn't even paid for it.

After a while, I began to argue with my boss. One day, there was a national storeworkers' strike, and I called to say I was going out on strike. My boss said, "What are you talking about?" So I just answered, "It's my work category." Then I began to refuse to do extra things. When I got married in 1976, they tried to fire me. I read over my contract and showed them that I couldn't be fired. I stayed on, but no one would talk to me, and they isolated me. They sent me to their other store and didn't turn on the heat. It was in the middle of winter, and I had to wear an overcoat and gloves. That kind of thing went on for seven months. Finally I quit. I was pregnant at the time.

After the baby was born, I was on the government placement list for the unemployed. I wanted a job, and Fiat was hiring. I didn't mind the idea of working at Fiat, but it all happened just by chance. Fiat called me and a friend of mine at the same time. We had our interviews and physical examinations, and when they said we were hired, we started hugging each other! I don't even know why. We were euphoric.

I work in the shop where they assemble the car doors. My job is to put a support bar inside the door. The handles are attached to this bar, and then it's welded. It's heavy work. I'm getting muscles in my arms! It's the heaviest work on the line, and we're all women who do it. At the end of the assembly line, there are some men who check over all the work. They say that's a skilled job, but it's not.

We've asked for a system of job rotation for everyone. That way we'd all have experience on different jobs. It would increase our skills and raise our job category. We'd also be able to share the lighter work. The department supervisor didn't want to let us do this. It was even hard to get the women to go along with the idea. They want to stay where they are. They say it's OK with them. A few of us decided to go talk to the supervisor, and he accepted our idea in part. So now there's job rotation, except for the final checking.

There's absolutely nothing difficult about the work at Fiat. You could learn any job in a couple of hours, except the machine maintenance and repair.

Women are oppressed in many ways, even in the family. But a lot of women at Fiat never rebel. Some of them don't even realize things are bad. Women are still inferior in the factory. There's good will on the part of some of the men workers, the comrades, but with the bosses, it's different. The woman–boss relationship is the same one that's existed for centuries. The bosses have power, and they make you feel inferior. They almost make fun of you. One of them always comes up to me and asks sarcastically, "*Signora*, how *are* you?"

When there's a strike, some women don't know what to do because there's this "intimate" relationship between them and management. Women have to feel free of this, and then we'll be able to work together. If Fiat hired a lot of women lately, there's a reason for it. They think it's easier to control us.

Our shop is new, and it's separated from the others. We work on the Fiat 138. People in other parts of the factory don't know how fast we have to work. The machines are new and very complicated. Fiat's technicians are still learning about them. The worker puts the door on the machine. It's very heavy, but then the machine does the rest. There are mechanical arms that move everything around.

Up to a month ago, the machines kept breaking down, so we were working less. Now the pace is really bad. The assembly line is supposed to do 2,250 doors every day, but we never do that much. It's impossible. About 1,800 is the most we can manage. Even then, the pace is so fast that if you have a cold, you don't have time to blow your nose.

Our factory council delegate has been at Fiat for ten years. He lives very far out, and so he's isolated. He does what he can, but he has 60 people on his work team. That's a lot. We want to elect a woman. I talk a lot with the other women, and they're beginning to feel a little stronger now and more willing to strike.

They've asked me if I would be willing to run for delegate. I'd love to do it! But I have personal problems. I have to find an apartment and take care of the baby. It's not easy to find a place to live. There're no vacancies in the buildings near Rivalta. I also need a day-care center. Then there's the problem of the shifts. How can I get up at five in the morning and leave for work with the baby? I asked for the special shift that starts later, but they told me that the only job I could have then was cleaning. That would just kill me because I wouldn't be in the shop anymore. I'd be isolated, and the important thing is being with the other workers.

I'm separated from my husband. He works as an electrical technician for a private company. Things changed between us after the baby was born. He became distant. When we were first together, he was everything to me. I suppose that wasn't good. I need to be loved, and I need tenderness. It was difficult when we first separated, but I feel stronger now.

Fiat is an experience. It's something you have to do all your life, and that's hard. But you find out about so many problems. You develop a class consciousness. One day my supervisor said to me, "Look, I feel the same way you do about things." I said, "What in the world are you talking about? You're in the armchair, and I'm in the shop! You give orders, and I carry them out. If you thought the way I do, you'd be in my place!" Do you know what he answered? "You're too profound. You think too much." I'm not saying you don't have to learn things in the factory. You have to be taught, but it doesn't have to be a power relationship.

In the next ten years, what I would like to see is real equality, with women active and politically conscious in society. That would be a great step forward. Women have to work side by side. If not, men won't go forward. I'd like to see better work conditions and the possibility of working more serenely.

But ten years aren't very much. We'll need much longer. After 30 years, I hope we won't have this kind of government. We're in chaos. It's crazy, especially in the government. There're elections all the time. The Christian Democrats haven't done much since the war. Things won't change with them.

I joined the Italian Communist Party last January, but I've always been a sympathizer. My father's in the PCI. He has some old ideas, but he's a committed comrade. I don't think the Soviet Union is communist. It's something else. Italy has a different history. We're more democratic. The PCI has shown that it doesn't want a head-on confrontation here.

I would have joined the PCI even if I hadn't gone to work at Fiat. I'd been thinking about it for a long time. I ended up sharing my father's ideas, but just by chance. I left my family, and I didn't want to adopt his views. I rebelled. I used to fight with him all the time. My political choices are my own. My father's influence has been moral, and I thank him for that. My mother isn't at all political. That's my mother's mistake—a woman who stayed at home.

Whoever has a class consciousness feels oppressed by terrorism now. In the factory, you work with people you don't know. You wonder who's next to you on the line. You can't work well like that. There've been threats against some of the factory council delegates. It's as though the terrorists want to stop our political work. No one really understands what's behind it all.

The young people at Fiat aren't bad. They're respectable, but they have another way of looking at life. Some of them rebel because they don't have a class consciousness. They have problems and can't fit themselves into any class. They turn to drugs. They aren't happy with anything. They're in the factory because they need jobs. But I think they hope to change things even if they won't admit it. They participate in the struggles even if they feel excluded and different. We have to give these young people confidence that things can change. It will take time for the workers to control the factory and to be autonomous in running it. But someday it will be possible.

Palmerio

I interviewed Palmerio one evening in Orbassano. The apartment building where he lived was modern, one in a long line of similar buildings at the edge of the street. There were no sidewalks and practically no trees. Inside, the hallway was clean and attractive.

Palmerio and his wife Vittoria showed me around their third-floor apartment. There were two rooms. In the first, a double bed took up most of the

An "immigrant" worker from Sardinia and his family at home in Orbassano, outside Turin.

space, and along the wall stood a child's bed and a crib. Four members of the family slept in this room. Across the hall, a smaller room was just about filled with a table, a large television, and a sofa. The two older children slept on the sofa. The kitchenette at the far end of the room could be closed off with a folding door. Next to this room was the bath.

Palmerio was quite short with bright black eyes, black hair, and a full beard. He was 35 years old. Vittoria, 28, was even shorter. She had a patient and smiling manner. The children, ages six, five, three, and two, all had the same shiny black eyes and silky hair. They sat in a line along one side of the table while I talked to their parents and would alternately play and then cry together as if on cue. After the interview, Palmerio, Vittoria, and I sipped their very strong, homemade grappa until it was time for the bus to Turin to come by.

I'm an unskilled worker. I insert rubber plugs using a kind of gun-tool. There's a robot about ten meters down the line from me doing the same thing. It's a tolerable speed, but it's monotonous. If there were skilled work for me, I'd be more interested and more committed. I've been doing this job for seven or eight months. Before this one, I did sealing, and that was more interesting. I've been at Fiat for nine years.

I come from Cagliari in Sardinia. We escaped. No, they made us escape. I was an agricultural worker. I left with my brother when I was 24. When it rained in Sardinia, there was no work, and you didn't eat.

When I arrived in Turin, I worked on the presses in a small independent factory. There were about 600 workers and three shifts. I worked nights. My brother went right to Fiat, and he was better off. I got married in 1971 to a woman from the same town in Sardinia.

VITTORIA: I would have liked to work, but with the oil crisis in 1973, there were no more jobs. Then the children came. Now I'm signed up on the government list, but who knows when something will come through. It's not easy for all of us to live on one salary. You have to give up certain "vices" and luxuries. But you go on living. What else can you do?

PALMERIO: We don't have any friends. We say "hello" to the neighbors, but people don't really know each other. They're all workers in these buildings. I'm a Communist. I don't know what the other people are. We did know one couple, but we were talking politics once, and it came out that I'm a Communist. He made a face, so we stopped seeing them.

There's no community. Workers come home, eat, turn on the television. Everyone stays inside. Home—work—home—party headquarters—home. That's my life. At first, it bothered me, but I don't think about it now. I see my comrades at the party headquarters. I dedicate my free time to the party. I can go and discuss politics there. My brother and sister-in-law live one kilometer from here, but we don't see them often. It's a pain to walk there, and gas costs too much. When we do go out, we go out with people who come from the same town in Sardinia. We speak the same language.

We've been in this apartment for eight years, first as newlyweds, now with four children. I take the town bus to the plant everyday along with everyone else. It takes 25 minutes.

VITTORIA: We hope to go back to Sardinia to live. Palmerio came to Turin talking about going back! It will change there. We'd like to do farm work, but modernized. We vacation in Sardinia every year.

PALMERIO: I joined the PCI in 1972. I wasn't very political when I arrived in Turin, but I voted Communist in Sardinia. My father didn't talk politics, but I saw that the PCI had a class line. So I voted for them. Even if I read *L'Unità*[7] only once a month, I knew how it was different from the boss's newspaper. We lived 40 kilometers from Cagliari, and you had to go ten kilometers to get a newspaper. I managed to read one about once a month.

I joined the struggles at Fiat right away. I missed the Hot Autumn of 1969, but there was still something going on when I began to work. I was a little disappointed because not everyone went out on strike. In the small factory where I first worked, when someone whistled, we all went out.

There was a strike this morning at Rivalta from 9:20 to 11:20. We marched around all the shops and chased out the scabs. We also blocked the road into the factory. In other departments, the disabled workers didn't go out. They didn't want to lose two hours' pay. The workers in the islands didn't strike either. The islands are worktables where one to three workers assemble parts. Some of them do their jobs sitting down. We won the islands for them, and now they don't even strike. Usually about 80 to 90 percent of the workers go out.

I think the new technology is positive. It does away with the worst jobs. We used to be like robots, and now robots can do that work. I don't think it will eliminate jobs or skills. There's no negative reaction toward it among the workers.

There're terrorist attacks in the city every day now. When we leave the factory, we tell each other that we don't know if we'll make it home or even across the street. I was threatened last year. A worker, about 30 years old, came up to me in the plant and said he'd be waiting outside to shoot me. It's because I'm one of the activists in the factory. I told my comrades, and they escorted me outside. For a few days, they escorted me to work and back home. But then it seemed OK so we dropped it. I told that fellow that if anything happened to me, he would be the first to be denounced. When I see him now, I don't even nod my head.

They've found Red Brigade leaflets in the factory. When there were strikes after the Moro kidnapping, some of the young workers who are part of Workers' Autonomy were shouting the slogan "*Né con lo stato, né*

con le Brigate Rosse" [Neither with the state, nor with the Red Brigades].[8]
They wanted to strike for the German terrorists too.

There've also been telephone threats to workers. One of my friends
found a note in his locker that said, "Berlinguer supporter,[9] it's all over
for you." It was signed by the terrorist organization *Prima Linea*. Since
then, comrades have been escorting him to work. Five or six travel with
him, and they change off cars.

I knew Matteo Caggegi, but not well. Just from riding the bus to
work. He lived in Orbassano. We found out he was in Workers' Autonomy when they handed out their leaflet at a rally organized by the antifascist committee. Caggegi was with them. But we didn't know he was a
terrorist. I'm glad the police killed him before he killed someone else. He
probably became a terrorist inside the factory, and there're probably
other terrorists inside.

I think the relations between men and women are normal at
Rivalta. The women protest and leaflet sometimes, but it's always the
same small group of Workers' Autonomy. Until recently, there was just
one woman on the factory council. Now there're two, but about 30 percent of the workers are women. I suppose there're so few on the council
because they do more work at home. But they participate in the strikes.

The important thing is to struggle. The bosses have their hands on
the levers now, but tomorrow we will. For us, the bosses are useless. We
can control production ourselves.

Massimo

*Massimo was 22 years old, tall, thin, and serious. We talked in one of the
cafés across the street from the PCI headquarters in Orbassano. When I stopped
by the headquarters earlier that day, some women from Rivalta were holding a
meeting to plan the PCI campaign strategy inside the factory for the upcoming
parliamentary elections. They had found out that I had visited Rivalta the week
before and were a little hurt that I had not gone to see their departments in the
plant. So they began to devise a scheme, which was never consummated, for
dressing me in a worker's uniform and sneaking me inside the factory.*

I was born in Pisa, in central Italy, but my whole family moved to
Turin in 1964. The salaries were lower in Pisa. My father was a metal-
worker but had been earning half of a Fiat salary. So he got a job at Fiat
Mirafiori. He still works there.

I graduated from a science high school, so I'm part of the diploma-
holding army—all the young people with diplomas and degrees who
haven't been able to find skilled work.[10] I wanted to go on to the univer-

sity because high school isn't enough to get a decent job. I studied medicine for a year, but I didn't do very well. Then I went into the factory. I've been at Fiat Rivalta for four months, but I'm also studying. I go to a school for marketing and personnel management in the evening.

I don't know what I want to be. I just know I don't want to be an unskilled worker on an assembly line. That's my only hope. Other than that, it's all pretty arbitrary. Right now, I'm young, so it's OK to work in a factory. But there's no future in it. I make 340,000 lire a month [about $400]. I can't have an autonomous life with that.

If I didn't go to school and do political work, I'd be a cretin in one year. I just put wheels on cars all day. Work and what I do for recreation wouldn't be enough.

In the factory, all you hear is swearing and stupid, obscene jokes. That's no way to spend your life. People do it because they don't know what else to do. You get bored, so you let go in the stupidest ways. It seems as though you don't have your brain in order. Everyone does it, but it's worse among those who've been in the factory for a while. When you first get there, you look around and say, "These people are crazy." Then without noticing it, you start doing the same thing. The more specialized workers do it less. Even the women are the same. In fact, some of them are worse. You come away with a certain impression of workers, that they're a mass of demented people. It's really bad because then incidents like the bombing at Piazza Fontana[11] can be blamed on the left if people have a low opinion of workers.

I've been in the FGCI[12] for four years, but I'm critical of the Communist Party. People don't have enough of a class consciousness, and that's the responsibility of the party. Workers don't have confidence in their own class. It's dangerous because it leads to depoliticization or an every-man-for-himself attitude. In 1920, that led to fascism.

I used to mythologize the Italian working class and how politicized they were. Part of the working class is like that, but part is also very different. They help the bosses or even stop others from struggling. They go around saying that if you go out on strike, you'll be worse off.

At Rivalta, a few workers can stop the whole assembly line. The strikes have 100 percent participation, but not many workers take part in the marches.

Relations among the workers are generally good. There's solidarity. Women are in the majority on my line. I think the relations between men and women are good. The old prejudices against women don't exist anymore. It was a woman, a 39-year-old mamma with children, who taught me how to put wheels on a car! There are women on every job, even the most difficult ones.

As far as I'm concerned, the whole idea of young people rejecting work is absurd. I want to take people who talk about that by the collar and show them the lists of unemployed people who've signed up for jobs. About 99 percent of them are young. It's just that young people want decent, secure work, not something completely stupid. We're making cars because there just isn't any decent work. If cars are rolling off the assembly lines, you have to ask who's making them. A lot of the young people who reject monotonous work but can't find anything else turn to drugs, heroin. There's also a high percentage of worker-students.

I joined the union right away. I believe in union unity, but it's difficult. At Rivalta, for example, there're conflicts between the PCI and the PSI within the union, and the workers get involved.

I live with my parents in Turin, and I'm afraid I'll be there for a long time. I can't afford to move out. I work the first shift and commute on the Fiat bus. It takes 20 minutes. I'm free from three to five in the afternoon. I call my girlfriend then, but I see her only on weekends. I have to be at school at 6:30 PM. It's not much of a life.

Tommaso

None was another farming village about a half-hour or so outside Turin. After the great wave of immigration and the opening of the Rivalta plant in 1967, None's population doubled. Today, half the residents are of southern origin, and a large number of the people who have jobs work at Fiat.

A young PCI functionary took me for a brief walk around town. None is tranquil, even deserted during the siesta hour. Some of the old streets are reminiscent of small Spanish towns. Stucco-covered buildings of two or three stories painted in pastel colors butt up against each other along narrow streets. The main sights seemed to be the billboards where the parties hung their election posters and the club where we had coffee. Some of the townspeople had organized this meeting place for themselves. There were tables for cardplaying in one large, rather dark room and a typical Italian bar setup and a pool table in the next room.

None was the only town in the entire area that did not have a left government. The Christian Democrats still dominated in None although the PCI had recently made some gains.

My guide, Petrossi, had grown up in None and still lived with his parents in a small house that had been recently remodeled and fitted with a modern bath. His father, retired by then, had worked as a blacksmith, first shoeing farmers' horses and later working for the riding stables. Petrossi had just returned from a cadre school in the Soviet Union. He was back at his job as head of the community-based local chapters of the PCI in the district around the Rivalta plant. Petrossi set up my interview with a Fiat worker from None named Tommaso and gave us his living room as a meeting place. When the interview was over, Petrossi's parents served lunch, including homemade ravioli, his father's specialty.

Tommaso was a large man, athletic and younger-looking than his 49 years. He was wary and nervous at first but lost his self-consciousness as he described his experiences in the factory.

Tommaso belonged to a vanishing breed of Fiat workers. He was of Piemontese origin and began to work at Fiat in the 1950s. A typical Fiat assembly-line worker of that era was the son of a small farmer in the provinces around Turin. Having access to a bit of land meant that there were vegetables and dairy products to supplement the low wages. The Piemontesi workers were called barachin *after the metal soup pails they carried to the factory each day. By the late 1970s, the* barachin *were gone, and the majority of the labor force at Fiat was made up of immigrants from other regions of Italy or the children of immigrants.*

I was born in Castagnole Piemonte, in the province of Turin. It's about four kilometers from here. My parents were tenant farmers. They did all right. They moved to None when I was still little. They did the same work and made some money. Things were fairly good for them.

I left the farm when I was 24 years old. You had to work too hard—too many hours, no vacations, no days off. There wasn't much mechanization in those days. We had a large family, and everyone worked together.

I married a girl from the country and went off with her to live and find work. She was 19 or 20. I did part-time jobs, nothing permanent. I lived here in None. I did woodcutting during the winter, drove a truck, did other jobs. I lived like that for two years.

I applied to Fiat several times, but it was difficult to get in during the 1950s. They weren't hiring much. You had to know someone. Fiat made sure it knew who all its workers were. A priest got me my job. His brother knew the manager who did the hiring at Fiat. This brother asked on my behalf, and I was taken immediately. I've never been a great friend of priests, but this one knew my family. I went to work on March 27, 1956. I'll never forget that date.

I did assembly work in the body shop at Mirafiori. I was on the line. You really worked hard. You couldn't stop, move, or talk. You couldn't arrive late. It was a dictatorship. If you complained, you had to leave. No politics. They fired anyone in the PCI. In 1957, the CISL won 50 percent of the votes. The bosses' union was put in later. I joined the CISL, but there were no strikes, no struggles until 1962. When the bosses' union came in, I wouldn't join. So I didn't have a union card for years.

There were good relations between the workers, but you couldn't talk. The bell rang, the line started, and that was it. There were three shifts for some departments at Fiat in those years. The supervisors were dictators. They weren't human beings.

There were already a few Southerners in the plant, but mostly there were natives of the Piedmont region, from the countryside. We weren't born workers. We were farmers. This was especially true on the assembly lines.

There weren't many other industries then, and there weren't enough jobs. You got a decent salary at Fiat compared to other factories. They used to say that getting a job at Fiat was like going to America. It was prestigious. You thought you were lucky to work at Fiat. My friends were making less money.

My wife did home labor. She made nylon stockings. She did it so we could have a little more money. One salary is never enough in Italy. Our boys were born in 1955 and 1959. My wife went to work at Indesit, an electrical appliance factory, in 1964. You know, they fired 19 workers there the other day for absenteeism.

The first real strike at Fiat was in 1962. It was supposed to last for eight hours, but only a few of us stayed out of the plant. The others all went in because it was dangerous to strike. The next time, we blocked the gates so no one could enter. We stopped everything. We threw rocks. We had to fight some of the other workers. They were the ones who owned houses and land.

There were seven of us in one work team who always went out on strike. They used to call us the "Magnificent Seven." When it was all over, we were afraid management would send us to different departments, and, in fact, they divided us up and transferred us. The contract we won that year wasn't so good.

In 1966, we negotiated a companywide contract and won a 44-hour week. I was always on strike, and management accused me of making other workers stay out. They said I was a hothead and told me I had to work the night shift. I asked to be transferred to the new Rivalta plant instead. Luckily I had a decent supervisor, and in 1968, I went to work at Rivalta.

The first workers at Rivalta came from Mirafiori. Then in 1969, thousands of Southerners came. They had really bad conditions and were extremely combative. The *Piemontesi* were doing all right by then. Relations between the two groups weren't good. The *Piemontesi* tried to avoid the Southerners. As far as I'm concerned, they're the same as everyone else, some good, some bad. Maybe they're a little backward.

In 1969, we had marches inside the factory and stopped everyone from working. There were some fights, and the supervisors were thrown out of their offices. The dictatorship of the bosses lost its hold after 1969, and then we could discuss politics. Each work team elected a delegate, and conditions changed—not completely but a fair amount.

I work in the mechanics department, assembling the suspension on the 126 model. I work alone at my own table. I haven't been on the assembly line for two or three years. The old lines are disappearing, and they're putting in these worktables. Six of us do the same job.

I do my seven hours' work in three and a half or four hours. I'm responsible for 78 pieces every day. I work the way I want and decide how to do it. When I finish, I talk or do crossword puzzles, even though we're not supposed to. I walk around. There's also a room for relaxing where we play cards. The supervisor knows all this, but he doesn't say anything. He doesn't come around unless something breaks. The others work more slowly than I do, but no one takes more than five hours to do the pieces.

Management doesn't react to what we do because of the union. The work times are agreed upon and that's it. In the 1950s and 1960s, there were timekeepers who checked how fast you were working. Now Fiat isn't allowed to do that.

Being off the assembly line and working at a table is much better. Each worker does an entire operation. A conveyor belt brings all the pieces. We assemble them and put the finished ones in a bin. Then they're taken away. Each piece I work on weighs 17 kilos [37.4 pounds]. We still work standing up.

After a while, you can do the work with your eyes closed, so it goes quickly. It's always the same thing. It's monotonous. You'd go crazy if you had to do it continuously for seven hours. But it varies from worker to worker. Some can't do the work at all in the time we're given. They don't have the ability or aren't used to the work. Not everyone can do it quickly.

In the 1950s, you had to work eight hours, and the supervisors tried to make you work even more. If the line stopped for 15 minutes because the electricity went off or because you ran out of material, they made you make up the time. Now they can't do that.

There've been a lot of new workers coming in since last September, almost all of them women. I don't like them very much. They're all young. They're different, lots of absenteeism, less desire to work. Before Fiat made us work too much, but with these kids, it's too far in the other direction.

They struggle even more than we did. Many of them are extremists, more than us. But as far as I'm concerned, they stay home too much. They stay at home for three days at a time on paid sick leave. If a lot of people are missing from one work team, management has to bring in people from other teams. That means those people have to work more because it's a new job for them. Management is always taking us off the 126 to work someplace else.

The relationship between men and women in the factory is good. I suppose it creates a little uneasiness. The women get lighter work sometimes, but there's no hostility. The women's movement is correct. They should be equal. I've always said we men are the weaker sex. Some men, Southerners, kept their women as slaves, but I'm for the women's movement.

We're all afraid of terrorism. You don't know where it comes from. Where I am, we haven't seen any leaflets. One delegate in the body shop was threatened, but only one. They shot a supervisor two years ago, an old type of supervisor. The workers were against the killing, but we didn't go out on strike.

I've been at home now for a month and a half. I cut a tendon in my hand bottling wine. With the national health insurance, I'll get my full pay for two months. But I don't like staying home. I get nervous.

In my free time, I usually bicycle, play cards or *bocce* or tennis, or go to the club. We organized the club ourselves. You can play pool there or cards. About 180 people belong—everyone. There's one movie theater, but we don't go anymore now that there's TV.

The young people in None work in the factories. There's enough work around here. None is 50 percent southern now. The young people do the same things we do in their free time. They go dancing in other towns too. A lot of them go dancing.

I rarely leave the village. I don't like Turin or other cities. I like the country. My wife still works in the factory. One son was in the army. He works now and then. The other one is a mechanic here in None.

If all goes well, I'll stay at Fiat until I can get my pension. That's eleven more years. I'll be 60 then with 34 years at Fiat. You need 35 years of work with papers to get a full pension, but I lost several years working without papers before I went to Fiat. The pension payments are taken out of your paycheck. A full pension is 80 percent of your pay.

I never thought about having a career. I didn't want any worries. I just wanted to do my work and that's all.

Industrial development has ruined everything. Ecologically, it's a mess. We live in smoke. There aren't any clear days anymore. Even food isn't natural the way it used to be. There's less taste than before. Everything we eat is full of chemicals. But I suppose if there were no industry, there would be no work and no jobs.

I think the new technology is OK. It does away with the hardest work. We don't have to be unskilled laborers anymore. Maybe it will eliminate jobs. Some workers think it will, so they're against it. Still, someone has to make the robots. One line at Rivalta had 250 workers. Now there're just robots and a few technicians. The workers were sent to other departments. Fiat is expanding production right now so jobs aren't being lost.

I don't belong to a party, but I agree more with the Socialist Party than the Communist Party. I'm a leftist. I joined the FLM in 1969, but I never wanted to join a party. Too many cards. I have a union card and that costs 25,000 lire a year [about $30].

I'm for change. Let the Communist Party go into the government and see what happens. I'm not afraid of communism. They don't eat people. My ideas are communist in the general sense. I don't want to see so many bosses. I'm not for the hard communists. They can be dictators too. But there are also "malleable" communists.

Liliana

May Day is a national holiday in Italy. All the workplaces close down. The unions in most towns organize marches and rallies. Turin is considered a workers' city, but for several years, the May Day celebrations had been disappointing, smaller than anticipated and somewhat dispirited. Then in 1979, the mood changed. About 50,000 people marched across downtown Turin, from Piazza Vittorio Veneto to Piazza San Carlo. The slogan chanting was loud, and the pace energetic. The streets were filled with red. There were thousands of flags and the huge banners of the factory councils, the PCI locals, and the smaller parties. Most of the marchers also wore something red.

Communist Party slogans and flags dominated the rally quantitatively, but the most beautiful banners were hand-painted, figurative works, similar in some ways to Mexican murals. They belonged to the Intercategoriale Donne CGIL-CISL-UIL, the union network that brings together women workers from many sectors of the economy (see Chapter 8).

After the rally, a group of women from the Intercategoriale had a May Day lunch at a restaurant run by leftists on the far side of the Po River. There were 34 women crowded around one long table covered with plates of food—anchovy salad, pasta fagioli, pasta asciutta, chicken, vegetables, and fresh strawberries. During the meal, I sat next to Liliana, 31 years old with dark skin and curly red hair. Like many of the other women, she had dressed up for the march. They all wore long print skirts and had pasted tiny multicolored metallic stars on their faces.

I went to work at Fiat Ricambi when I was 16. The plant is in Volvera, near Rivalta. It's where the spare parts are packaged and sent out. There're about 1,400 production workers and 600 white-collar workers.

My father worked at Fiat Ricambi too before he retired. He was in production. I went to work in one of the offices. My mother is a housewife, and my grandparents were peasants in Asti, southeast of Turin.

The 1960s were difficult years. The union for the white-collar workers was the UIL. If you were a Communist, you really had to hide it. I think it was even worse for us than it was for the production workers.

Then everything exploded at Fiat Ricambi in 1967 around the issue of pensions. The production workers went on the first marches inside the factory. They came through the offices and shut them down. At first, relations between the office workers and the production workers were very tense, although not as bad as they were at Mirafiori where the production workers attacked the office workers. The bosses had always used the white-collar workers as a buffer between themselves and the production workers.

I joined the union right away and was active in the old internal commission, but after 1968, I became much more involved. I was appointed by the union to be the delegate from my office to the factory council. My office was so backward politically that the union was afraid to hold regular elections. They were afraid a conservative would be voted in. The situation's better now so they should be having a regular election soon.

The women's movement is what really changed my life. I was already political and active, but choices for my personal life, relationships with people, and how I live were all influenced by the women's movement.

I live on the outskirts of Turin, on the opposite side from the factory. I take the Fiat bus to work every day. It takes an hour and a quarter each way. I didn't want to live near the factory because it's a miserable neighborhood. There's nothing there. If you want to live in the city, you have to take whatever's available. There isn't enough housing.

I was married, but now I'm separated. I don't have children. I spend my time working as a factory council delegate and for the party section in the factory. I joined the PCI in the wave of 1975.[13] I don't have any free time. By the time I get home, all I want to do is go to sleep.

The young women workers are different from the older ones. They've had more education and are more politicized even if it's not within an organizational context. They've absorbed a lot of feminism even if they haven't been active in the movement. They're more open than the older women, and they work openly on women's issues.

Maybe the young workers are impatient because they don't know that it was even worse at Fiat before. They don't know how much has been done, and they're angry at how things are now.

I think the rapport between men and women is very bad, even within the factory council. Men are hostile toward women coming in and raising new issues. They take the attitude that if women want to work, they'll have to suffer the bad conditions.

Telesca

A factory council delegate from Mirafiori took me to one of the blocked entrances to meet some of the workers on strike. In all, about 30 stood around talking just inside the wall or sat on the grass playing cards and reading. Only four of them were women. The red FLM banner flew from the top of the gate.

The union had organized the strike action so that workers took turns blocking the entrances. Every two hours, a new group would relieve those outside, and the first group would go back into the plant. In this way, no worker lost more than two hours pay, and yet the occupation could continue around the clock.

From inside the gate, there was a partial view of Mirafiori which looked like a crowded city of hangars, buildings, and roadways. There were trucks everywhere. I sat down on the grass with Telesca—36 years old, serene, and self-confident. We spoke until it was time for her shift to reenter the plant. I stayed where I was for a few minutes, going over my notes. When I looked up, there was a ring of workers surrounding me, demanding to know who I was and what I was doing. When I said I was from the United States, one older worker accused me of being a CIA agent and then launched into his harangue. "For 30 years, you've been strangling us," he shouted. "We'd be fine if the Americans would just get out. As far as I'm concerned, the Americans are as bad as the Fascists. No, they're worse!"

Some of the workers standing there seemed embarrassed. Others were just curious. A young soft-spoken Sicilian offered an apology and then began to describe how the workers at Fiat were not earning enough money to make ends meet. This turned into a discussion among a half-dozen of them, all from the South, about the scarcity of jobs, political payoffs, and the widespread corruption in their home regions. Yet, without exception, they said they hoped to go back some day. They wanted to know the salaries of auto workers in the United States and calculated that the figure I gave them was about three times their own salary. After a while, a whistle blew, we shook hands, and they went back into the plant.

I was born in the South, in Lucania in the province of Potenza. The area where I lived was strictly agricultural. Italy was an agricultural nation 30 years ago, even if people didn't think of it that way. I came to Turin to find work in 1960, when I was 17. My sister and brother came also. They were my age.

You feel physically sick when you leave your own village. I still feel it as though it was just two days ago, even if we've created our own way of life here with our own people. It's your birthplace and your traditions that you miss. When I left, I knew there was no future there. The South was a colony of the North. Even after 30 years, nothing has changed. The decision to leave was forced on us. To stay meant no possibilities. We left with the hope of finding a better life, but it was just a hope because we don't have it even now.

When I first came, I worked in a paper factory. We made the little paper cups you put pastries in. It paid badly, and I didn't have work papers. I was there up to 18 hours a day. We did piecework, and there was no union. We were all girls under 18.

Then I worked in a chemical factory for seven years. There was a union, but in an embryonic stage. It was just coming out of hiding. The conditions were very repressive for the workers. You couldn't eat a sandwich, you couldn't go to the bathroom, you had to ask permission to get a tissue.

I met someone from the South and got married. It's the only happy thing in 20 years! My husband had no family. We were married in 1965, and our children were born in 1966 and 1968. We have two boys. I left work because there were no day-care centers, and I couldn't pay for a baby-sitter. For ten years, I was a housewife.

I began to work at Fiat last year. I work second shift, and my husband works first shift. We live through telephone calls and notes. There're immense sacrifices, running from morning to night. And for what? Not for the satisfaction I get in the factory! The boys were growing up, and we had more expenses. We want our boys to have a better life. We have to pay for this, so I'm back in the factory.

At first, my sons didn't want me to go to work. They said they'd rather give up certain things and have me around. They suffer from the oppression and authoritarianism in school, so they understand what I go through at Fiat. One day, my older son said to me, "At school, we don't even have a union." They've developed a political consciousness, so now they accept the fact that I work.

Free time? It doesn't exist! I can relax for a half-day on Sunday when my husband helps me in the house. He and my sons all help. I can take the whole day on Sunday if I want to live in chaos for the next week.

When I was a housewife, I wanted to learn a skill and get a decent job. I took a course to be a herbalist, but there're chemists without jobs now. So what could I do? I had wanted some freedom in my work. Here at Fiat, I'm a cog in the machine. You're not indispensable at Fiat. They don't need you. If you leave, there'll be someone else to take your place.

I work in the body shop, on an assembly line. We put together the sides of the 131 model and then send them on to be welded. There're no robots on our line. It's hard work and dangerous. We have to wear gloves and heavy shoes and be on our feet for seven hours a day. It's continuous, repetitious, monotonous. There're still accidents, but the rhythms are better than they were before.

I know it was hell in there ten years ago. The workers who have been at Fiat for a while think it's better now, but I've just come in, and I find it very hard. There's a lot to do, a lot to change.

I've been in the PCI since 1962. My husband's also in the party. I joined the union my first day at work. As a housewife, I wasn't ignorant of what was happening. I went into the factory knowing I'd have to struggle. I was born with a political consciousness, rebelling. Even in the South, I rebelled. My brothers tried to order me around. They'd tell me to get them a glass of water. "What's wrong with you?" I'd answer. "Get it yourself."

Male–female relations are generally good in the factory. But the situation for a woman depends on her preparation and her level of emancipation. A secure woman doesn't fear anything or anyone. It depends on her level of consciousness outside the factory.

I agree with the feminists. I am a feminist. But I want to be next to men, not under them or over them. I see other women workers acting subordinate to men. I fought this as a little girl with my father and brothers. I saw injustices toward women even then. I had to be quiet because I was a girl. My brothers could study but I couldn't. Women had to obey. I couldn't go out; my brothers could. I couldn't buy anything without asking first; they could.

My husband and I are comrades, not just husband and wife. Because of my personality, he's never tried to put me down. He even brings home the feminist newspapers for me. The word "wife" doesn't have any sense for me. Equality is something you have to feel inside. But men have to change if women are going to have real equality.

Women have to struggle outside before they come into the factory. Many of them are still persecuted by their husbands, so they suffer in the factory too. They're quiet. Of the 20 women where I work, all of us go out on strike, but I'm the only one who goes out to help block the gates.

The physical conditions at Fiat are terrible for women. There're no showers, no toilets, not even an infirmary, and thousands of women have come into the factory over the last year or so. How can they do this? It's like trying to run a factory without electricity. So what happens? The women rebel. They put women on heavy jobs to make them eat their equality, and the women have to keep quiet. Equality is held over their heads.

There was a women's march inside Mirafiori the other day to protest the lack of facilities. The women have to take turns changing clothes, screening each other. There're only two toilets. So the women formed a

Three workers at Fiat Mirafiori. In 1978 and 1979 the company hired thousands of new workers, many of them young women.

line, shouted slogans, and marched to management's offices to talk. It was spontaneous, mostly newly-hired workers. The office doors were closed. It's like a fortress. Later on, management met with a delegation and gave the usual answer: "We'll look into the problem." Nothing's happened. We'll wait 15 years, until the building falls down and we retire. Then they won't have to do anything about it. The only positive thing is to hope to change things for those who come after us.

Marcello

I had heard about Marcello from a number of union and left activists. He had the reputation of being a very politically sophisticated and dedicated factory council delegate. I met him on May Day in Piazza Vittorio before the workers' march began. He said he would be happy to talk and invited me to his home for dinner the next evening.

Marcello and his girlfriend lived near the center of Turin in an apartment filled with books, ceiling to floor. After dinner with two relatives from out of town, Marcello and I talked for several hours in spite of the fact that he had to be at Mirafiori by six the next morning.

I saw Marcello a few more times at Fiat demonstrations and at campaign rallies. He seemed to spend 20 hours a day on politics. He had factory council and union responsibilities and was also an activist in one of the small left parties. Marcello was taller and more muscular-looking than most Italian men, but his political work over the previous six years had taken its toll. He was in his mid-30s and looked worn.

My father was a successful businessman, but the family was always concerned about social justice and even open to communism, although not in an ideological way. These attitudes led me to the Third World. I spent two years in India, but I found that human justice wasn't the issue. I began to think in terms of causes. I saw the metal and mechanical workers' struggles here and the German student movement. I knew about the movement in Berkeley, California. I went to Berlin and Paris.

From all this, I realized that the most real and positive experience, the one with possibilities, was the Italian workers' movement. The German movement was very sectarian. The Italian movement, because of its history, Fascism, the Resistance, its capacity to reproduce vanguards, was the most favorable situation. So I went into the factory.

I began to work at Fiat in 1973. I went in with great myths about workers in general and about the metal and mechanical workers and the FLM in particular. My ideas were presumptuous. I found I couldn't talk to workers in general terms. There was a gap between my abstractions and the everyday problems of workers like salaries and family. Their focus wasn't just revolution and ideals. It included insecurities of bourgeois life and the need for guarantees of material security. These were givens for me so I could reject them.

The traditional vanguard, the PCI cadres, didn't trust me at first. They saw me as an intellectual. Their notions were based on a hypothetical conquest of power on the model of the Soviet Union. But at the same time, they were caught up in everyday problems. I wasn't part of the old conception of the Winter Palace.[14]

I got along right away with the ordinary workers. I was part of a team in the body shop that wasn't interested in politics. The supervisor was involved in management's effort to put in the fascist union. The team was known as the "black hole" of the body shop. During the 1969 strikes, they had scabbed. Six months after I began to work, they left the fascist union, and everyone joined the FLM.

It wasn't because I lectured them. We discussed issues like social justice, human dignity, and liberty that didn't have an overt class content. The workers had been manipulated by the supervisor, and I presented an alternative kind of authority that split the work team. They realized that they were seen by the other workers as mentally underdeveloped. I helped bring up what was underneath, and we began to be known as a superior team, one that went out on strike for other workers.

Gradually I began to talk about class and explained that what was going on in the factory wasn't a question of good or bad. The workers began to join the PCI. I had gone into the factory on September 24 and the next day had joined *Il Manifesto*.[15] But I thought it was better for the other workers to join a mass party and not a small party of cadres. Joining the PCI is a class choice, not a choice for activism or militancy. You can't translate rebellion directly into militancy. It's too difficult for workers to break with the bosses and with the traditional left at the same time.

In 1973, I was the only member of *Il Manifesto*. Now there're 20 of us in the body shop, and we're an important influence. In 1973, I didn't understand the contract negotiations. In 1975, I helped write the contract. Some of the other New Left groups just blamed everything on the betrayal of the PCI and the unions. They didn't construct anything positive.

It's been over ten years now that the workers have been challenging Taylorism and struggling for control and a change in production relations in the factory. I chose to struggle on this terrain, but it requires a great deal of work. The process of restructuring by management goes on constantly, so there has to be continual surveillance. It puts the factory council delegates on the front line all the time. After a while, this fatigues and eats away at them. But if they let up, they'll lose the confidence of the workers.

I haven't withdrawn, but I feel like I can't do it alone. There have to be many of us. If it's done by just a few, it becomes demagogic. But there aren't many right now. It's a political choice to take on this work. When I enter the factory every morning, it's like entering another planet. It's a different world. Other workers experience the same split, but for them it's more a split between their families and their friendships inside the factory.

The composition of the labor force has changed at Mirafiori recently because of the new workers. They're starting out at a level of consciousness that in certain respects is higher and different from what we began with. They have a stronger conception of individual worth, more self-respect, and a desire for satisfying work. They reject arbitrary authority. They join the union right away and struggle. They also have everything we've done and won to build on. But what they don't have is a sophisticated class consciousness and a concept of how to maneuver and present positive alternatives, how to operate on an institutional level in the union and with management.

If you swept away all the present delegates and put in these young people, within three to six months management would have regained control. Management might be able to co-opt them just by establishing more civil relations. It's also true that the bosses could make mistakes. These young people will rebel against authoritarianism. But the possibility of winning them over is there.

The contract struggle is teaching them a lot. You learn inside the factory. The factory is the best school. The new workers are already showing a different level of consciousness. They won't be the same after these struggles.

The key point for party and union cadres now is to offer a positive alternative, not just in terms of better working conditions but also in terms of a better way of producing. We have to show the workers that we can organize production better than management. This is the only way to build a consensus and gain credibility. If all you do is oppose what management does, you may win in the short run, but you lose in the long run.

The anomaly of the Italian working class is that it won so much in terms of control over production and over work conditions. The working class at Fiat has established its own control. Workers listen to what the delegates say. They don't obey the supervisors anymore. The contradiction is that the situation in society at large doesn't correspond to this workers' control in the factory. There's a gap.

There's no chaos in the factory. There's control and conscious organization by the workers and the union. They have the situation in
hand. As soon as there's chaos, management regains the upper hand.

Here's an example of the kind of control we've won. Every time Fiat
changed a model, there was new machinery to produce it. Each new
setup included elements of the previous one and some new, more advanced technology. Then came the 131 model which was a leap forward.
It used more robots, numerical control, and a centralized computer.
When they were putting in the 131 line, there was a long period—several
months—when the workers just sat around for eight hours a day. After a
while, they began to worry about their jobs. This was in 1975. Another
delegate and I came up with a contract demand around production data.
We demanded that Fiat set up a production program for three months
and tell the workers what was going to be produced and how much. Then
this program could not be changed for three months. Management was
no longer allowed to switch workers around from line to line.

When Fiat decided to enter the foreign market in a more aggressive
way in 1978, it meant changing production more frequently—producing
more of one model, less of another. This meant switching workers
around, which is what we call labor mobility. The union had fought
against this with the contract clause on production data.

The work schedule is going to be an important card for the union to
play in the future. Reducing the work week to 36 hours—six hours, six
days—was first proposed in 1972. Fiat was willing to accept it then, but
the workers objected because it meant working six days a week. Now the
workers are beginning to accept the idea, but Fiat opposes it. A five- or
six-hour workday, six days a week implies new relationships between the
worker, factory, city, and society. If this change goes through, a lot of
other things like social services will also have to change.

Notes to Interviews with Fiat Workers

1. This was true until the mass layoffs at Fiat in October 1980 when man-
agement dismissed many disabled workers as well as union activists and women.
In the early 1980s, these groups were often the first to lose their jobs in many
Italian companies.

2. A political movement of the far left (see Chapter 6).

3. Without work papers (*libretto di lavoro*), labor is illegal and unprotected by law (*lavoro nero*).

4. Once an independent automobile company, Lancia was bought by
Fiat in 1969.

5. According to the union, demanding higher pay for certain job categories was part of the program to upgrade the qualifications and material conditions of all workers over time. The union hoped to win this demand and then move large numbers of workers into higher categories. Those who disagreed with the policy argued that it was less egalitarian and less democratic.

6. Workers wrote in their choices for delegates on a blank ballot rather than select them from a list of nominees. Many workers considered this procedure to be more democratic.

7. The daily newspaper of the Italian Communist Party.

8. After the Red Brigades kidnapped Aldo Moro, president of the Christian Democratic Party, in March 1978, there were unitary protest demonstrations all over Italy. Many of the political forces (the Communist Party as well as the Christian Democrats) used the demonstrations as a show of support for the state and as a protest against the forces working to destroy it.

9. Enrico Berlinguer, secretary of the Italian Communist Party.

10. The Italian expression *esercito diplomato* (literally, "diploma-ed army") is a play on the Marxist term "reserve army of labor," which refers to unemployed workers who exercise downward pressure on wages as they compete in the labor market for jobs.

11. The December 1969 bombing in downtown Milan killed 16 people. The police first blamed the crime on anarchists, but subsequent investigations showed that two neofascists and a member of Italy's secret services were responsible for the massacre.

12. *Federazione Giovanile Comunista Italiana*, the youth organization of the PCI.

13. In the mid-1970s, the credibility and popularity of PCI increased throughout Italy.

14. In 1917, Bolsheviks and supporters seized the Winter Palace in Petrograd, seat of the Russian government. The expression "seizing the Winter Palace" refers to a revolutionary seizure of state power by force.

15. *Il Manifesto* was a political organization of the New Left in Italy. Founded at the start of the 1970s, it did significant work in political theory, ran candidates in elections, and published a daily newspaper also called *Il Manifesto*. After a series of organizational transformations and splits, the newspaper became independent of any political party.

Interviews with Others in Turin

Carlo Besusso

Just as the phrase "the White House" has come to mean the president of the United States and his administration, the words "Corso Marconi" (Marconi Boulevard) translate automatically for Italians into Fiat's top management. The company's executive offices are housed in an austere white marble building that dominates Corso Marconi in downtown Turin. On one of the upper floors was the suite of Carlo Besusso, head of industrial relations and a lucid spokesperson for Fiat.

Besusso was about 50 years old, an intelligent and unpretentious person. Unlike one younger man in the press relations office who assured me that there were no labor problems at that time and none foreseen for the future, Besusso spoke candidly and at length about management's struggle with labor over control in the factory. Even as we spoke, the workers at the Mirafiori plant had begun another "occupation," blocking all the gates to the factory.

My conversation with Besusso covered the new technology at Fiat as well as the nature of the labor force and management's efforts to reestablish its authority. Besusso began talking about robogate, *the completely automated welding department at Fiat Rivalta.*

You can't understand *robogate* simply by comparing it to the old auto-making technology. Over the years, there've been various stages of automation. Technological development is a long process of successive phases, and *robogate* is the most advanced point so far of a certain part of the process. The assembly line for our 131 model, for example, is highly automated, but it uses different machines and technology from *robogate*. There's also the automatic *mascherone*, a machine that does a large number of welds at one time. It's just as automated as a robot, but it's built to weld one particular car model. When the model changes, the machine can't be used. We had to scrap about two billion lire worth of those machines when we changed models.

Robogate can handle four different models at once, and the machinery is only 30 percent specific to those models. So if we change models, only 30 percent of *robogate* has to be rebuilt. As far as welding goes, there's nothing more advanced than *robogate*. It's the vanguard of the vanguard.

Now all new forms of labor organization pass through new technology. Technology is going through giant changes today.

In general, robots are very flexible. A computer controls the pattern of work. You can change the computer program completely in a short time. Robots have great possibilities in the auto industry, but I also have reservations about where they can be used. I can see them painting and welding but not doing everything in the factory. Third-generation robots will have sight and a sense of touch and will be able to correct their own mistakes. But all that is still in the experimental stage.

We spend a lot of money to develop our technology, so we want to sell it to other auto companies. Peugeot and Volvo have bought our 131 line, and Chrysler bought *robogate* for its Belvidere plant. We're slowly picking up again in terms of sales, and we ought to continue to improve unless there's an even worse energy crisis that cuts into the auto market. But the sales levels of 1974 are still far off. We won't reach them for a while. Some markets are closing because many Third World countries are making their own cars. Fiat built factories in Brazil, Turkey, and the Soviet Union. Now they're exporting cars.

You'd need a crystal ball to know what will happen next. I think the 1980s will be pretty much the same in terms of technology. There're no practical solutions at the moment for automating certain phases of production. But there will be increased use of the existing automation at Fiat. It's inevitable because of the company's problems. We have the lowest worker productivity of any auto company in the world. Our employees work fewer hours, and they work slower. So we have no choice but to substitute men with machines. It's necessary for our competitiveness. We also need the new technology to make a better product. We have to offer better working conditions in terms of less monotony, less danger, and greater skills. But the fundamental point is to increase productivity. It's essential for us to follow this road.

Actually intensity of work is a more correct term than productivity. Productivity can refer to machines, workers, or whatever. What I'm talking about is fewer days worked per year, fewer hours per day, and less intense work each hour. Fiat employees work 37 percent less than auto workers in other European countries, especially Germany.

During the economic crisis of the mid-1970s, Volkswagen laid off 17,000 workers. We didn't hire anyone new, but we tried hard to keep our workers.[1] Total employment at Fiat dropped through attrition. During that time, the workers got used to doing less. Three were doing the job of two. Now it's hard to go back.

Not long ago, I saw an assembly line in a German factory going at a frenetic pace, but there were no Germans on the line. There were Italians, Spaniards, and Turks. There, they want to do piecework. The Turks, for example, work as hard as possible for a short time and then take their money back home. Our workers wouldn't put up with that pace or the conditions in American auto plants for one minute. The salaries of Italian workers used to be low. They've gone up a great deal although they're still lower than in Germany. But our productivity is low, and the workers want it even lower.

It's difficult to say why. There's the political and social maturation of our workers. In the 1950s, we had an uneducated labor force. A third-grade education was common among the workers, and the tasks were geared to this unskilled level. The workers couldn't do more. Now the opposite is true. At Fiat, we have high-school graduates with specialized diplomas just the way they have college graduates in the Volvo plants. We have to upgrade the level of work. Otherwise we'll face a general rejection of work. But specialization and the use of skills also depend on what is being produced. Putting together a car is always going to be unskilled work. You can't upgrade it beyond a certain point.

Another major problem is the orientation of the unions. They have a different conception of labor, one in which the workers have more power, more responsibility, and more autonomy over the work process. In Italy, the unions are class unions. They're challenging the capitalist system. They don't agree with the perspective of participating with management in solving the problems of the company as they do in Germany. Our unions want more information on management's decisions before they are implemented. The unions want to be able to decide ahead of time what they'll accept. This means that management stops being management! The union has a right to know where we're going but not to control the process and not to make the decisions.

Installing new automation is definitely tied to the question of control. Control means greater productivity. It means no strikes and who decides what in the factory.

The unions did worry at first about a loss of jobs because of the new automation. Then they saw that rather than do away with workers, automation changes the type of work done by humans. It becomes more a question of checking what the machines do. As the quality of the product goes up, it's more complicated and takes more workers to produce. So there isn't really a loss of jobs. Also the process of automation is slow. It won't change things dramatically, and it won't affect all the workers. It's true that there will be a less rapid development of employment. But now we export technology. New employment will be created this way.

The worst thing we have to deal with are the limits the union puts on the use of workers. Last summer, for example, we unexpectedly had a large order for one model. We needed to make 5,000 more cars, and we asked the workers to do overtime. The union stopped this by picketing and using violence. They asked for new workers to be hired instead. But it was for a limited time, just a few weeks. It was like a restaurant having to prepare one wedding banquet, and rather than asking its personnel to work overtime, it hires ten new cooks. We lost a good market opportunity last summer because of the union's inflexibility.

Here's another example. The 127 and 131 assembly lines are close together in the factory. When the orders for the 127 fell and those for the 131 went up, we asked the union for a few workers to move 20 meters from one line to the other. The union refused. The union doesn't want the work groups broken up. It claims this will impede its work. The great fault of the union is to refuse all overtime and to be absolutely inflexible on the use of labor.

The unions have a particular ideological and political matrix and a confrontational spirit. They're always in opposition to a point that ultimately hurts the workers. Fiat has to be competitive. To distribute wealth, you have to create it. To create jobs, you have to be competitive. If we don't raise productivity to the level of other companies, we'll be committing suicide. We'll lose all the jobs. Our fundamental point is that we're a private company. We're not subsidized by the government. Either we succeed or we go under.

I've never seen the union call a strike that didn't lead to violence—workers beating up others to make them go out on strike. I'd like to see one strike without violent picketing. The unions should let those who want to work stay and work. They call me a provocateur for saying this. They claim that management will punish the workers who do strike, that there will be reprisals.

The union itself admits that it doesn't have complete control over the workers. There're extremist groups that strike without the union's supervision. These workers are even more violent and more intransigent than the unions. Today the union sent out a flyer asking the workers not to strike. They said a strike would make the situation worse. The workers went out anyway.

The union is asking for new plants in the South right away. We say we won't build new plants in the South until those in the North are used to full capacity. Since 1970, all new Fiat plants have been built in the South. The North can't support any more. The labor market is tight here. More investment in the North would mean an influx of immigration from the South and from Africa that couldn't be dealt with socially.

The recently hired young people reject work. It's ideological. This rejection of work exists all over Europe among young people. The only place where they're willing to work is the Peugeot factory in France, which is a Calvinist enclave. Young people want to work less and live better. That's understandable. Who doesn't want that?

The reduction of the workweek is being pushed all over Europe, but it has to be implemented everywhere, not in just one factory. If we do it just at Fiat, we'll have to close down. I think the reduced workweek will come in the not too distant future.

For the future, I see a slow process of maturation on both sides, industry and the workers. The events of 1969 brought a harsh reaction by capital. Now there's a better equilibrium. That's my hope. The old conception of the boss who beats and fires workers no longer exists. Things have changed. All in all, there's a willingness to find a position of equilibrium.

Fogolin

The press relations office at Fiat made arrangements for me to see the Rivalta plant, but management would not allow any outsiders into the factory when there were strike actions. So the visit was put off day after day for a week. Finally one afternoon when there were no planned work stoppages, I spent several hours walking around robogate and the nearby departments. My guide was the department supervisor, Fogolin, who described how robogate worked and then showed me the stages of production that immediately preceded it.

That entire section of the factory was highly automated. The side panels of the car bodies moved along a conveyor belt, each one on its own carrier. They were welded automatically and then went on to a station where two human workers placed supports into position. When the workers pushed a button, the carriers moved on. Next the sides met up with the other components of the car body. At two more points along the conveyor-belt journey, there were human workers. One positioned the components and the other knocked them into place with a single blow of a mallet. Then the car bodies were lifted up one at a time by a clamp that looked like a giant spider carrying off prey. The clamp lowered the bodies onto the automated carriers inside robogate.

In contrast to robogate, the other sections of Rivalta were packed with machinery, transport vehicles, cables, individual worktables, and long assembly lines. A tier of thick conveyor chains transporting car parts winded around endlessly overhead. Behind glass walls were rooms of computer equipment, and just beyond robogate was a repair shop where two women were reassembling and testing welders. Fiat originally designed Rivalta to produce 1,600 cars a day. Actual production when I was there was 850.

Fogolin was proud of his department. He enjoyed working with the new technology and seemed to have amiable relations with the workers. A factory council delegate told me later that Fogolin was considered a good supervisor and easy to work with. After he showed me around, Fogolin talked a little about his job. He was a large man in his late 40s.

I've been at Fiat for 20 years, first at Mirafiori, now Rivalta. I've been a department supervisor for just one year. This entire part of the factory, including robogate, is my responsibility.

My work is difficult. I'm squeezed between the workers and management, like all the supervisors. But I have a good relationship with the workers. They come to me with their personal problems, problems about their children or their wives or husbands cheating on them. I have to give them good advice, otherwise they'll lose confidence in me.

As far as I'm concerned, the labor problems are due to the union. It's not that the workers are so tied to the union, but they're dragged along by it. The supervisors have been replaced to some extent by the personnel directors. They deal with the union, and we have less authority now. This change began about eight years ago.

It's not that I believe there shouldn't be a union. It's only right that the workers be represented. But these unions are too political. They don't stick to the job of just representing the workers. Everything's too political now.

I think it has worked out well having women in the factory. The women in the repair department are really good. They're more meticulous than the men in this kind of work. Maybe they can't do the heaviest work, but they do other things even better.

The young people don't want to work, but I don't blame them. It's not their fault. Even in the schools, they don't learn to work. There's nothing for them to fit into, no structures. But in my department, they work. I've taught all of them skills. I help them.

I get along with all the workers, even the Communists. I'm a Socialist. I've been a Socialist since before I came to the factory, and I say so openly. [Pointing to a worker] There's a Communist over there, a factory council delegate. He's an exceptional person, a unionist, but he's an ideal of honesty and correctness. He treats people well. He knows how to talk to them. We're like brothers. If the world were filled with people like him, it would be ideal.

Marco Revelli

Marco Revelli taught the 150 Hours course for Rivalta workers that I attended. During the first half of the 1970s, he had been active in one of the New Left groups called Lotta Continua *(Struggle Continues), which ceased to function as a national organization in 1976. Revelli wrote for a number of left publications and taught at the university. Much of his work at that time focused on the organization of labor and the composition of the labor force at Fiat and in Turin. He was in his mid-thirties, an affable and generous person.*

The young workers in my course have all had difficult lives. They're much older than their years. The girls began working without papers at 12 or 13. They've all had difficult family situations.

Politically they're not developed, not polished. Ten years ago, they would have been political cadres, but the social context has changed, and now they're just uprooted. The political world they know is the last three years—the PCI going into the national government and playing an authoritarian role, young people being killed by the police. They don't know the history of the working class and the political struggles of the past.

The terrorist groups often recruit from the autonomous collectives. They choose a young person they think is a good possibility and then convince him or her to carry out an action. They use flattery like "you're braver than the others. You wouldn't be afraid to use a gun." They recruit more in the community organizations than in the factory collectives. It's the same technique that's used in drug pushing.

The reaction in the Rivalta plant to the Caggegi shooting was a witch-hunt.[2] It was pushed by the PCI and the unions. Anyone who was friends with Caggegi was suspect. People were afraid to talk to each other. The PCI's attitude is that Caggegi was the son of a Mafioso and therefore a delinquent. In general, they see these young people as born crazy or evil. Their solution is to put them in prison before they kill someone. I think you have to go to the root of the problem, to the social conditions that produced these people.

What's significant is that it's not like 1968 when the working class was united as a whole and when there was a category called workers. Now the factory just isn't homogeneous. Sex, age, and family situation define behavior. The factory council delegates no longer represent unified groups. I think it's reactionary to try to put one hat on all these diverse groups. The diversity is fertile.

Last week there was a march of 1,000 women inside Mirafiori. They sacked the lunchroom of the white-collar workers, took food—ham, cheeses, everything—and ate it in the factory. They were demanding dressing rooms, but they're angry about the entire situation. Another time, they held an assembly, a strike against the strike, because the men were acting like pigs. The greatest obstacle for them was the men's behavior. They refused to do anything for the strike until the men kept their hands to themselves.

Some of the younger women have a contradictory consciousness. One was telling me that she's against feminism and separatism and that feminism is bourgeois. She also said that when she and the others struggle, they struggle as women. There's often a split between their consciousness as workers and then as feminists.

The political cadres in the factory are completely different from the other workers. They're a minority. They speak a different language. Often their high level of consciousness is just babble, and they use their power against the other workers. The delegates can exercise a repressive kind of authority.

In the 1960s, Southerners discovered the North and industrial society through the factory. Now the younger people have grown up here. Before, work conditions were so bad that everyone was united. Young workers today are much freer in the factory. They don't define themselves as workers. They say, "I'm a student" or "I like jazz" or "I play the guitar." They hate factory work and resent the time they have to spend there. One of the workers in my course once said, "Every day when I leave, I say to myself, I've lost eight hours of my life."

There's a positive aspect to all of this, but it means that the objectives and the whole way of organizing in the factory must change. There's a crisis in both union and political participation. Absenteeism is a problem for the union. About 30 to 40 percent of the workers use their sick leave and get a doctor's signature when there's a strike. That way they don't lose any pay. They won't scab, but they don't really strike either.

The union finally decided not to tell the workers about the strikes ahead of time. In the 1960s, absenteeism was low when the number of strikes was high. Now it's the opposite.

In the 1960s, the large factories in Italy were the motor of the economy and defined the consciousness of workers. Since then, production has been decentralized, and there're tens of thousands of little factories now. Women used to make gloves and umbrellas at home. Now they put together carburetors and motor parts. It's a new kind of black labor. Fiat uses it. It's the submerged economy that's growing in Italy.

The 1950s and 1960s were the Tayloristic phase. Workers knew how much they produced. Controlling this by slowing down or stopping was their power. Now with centralized computer systems and robots, the Tayloristic phase is over. The worker produces so much more that all perspective on work is lost. Between 1973 and 1979, the work time required to produce a car was cut by 50 percent.

Gino Anchisi

A member of the provincial-level secretariat of the PCI put me in contact with Gino Anchisi, who was one of the full-time party functionaries in the area around Rivalta. Anchisi was young, still in his twenties, but had been politically active for a decade. At the time I met him, he was rather drained by his work and by the tensions of that period. He had also had a few minor run-ins with the party bureaucracy. Anchisi set up several interviews for me in Orbassano and drove me out there a few times. We had long conversations, and I always found him to be clear-thinking and flexible, not at all a "follow-the-party-line" functionary.

For its organizational structure at the local level, the PCI divides an area into zones. The zone here includes Orbassano and several other towns. It has 2,300 members. A zone is divided into neighborhood chapters [sezioni] and factory chapters. If a factory is small, it will have a party cell that affiliates with a larger chapter. I head the factory chapters in this zone.

I grew up in a small town on the other side of Turin and became politically active when I was about 18. I organized a party in my town. Until I began working full-time for the PCI, I had a job at Fiat in one of the administrative offices.

I get really fed up with the hardheads in the party and end up having arguments with them. Last winter, at a federal committee meeting,[3] I objected to the questionnaire on terrorism that the party was going to have members fill out. A few days later, I got a letter calling me down for what I said. I complained and threatened to leave, so they apologized. It irritates me all the more because my zone was the only one that maintained its membership level last year. I have a job waiting for me at Fiat. Since I'm a member of a town council, they have to hold it for me. The party knows that I'll leave if I get too fed up.

I don't agree with all the old ways of doing things within the party. I want to involve people more in political debate. There's too much emphasis on just getting votes without the policies and political debates that win more votes. We spend a lot of time on organizational work—membership drives, selling the newspaper—and yet if the PCI didn't do this kind of work, it wouldn't exist the way it does today.

The PCI has to do much more to involve young people and to respond to their needs inside the factory and outside. In some ways, this younger generation has a more positive relationship to work. In part, they reject it, but they also organize spontaneously on the job. They switch tasks to break the monotony. This isn't just a rebellion. It has great potential not only for work conditions, but for control and power. We should be using it.

I think young workers expected to find something different and better in the factory. They heard so much about 1969, but instead, they found it's still a miserable place with assembly lines. Some of the older workers who've been at Fiat for ten years or more are satisfied with what they've won. The PCI keeps talking about "historic memory" and pointing back to 1969. This just isn't sufficient today. It could even become something reactionary. The current delegates are from the 1969 generation, and they've been squeezed dry. Now it's time to use younger people, to involve them. If not, there'll be space for Workers' Autonomy and terrorism.

The union and the PCI should also be doing more about changing the organization of work inside the factory. One change should be work islands instead of assembly lines. But politically, the work island is still an open question. A few workers can stop an entire assembly line fairly easily. It's not as simple to block production when there are islands. Then there's also the problem that certain jobs can be done economically only on assembly lines. So eliminating the lines at Fiat here probably means doing those jobs in the Third World.

The work islands also require much more space. Where is that space going to come from? The local government doesn't allow Fiat to expand at will anymore. But what's more important is that islands would mean greater skills and control for the workers. The islands imply all sorts of political, economic, and social changes. The greatest cost to management would be giving up control and changing the hierarchy. From their point of view, it's risky.

Gianni Montani

Gianni Montani has had a long and varied relationship with Fiat. For several years, he worked on the assembly lines. Then in the early 1970s, he became the Turin correspondent for the newspaper Il Manifesto. *For most of that decade, Montani reported regularly on his former place of employment. At one point, he decided to go back to work in the plant, but after three days on the job, management realized who he was and fired him. Montani sued and won. In 1978, he went to work for the CGIL and continued to monitor changes in the labor process at Fiat.*

We met during my 1978 trip to Turin. It was Montani who first told me about robogate *and arranged a tour through his contacts in Fiat's press office. Montani was in his late thirties, soft-spoken, and balanced in his opinions. During both my stays in Turin, he proved to be a model of patience and answered questions for hours, puffing thoughtfully on his pipe.*

Most workers see the new technology as positive. Their jobs are less dangerous and less tiring. How could they take the position that the technology is completely negative? They're the ones who have to do the work. A simplistic position against the new technology falls into Luddism.[4]

The negative aspects depend on when the new technology is put in, who controls it, and how it divides the working class. Right now, Fiat has installed it just in small sections of the factory. Only certain workers use the new technology, and they're usually seen as privileged. This can create competition and divide the workers.

The union has to begin to take the initiative on technology. For example, at Rivalta, there's *robogate*, which is completely automated, but there's no *digitron*. This means the workers still install the mechanical parts into the body shell with their arms raised. The union should demand the *digitron* system at Rivalta.

The new technology also brings up the problem of the division between manual and intellectual labor. With computerization, machines can produce parts by themselves. The worker just stands and looks at the machine and waits to see if a red light goes on, indicating that something is wrong. There's complete isolation. One worker's in front of a machine, and 30 meters away, there's another worker. They can't talk. It leads to nervous disorders and new kinds of hazards related to work conditions. The solution is for workers to design programs as well as carry them out. They should also learn how to maintain and repair the equipment.

There's one machine maintenance crew at Mirafiori that demands instruction whenever new technology is introduced. They want to learn how it functions and how to repair it. That way, they increase their skills and protect their jobs.

There was another work team at Mirafiori doing finishing in the body shop. Each worker went over just one thing, for example, smoothing over welds. At the end of the line, there was a worker who checked over the entire frame. That worker was in a higher job category. The work team struggled for several months to get management to allow each worker to learn every job. They wanted to raise their qualifications. Management finally agreed. The more highly skilled workers objected at first because it meant that they would have to rotate back to other jobs.

When some of the younger workers switch jobs with each other spontaneously, they do it to keep from getting bored. Yet, it shows how the authority of the supervisors has decreased. The switching is tolerated now because it happens just here and there. The union should get behind it before it becomes chaotic and before the young people become frustrated.

I think one of the most important factors for understanding young workers today is the period of socialization they go through. It's a new phenomenon in Italy. It used to be that the children of workers or peasants went to work themselves at the age of 12 or 13. They identified with being workers. Now most young people go to school until the age of 18. For five years, they live in the *mondo dei giovani* [the world of young people]. This world didn't exist in Italy 15 years ago. It was imported from the United States or England. Now it's an Italian phenomenon, and it's created a different mentality in young people. They deny or hide being workers.

Another change that's taking place is the role of the work team and the department supervisors. As the workers gain more control and acquire skills, the supervisors become useless. So they're often the ones to oppose innovations.

Fiat is always changing its top management. In the early 1970s, there was a new, more progressive generation. They were young people trained in the universities in the 1960s. They were influenced by the struggles and brought more progressive ideas into management. Most of them are gone now. When a contract goes badly for management or whatever, a whole generation of Fiat middle management is fired. A few of the current personnel directors are still more open and enlightened. They're on the other side, of course, but they're open to change.

Taxicab Driver

The taxicab drivers in Turin had a small but telling role to play during the years of the mass immigration to the city. Most of the drivers were Piemontesi, the sons of peasants and workers. They drove long hours, and a large part of their regular fares went to the cab companies. They would wait at Porta Nuova, Turin's central station, as the trains from the South pulled in. Every day hundreds of immigrants, carrying their cardboard suitcases and boxes, got off the trains. The taxi drivers would put large luggage racks on the tops of their cabs and charge an additional fee for every bag. When the cabs were full, they'd drive the immigrants to the boardinghouses and shantytowns.

Turin was rapidly transformed. As the population swelled and the original inhabitants found themselves in the minority, racism took root. It is by no means true that all Piemontesi direct their anger and prejudices against the immigrants. But racism is widespread, and many people make no effort to hide their sentiments. One of these was the taxi driver who took me to the airport at the end of my stay in Turin. He was in his mid-forties.

I was born in the area of Biella, northeast of Turin, where the textile factories are. I worked as an independent truck driver for years, and then I began driving a cab.

Turin has changed completely. It used to be a small, quiet city, like a Swiss city. Now it's chaotic. Frankly, I liked it better the old way, the way it was before the immigrants came. They brought different life styles and different customs.

Our biggest problem in Italy is the South and the Southerners. They're a mixture of races. The South was invaded so many times, and what's come of it is a *razza malfatta* [a badly made race]. It's not their fault. It's just the way they are by nature. They're deceitful and crafty and mean. The Mafia is all southern.

In the United States, you have a lot of racism. It's terrible. Look at the way blacks are treated. We're not racist here toward Southerners because we know they're just a bad mixture and they're that way by nature. That's not racism.

I don't think the Fiat workers should be out on strike. They just sit around the factory all day. They don't work. Then they ask for higher salaries, and the cost of cars goes up. The price of everything goes up. As far as I'm concerned, the economic crisis is due to the Fiat workers. It all begins there. Now they want a shorter workweek. Fiat workers have it pretty good. There're a few jobs like working in the foundry that are still bad, but the rest is OK.

Italy's a poor country. We have no resources. Our only resource is work, and people don't want to work today. They want to be given houses and money without working. If I work and build a house, why should someone else get to live in it without working? If you need a skilled laborer, a plumber or a machinist, there aren't any. But these people don't want to learn skills because they don't want to work. They want civil service jobs that pay well and let them sit around without doing anything all day.

The Communists have made a mess of things here in Turin. They came in saying they would transform the city. But it's worse than before. All politicians are thieves at best. The Communists are the same. There's not one party that's worth anything. It's all payoffs.

I vote for the Christian Democrats but not because I like them. The little parties don't count for anything. There's only the DC and the PCI. Sure, if you could vote the PCI into the national government for five years and see what they could do, fine. But you'd be crazy to think that you could vote them out again. There wouldn't be elections or there would be just one party to vote for. As long as the Communists are Marxists, people are afraid of them.

Diego Novelli

From 1970 to 1975, the Christian Democrats in Turin were unable to maintain a stable government. There were seven elections for mayor, nine for the giunta (the municipal equivalent of a cabinet), and 22 months of governmental paralysis. With this kind of DC performance and with the rising popularity of the Communist Party, the left in Turin hoped to make gains in the 1975 local elections. But they did not expect to win a majority. The day after the voting, the government was in their hands. The PCI and PSI set up a majority coalition, and in mid-July, Diego Novelli became mayor.

Novelli had served on the city council for 15 years, but his life's work was journalism. He headed the Turin bureau of l'Unità, the official daily paper of the Communist Party, and had chronicled the transformation of the city and its inhabitants. Novelli had not anticipated becoming the city's top official in 1975, and he claims he was unprepared psychologically for the job. Yet he soon established himself as Italy's most popular mayor. When the PCI increased its share of the vote in Turin in the 1980 local elections, many commentators described the vote as being "Americanized," meaning that people had voted for an individual—Novelli—rather than for a political ideology or a party's policies.

This explanation may be valid, but it's also true that the left coalition government provided Turin with a stable administration and a long list of concrete improvements: 21 day-care centers, 121 nursery schools, more public transportation, free bus travel for older people, restoration of sections of the old city, transformation of an exposition hall into a public sports club, new libraries, meeting places for young people, swimming lessons for children, public concerts, and art exhibitions.

This was Novelli's program to "give Turin a human face." Critics complained that it was easier to find an art exhibit in Turin than an apartment, but most agreed that the city administration was shackled by the ongoing instability and ineffectiveness of the national government which had to approve and fund many local projects.

Novelli was in his late forties. His personality was considered to be typically Torinese: reserved, suspicious, even hostile at first. He evaluates his interviewer carefully. Then if extreme caution does not seem necessary, the chill wears off, and the mayor is likely to become more open.

I interviewed Novelli in his large office with its high ceilings, frescoed walls, antique furniture and rugs. He sat in one corner of the room behind a tremendous desk, half of which was covered by a handbell collection. For the first ten minutes, Novelli signed a stack of papers while he spoke and never once looked up. By the time I left, something like the start of a smile had pulled at the corners of his mouth a few times. At the end of the interview, he talked about how he found his job personally oppressive. He was no longer free to roam around the city but was chauffeured in an armored car. There was some incident every day to remind him of the desperation of Turin's population. Yet he knew of no short-term solutions. A few days before our conversation, a young immigrant worker mistakenly thought that he and his family were being evicted from their apartment. He made his way to city hall and set himself on fire under the windows of the mayor's office.

The relationship between the city government and Fiat is a civil one. We made this our policy in 1975. We said our attitude would be neither hostile nor punitive but one of reciprocal respect and autonomy for each of us. For decades before that, the city government functioned pretty much as a notary public for Fiat. When Fiat telephoned the mayor's office, everyone stood up. Of course, I wasn't around then, but I imagine it was like that.

Up to now, our decisions and choices have coincided with Fiat's. There've been quantitative not qualitative differences. For example, around the issue of land, Fiat wanted to expand, and we said *no*. After a few months, Fiat gave in. We want Fiat to invest in the South, and they refuse. It's a situation of continual bargaining. Fiat isn't the devil. We have to stop seeing the company that way.[5]

The PCI hasn't seized the Winter Palace in Turin. Outside city hall, you don't see a red flag. You see the flag of Turin. I'm the mayor of the entire city, not just the left, although that's not to say that I leave my political baggage outside the door when I come to work in the morning.

It's true that Fiat brought about the city's worst problems 15 years or so ago. The company's growth was completely unchecked, and there were waves of immigration with no effort to provide the needed services. In 1971, Fiat actually tried to put up shanties for the workers. Can you believe that? Shanties in 1971, not 1871! The political and cultural hegemony of large industry over the city was total. Industry didn't develop as a function of Turin. It used and fed off the city. The relationship was turned upside down.

When a city reaches a certain size, there're problems. Turin suffers from the same problems as all large cities. It's just that here they've taken on the proportions of a laboratory for human pathology. Turin is Italy's automobile city, but we don't want to become Detroit. We could get there soon, but we're not there yet and hope never to be. We don't have neighborhoods that the police are afraid to go into.

Statistically Turin is the third largest southern city in Italy. After Naples and Palermo, we have the largest number of Italians who were born in or whose origins are in the South. The old *Piemontese* fabric has been stretched completely out of shape, and it hasn't been substituted by a new one. The city no longer has its own identity. It's neither northern nor southern, and the biggest problem is that there don't seem to be many possibilities for developing a new and different connective tissue.

The system of production inside the factory is reflected in what goes on outside as well. Think about the assembly line. Every worker completes one operation and keeps repeating it without knowing what happens before or after his task. In the neighborhoods where the workers live—and not only in those neighborhoods—everyone is shut in an apartment without knowing the other inhabitants of the same building. You discover who lives upstairs only when a sink clogs up and the water from the ceiling drips on your head.

This administration has already changed the city to some extent. We've doubled the park space, put in bicycle paths, built day-care centers and schools. The children use everything in Turin—museums, government offices, service agencies—as learning facilities, and the university students in urban planning can treat the city as a laboratory. We plan to use their studies in setting up our programs.

Unemployment itself isn't the major problem. It's intellectual unemployment. The work available doesn't correspond to the aspirations of young people. This leads to protests, rebellion, drugs, and suicide. The city just can't resolve all this alone. There have to be changes on the national level. We've already gone beyond our jurisdiction here. When we took over, there were firemen who didn't have a fire station. If you

Striking workers with their union banners outside Fiat Mirafiori in May 1979.

248

were accused of a crime, you had to wait two or three years for your trial to come up. The prisons date back to the nineteenth century.

Today many of our problems are outside the factory. In the 1960s, Fiat set things up in the plants, paid the workers, and then couldn't understand why they revolted—as if there was just the factory! On the third of July 1969, there was a general strike of all workers in Turin because of housing problems. And what do you know! Fiat discovered that there's life outside the factory.

The economic theorist J.A. Schumpeter wrote about the necessity of continuing to invest where previous investments were already made so as not to weaken the initial capital. This law has dominated urban industrial development for more than two centuries. It's the origin of severe regional disequilibriums and frightening obstructions within the most developed areas and the large cities of the world. It's the law of capitalism in its untamed state. It's robbed man, who originally produced capital, of his role as subject. Today this law of Schumpeter's must be rejected. Wherever it continues to be applied, it throws capital into crisis as well as man.

The current contract struggles at Fiat are like many others in the past. Management never gives anything without struggles. If there had been no struggles until now, the workers would be no better off than my grandmother was, in a factory at the age of ten, standing on a stool to reach the loom.

The factory and this city are completely tied together. If Fiat goes into crisis, Turin does too. Fiat is important for the future. In the short run, there're margins for satisfying the needs of both Fiat and the workers.

Notes to Interviews with Others in Turin

1. During the economic crisis, the workers at many organized Italian plants including Fiat prevented mass layoffs by striking or occupying the factories.

2. Matteo Caggegi was the young Fiat worker killed by the police (see interview, 150 Hours Course).

3. At the provincial level, the policy-making body of the PCI is the federal committee. It parallels the regional committee at the regional level and the central committee at the national level.

4. The Luddites were English workers in the early nineteenth century who protested the elimination of jobs and lower wages by destroying the new, labor-saving textile machinery. The term Luddism is now used to designate workers who oppose technological innovation and focus their protests against machinery.

5. The relationship between Fiat and the city government was not without serious conflict after the time of this interview. In fall 1980, Novelli vigorously opposed Fiat's attempt to fire 14,000 workers. The mayor applied whatever pressure he could, including a visit to the president of the republic. Novelli argued that by struggling against the firings, he was acting on behalf of the welfare of the entire city.

Bibliography

Aaron, Benjamin, and K.W. Wedderburn, eds. *Industrial Conflict: A Comparative Legal Survey.* New York: Crane, Russak & Co., 1972.

Accornero, Aris, ed. *Problemi del movimento sindacale in Italia 1943–1973.* Annali, vol. 16. Milan: Feltrinelli, 1976.

Allum, P.A. *Italy—Republic Without Government?* New York and London: W.W. Norton, 1973.

Armeni, Ritanna. "Una femminista che vince." *Pace e Guerra,* March 31, 1983, pp. 34–35.

Ascoli, Giulietta. "L'UDI tra emancipazione e liberazione (1943–1964)." *Problemi del socialismo* 17, no. 4 (October–December 1976):109–59.

Barbagli, Marzio, and Piergiorgio Corbetta. "Partito e movimento: Aspetti e rinnovamento del PCI." *Inchiesta* 8, no. 31 (January–February 1978):3–46.

Barkan, Joanne. "Eight Hours a Day at Fiat: Conversations with Italian Auto Workers." *Radical America* 14, no. 4 (July–August 1980):23–39.

———. "Italian Communism at the Crossroads." In *The Politics of Eurocommunism: Socialism in Transition,* edited by Carl Boggs and David Plotke, pp. 49–76. Boston: South End Press, 1980.

———. "The Italian New Left in the Seventies." *Socialist Revolution,* no. 36 (November–December 1977), pp. 94–104.

———. "Italy: Working-Class Defeat or Program for a Transition?" *Monthly Review* 29, no. 6 (November 1977), pp. 26–36.

———. "Robot the Riveter." *Attenzione,* March 1981, pp. 34–37.

———. "Worker Turmoil in Italy." *The Progressive,* June 1979, pp. 46–49.

Berlinguer, Enrico. *After Poland: Towards a New Internationalism.* Edited and translated by Antonio Bronda and Stephen Bodington. Nottingham: Spokesman, 1982.

———. *Reflections After Events in Chile.* Reprint from *The Italian Communists, Foreign Bulletin of the PCI,* no. 5, 1973.

Blackmer, Donald L.M., and Sidney Tarrow, eds. *Communism in Italy and France*. Princeton: Princeton University Press, 1975.

Brandini, Pietro Merli. "Italy: Creating a New Industrial Relations System from the Bottom." In *Worker Militancy and Its Consequences, 1965–75: New Directions in Western Industrial Relations*, edited by Solomon Barkin, pp. 82–117. New York: Praeger, 1975.

Caldwell, Lesley. "Church, State, and Family: The Women's Movement in Italy." In *Feminism and Materialism: Women and Modes of Production*, edited by Annette Kuhn and AnnMarie Wolpe, pp. 68–95. London and Boston: Routledge and Kegan Paul, 1978.

Cantelli, Paolo. *L'economia sommersa: Industria manifatturiera e decentramento produttivo*. Rome: Riuniti, 1980.

Centro Studi Investimenti Sociali. *XIII Rapporto/1979 sulla situazione sociale del paese*. Rome: CENSIS, 1979.

Cinato, Ada, Cristiana Cavagna, and Francesca Pregnolato Rotta-Loria, eds. *La spina all'occhiello: L'esperienza a Torino dell'Intercategoriale Donne CGIL-CISL-UIL attraverso i documenti 1975–78*. Turin: Musolini, 1979.

Commission of the European Communities, Directorate-General Information. *Women in Statistics, Women of Europe*. Suppl. 10, Brussels: 1982.

D'Antonio, Mariano. *Sviluppo e crisi del capitalismo italiano 1951–1972*. Bari: De Donato, 1973.

"Economic Crisis and Political Response in the Auto City: Detroit and Turin." Papers prepared for a conference in Detroit, 10–13 December 1981. Cambridge: Center for European Studies, Harvard University, 1982. Mimeographed.

Ergas, Yasmine. "1968–79—Feminism and the Italian Party System: Women's Politics in a Decade of Turmoil." *Comparative Politics* no. 3 14 (April 1982):253–79.

Faenza, Roberto, and Marco Fini. *Gli americani in Italia*. Milan: Feltrinelli, 1976.

Foa, Vittorio, ed. *Sindacati e lotte operaie 1943–1973*. Documenti della storia, no. 10. Turin: Loescher, 1975.

Forcellini, Paolo. *Rapporto sull'industria italiana*. Rome: Riuniti, 1978.

Frogett, Lynn, and Antonia Torchi. "Feminism and the Italian Trade Unions." *Feminist Review*, no. 8 (Summer 1981), pp. 35–47.

Fuà, Giorgio. *Occupazione e capacità produttiva: La realtà Italiana*. Bologna: Il Mulino, 1976.

Gianotti, Renzo. *Trent'anni di lotte alla Fiat (1948–1978): Dalla ricostruzione al nuovo modo di fare l'auto*. Bari: De Donato, 1979.

Giugni, Gino. *Il sindacato fra contratti e riforme 1969–1973*. Bari: De Donato, 1973.

Graziani, Augusto, ed. *L'economia italiana dal 1945 a oggi*. 2d ed., rev. Bologna: Il Mulino, 1979.

Guidi, Eugenio, et al. *Movimento sindacale e contrattazione collettiva 1945–1970*. 2d ed., rev. and enl. Milan: Franco Angeli, 1971.

Harrington, Michael J. "The U.S. in Italian Democracy." *The Nation*, July 3, 1976, pp. 16–18.

Hildebrand, George H. *Growth and Structure in the Economy of Modern Italy*. Cambridge: Harvard University Press, 1965.

Horowitz, Daniel L. *The Italian Labor Movement*. Cambridge: Harvard University Press, 1963.

Italian Communist Party. *Proposta di progetto a medio termine*. Rome: Riuniti, 1977.

Joseph, Paul. "American Policy and the Italian Left." In *The Politics of Eurocommunism: Socialism in Transition*, edited by Carl Boggs and David Plotke, pp. 335–74. Boston: South End Press, 1980.

Kogan, Norman. *A Political History of Postwar Italy*. New York: Frederick A. Praeger, 1966.

———. *A Political History of Postwar Italy: From the Old to the New Center-Left*. New York: Praeger, 1981.

Lange, Peter, George Ross, and Maurizio Vannicelli. *Unions, Change and Crisis: French and Italian Union Strategy and the Political Economy, 1945–1980*. London: George Allen & Unwin, 1982.

LaPalombara, Joseph. *The Italian Labor Movement: Problems and Prospects*. Ithaca, NY: Cornell University Press, 1957.

Low-Beer, John R. *Protest and Participation: The New Working Class in Italy*. Cambridge: Cambridge University Press, 1978.

Luraghi, Raimondo. *Il movimento operaio torinese durante la Resistenza*. Turin: Einaudi, 1958.

Magri, Lucio. "Italy, Social Democracy, and Revolution in the West." Interview with Joanne Barkan. *Socialist Revolution*, no. 36 (November–December 1977), pp. 105–42.

Mantelli, Brunello, and Marco Revelli, eds. *Operai senza politica*. Rome: Savelli, 1979.

Mattera, Philip. "Small Is Not Beautiful: Decentralized Production and the Underground Economy in Italy." *Radical America* 14, no. 5 (September–October 1980):67–76.

Neufeld, Maurice F. *Italy: School for Awakening Countries*. 1961. Reprint. Westport, Conn.: Greenwood Press, 1974.

Niethammer, Lutz. "Structural Reform and a Compact for Growth: Conditions for a United Labor Union Movement in Western Europe after the Collapse of Fascism." In *The Origins of the Cold War and Contemporary Europe*, edited by Charles S. Maier, pp. 201–43. New York and London: New Viewpoints, 1978.

Novelli, Diego. *Lettere al sindaco*. Edited by Piero Giordanino. Turin: Società Editrice Internazionale, 1979.

Organization for Economic Co-operation and Development. *Italy. OECD Economic Surveys*. Paris: OECD, 1980.

Organization for Economic Co-operation and Development. *Italy. OECD Economic Surveys*. Paris: OECD, 1981.

Penniman, Howard R., ed. *Italy at the Polls: The Parliamentary Elections of 1976*. Washington D.C.: American Enterprise Institute for Public Policy Research, 1977.

Penniman, Howard R., ed. *Italy at the Polls, 1979: A Study of the Parliamentary Elections*. Washington, D.C.: American Enterprise Institute for Public Policy Research, 1981.

Pinnarò, Gabriella, ed. *L'Italia socio-economica 1976–77*. Rome: Riuniti, 1978.

Pizzorno, Alessandro. *I soggetti del pluralismo: Classi, partiti, sindacati*. Bologna: Il Mulino, 1980.

Pizzorno, Alessandro, et al. *Lotte operaie e sindacato: il ciclo 1968–1972 in Italia*. Bologna: Il Mulino, 1978.

Przeworski, Adam. "Social Democracy as a Historical Phenomenon." *New Left Review*, no. 122 (July–August 1980), pp. 27–58.

Regini, Marino. *I dilemmi del sindacato: Conflitto e partecipazione negli anni settanta e ottanta*. Bologna: Il Mulino, 1981.

Romagnoli, Umberto, and Tiziano Treu. *I sindacati in Italia dal '45 a oggi: Storia di una strategia*. 2d. ed., rev. Bologna: Il Mulino, 1981.

Sheehan, Thomas. "Italy: Terror on the Right." *The New York Review*, January 22, 1981, pp. 23–26.

Il sindacato di Eva: Documenti 1978–81. Turin: CGIL-CISL-UIL Piemonte, 1981.

Spesso, Ruggero. *L'economia italiana dal dopoguerra a oggi*. Rome: Riuniti, 1980.

Templeman, Donald C. *The Italian Economy*. New York: Praeger, 1981.

Togliatti, Palmiro. *Discorsi alla Costituente*. 2d. ed. Rome: Riuniti, 1974.

Treu, Tiziano. "Italy." In *International Encyclopaedia for Labour Law and Industrial Relations*, suppl. 5, edited by R. Blanpain. Deventer, The Netherlands: Kluwer, 1978.

Turone, Sergio. *Storia del sindacato in Italia 1943–1980*. Rome: Laterza, 1981.

Wharton Econometric Forecasting Associates. *World Economic Outlook* 4, no. 1 (May 1982).

Wiskemann, Elizabeth. *Italy Since 1945*. London: Macmillan Press, 1971.

Woolf, S.J., ed. *The Rebirth of Italy 1943–50*. New York: Humanities Press, 1972.

Index

abortion, 34, 132; feminist campaign for, 133–135; national referendum on, 136
absenteeism, 88, 169
ACLI. *See* Christian Associations of Italian Workers
Aeritalia. *See* Fiat Aeritalia
Afghanistan, Soviet invasion of, 163
agitation committees, 15–16
Agnelli, Giovanni, 165
agricultural sector, 2–3, 9, 10; CGIL and, 42, 45; in early postwar years, 18, 36, 37–38; land reform and (*see* land reform); modernization of, demands for, 96, 125; shift away from, in 1960s and 1970s, 51, 94; women in, 10, 141; workers' revolt of late 1960s and, 70, 75
Alfa Romeo, 127, 152
Allende Gossens, Salvador, 117
Amato, Mario, 108
Anchisi, Gino, 239–240
anticommunism: center-left coalition of early 1960s and, 57–60; and coalition politics in 1950s, 38–40; in the workplace, 46–48; in reconstruction period, 16, 18, 26, 27
ASAP (employers' association for the state-controlled companies of ENI), 9, 53
assassinations, 108, 109
assembly-line speeds, 41, 62, 71
atomic bomb, strikes against, 42
automation, 54, 62; in 1970s, 148–153
automobile industry, 3, 11; growth in, 37, 51; robots in, 149, 150, 151, 152, 231–232
autonomous unions, 3, 5, 28, 127
autoriduzione (self-reduction), 102
Azzaroni, Barbara, 200

balance of payments, 61, 95
Basile, Carlo Emanuele, 59

Benvenuto, Giorgio, 168, 170
Berlinguer, Enrico, 116, 122, 162–163, 164, 166
Besusso, Carlo, 231-235
birth control, 34, 132
Bologna, 115
bombings, terrorist, 106–108
bonuses, production, 56
Brazil, Fiat in, 232
Bretton Woods accord, 16, 94

Caggegi, Matteo, 201, 214, 237
Carniti, Pierre, 168
Carter, Jimmy, administration of, 126
Casalegno, Carlo, 111
cassa integrazione (wage supplement fund), 101, 168, 171
Cassa per il Mezzogiorno (Fund for the South), 37–38
category unions, 3, 41; collective bargaining gains in late 1950s and early 1960s, 55, 56, 57
Catholic Action, 22; female branches of, 31
Catholic Church: anticommunism and coalition politics in 1950s, 38, 39, 46; CISL and, 3; reorientation in early 1960s, 64
CGIL. *See* Italian General Confederation of Labor
chambers of labor (*camere del lavoro*), *see* provincial-level intercategory structures
chemical industry, 3, 10, 37; confederation membership distribution, 45; workers' revolt of late 1960s and, 75
child-care leave, 140, 145
Chile, coup in, 117
Chinese Cultural Revolution, 65
Christian Associations of Italian Workers (ACLI), 22, 37; leftward movement in 1960s, 64

257

About the Author

Joanne Barkan works as a writer and editor in New York City. She lived in Italy for several years and has since made frequent trips there as a journalist. In addition to her study of the Italian Communist Party, published in *The Politics of Eurocommunism* (South End Press, 1980), Ms. Barkan's articles on politics and social movements in Italy have appeared in many American journals and magazines. She was a regular contributor to the Italian daily newspaper, *Il Manifesto*, writing on events in the United States.

Ms. Barkan holds degrees in French Literature from Goucher College (B.A.) and the University of Wisconsin (M.A.) and did further graduate study in Romance Languages at the Johns Hopkins University.